Praise for *A Place Near Heaven*

Enright takes us on an enchanting journey . . . It is at once a diary, a natural history and an astute observation of rural life . . . Poet Edmund Spenser was also a blow in . . . Both men are inspired by the beauty of the ever-changing landscape and the spectacular abundance and variety of wildlife.

Martin Noonan, *The Irish Times*

. . . likely to become an instant classic — powerfully evocative, lyrical, funny and moving.

Walking World Ireland

Filled with quiet observations of the natural world written like a diary, it will draw readers into a more meditative space.

Sylvia Thompson, *The Irish Times*

This is a book of months and holds within its chapters real people, animals and happenings of everyday life as well as the poetry of nature and the chronicling of the passage of migratory birds and the tragedies of dolphins that die alone on muddy banks and lonely shores. It could lie around for years and, when you eventually come upon it, would be as freshly minted as the breeze trilling in from Courtmacsherry.

Irish Independent

Every page is suffused with the love Enright feels for the part of West Cork. Every sentence is awash with the sensual pleasure.

Sunday Independent

First rate nature writing and fresh, enthusiastic observation.

Alannah Hopkin, *The Irish Times*

From road-bowling in October to sulky racing on the strand on a hot August day in Inchydoney, *A Place Near Heaven* evokes the serene beauty of the landscape. We are all the richer for it.

Irish Examiner

Poetic sentences and passages which sing with a love of the land . . . a master of the art of evoking a landscape and its people in lyrical sentences.

Evening Echo

A vivid picture you won't find in travel guides . . . sharp and humorous observations about mankind. Ireland's living culture shines through his stories.

The Irish Letter

Beautifully written, it is a work in the finest tradition of writing on rural life and nature, inspiring and suffused with a sense of place.

Inside Cork Heritage Watch

He writes like an angel . . . a delightful book that will not only give you great pleasure as you read it but one that will give you lasting joy. Every month brings its own beauties, regardless of the weather.

Irish Farmers Journal

The Kindness of Place

Twenty Years in West Cork

~

The Author

Damien Enright is a journalist, television writer-presenter, broadcaster and published poet. For more than twenty years, he has written a weekly outdoors column in the *Irish Examiner* and, in 2004, Gill & Macmillan published *A Place Near Heaven*, his much-acclaimed book on West Cork to which this volume is a follow up.

He has also written and presented television programmes for RTÉ, including the well-regarded three-part series 'Enright's Way'. Other works include six walking commentaries on West Cork and its offshore islands, travel writing for Irish and overseas magazines, a memoir published in 2010, and *Scenic Walks in West Cork*, published in 2011.

With happy childhood memories of West Cork, he returned there with his family in 1990 after spending thirty years overseas. Since then, it has been his permanent home.

The Kindness of Place

Twenty Years in West Cork

~

Damien Enright

Gill & Macmillan

Kenmare

CAHA MOUNTAIN

Glengarr

KENMARE RIVER

BEARA PENINSULA

Allihies • Castletown
Berehaven •

BANTRY BAY

• Durru

BERE ISLAND

Ahakista •

DURSEY
ISLAND

Ballydehob

MUNTERVARY
OR SHEEP'S HEAD

DUNMANUS BAY

Schull •

ROARINGWATER BAY

SH

MIZEN
HEAD

CAPE C
ISLA

"Suer it is yett a most bewtifull
and sweete Country as any is under Heaven,
seamed thoroughout with many godlie
rivers, replenished with all sortes of fishe
most aboundantlie... "

Edmund Spenser, Poet and Planter, County Cork, 1596.

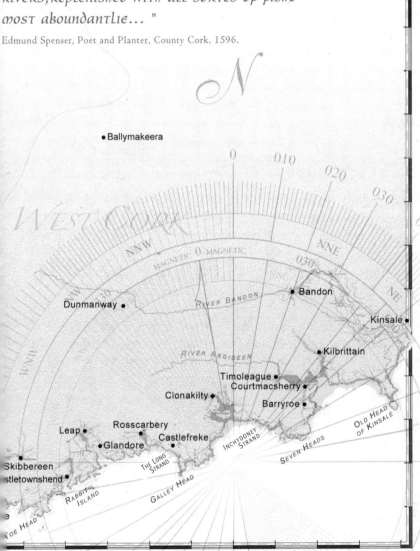

To my wife, Marie, best friend and fellow voyager; to my children
and grandchildren, for the joy they've brought me;
to Peter Wolstenholme for answering bird questions;
to Kevin Hanly, for pointing out things;
to my *Irish Examiner* readers for their encouragement;
to Jonathan Williams, my agent; and to Fergal Tobin who made this
second West Cork book possible.
And, finally, with thanks to my neighbours,
the people of West Cork.

~

Gill & Macmillan
Hume Avenue, Park West, Dublin 12
with associated companies throughout the world
www.gillmacmillan.ie

© Damien Enright 2012
978 07171 4864 6

Illustrations by Nevil Swinchatt
Design by DesignLab, Dublin
Print origination by O'K Graphic Design, Dublin
Printed in the UK by MPG Books Ltd, Cornwall

This book is typeset in Venetian 301BT 11pt on 15pt.

The paper used in this book comes from the wood pulp of managed forests. For every
tree felled, at least one tree is planted, thereby renewing natural resources.

A CIP catalogue record for this book is available from the British Library.

1 3 5 4 2

The lines from 'A Christmas Childhood' by Patrick Kavanagh are reprinted by kind
permission of the Trustees of the Estate of the late Katherine B. Kavanagh,
through the Jonathan Williams Literary Agency.

Contents

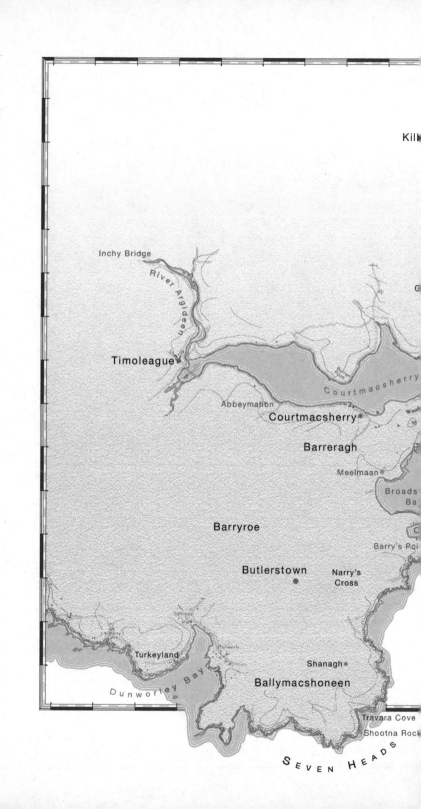

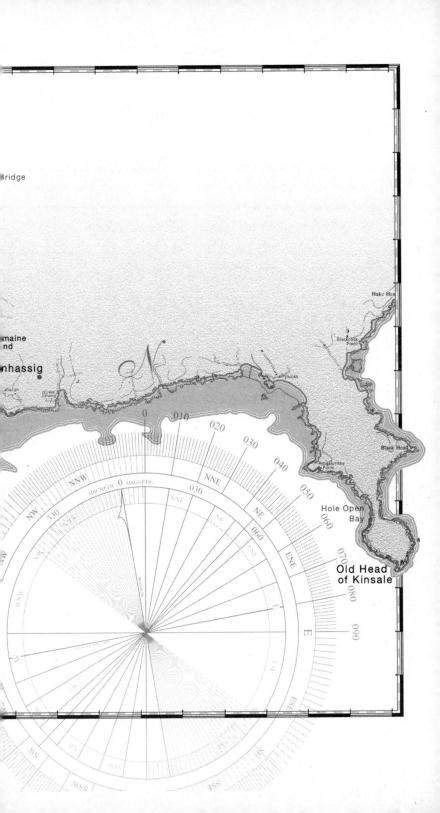

Author's Note

The following pages include extracts from my *Irish Examiner* newspaper columns, my walk books of West Cork and other writings. They owe everything to the late Seán Dunne, poet and editor, who first suggested I set down a calendar of these precious West Cork days.

Introduction

It is twenty years since we came to live in West Cork and I now know all sorts of things I didn't know before I came. This temperate coast is an amateur naturalist's dream acre. When I first arrived, intoxicated with the huge bay in front of our house, the vast plains of sand and the big skies over them, I spent hundreds of hours, in all seasons, on the shoreline, scouring rock pools and turning over stones. My sons willingly joined me and my wife was suitably impressed when we showed her a fine butterfish or goldshinny wrasse, for who would have imagined that such exotica, in their tropical hues, lived on the Irish shore! Within a year, everybody in this house knew a tompot blenny from a plain shanny, and a strawberry from a dahlia anemone.

Concurrently, I learned about the shore birds, the vast flocks that arrive in autumn and leave in early spring. I knew a bit about birds already — my bank-manager father had handed on the knowledge of a boy born on a farm. However, the migrant birds of the bay were, in most cases, new to me. I can now recite their names in litany, and recognise most of them at a passing glance. Such trivia are the wages of the indolent mind.

Wild plants next took my fancy, and meanwhile all common and curious things in nature engaged my attention as and when I set eyes upon them: all manner of things that crawl on the earth, swim in the water or fly in the air. Over the years, many of these also came to be recognised, named and admired — admired all the more for knowing a little about them, just as one enjoys better the quality of music, poetry, art or Clonakilty black pudding for knowing about them. I do not include mushrooms in my recent education — the chance of finding edible varieties had set me to studying them long before we moved back to Ireland, from which I was absent for over thirty years. Regarding trees, their names, their beauty and their properties, it is an ongoing study; while I have been an attentive hedge-scholar, there are still many gaps in the hedge.

Butterflies came next, the summer's lease of painted ladys from North Africa, the autumn glory of red admirals, peacock and fritillaries, and, as I admired the butterflies of the day, I enjoyed the moths of the night arriving at our lighted window out of the dark of the woods and fields around. Simultaneously, I could not but be enthralled by the dragonflies, demoiselles and darters, the bumblebees, honey bees and cuckoo bees, horseflies and hover flies — the whole glittering panoply of nature's wonderments set before our eyes in this fortunate corner of this fortunate isle.

Here, also, history and prehistory have, for the first time, engaged me. It is everywhere on the landscape. One cannot travel a mile but pass a ruin of the near or deep past. The built walls crumble but the standing stones, unbowed by time, abide. Twenty years on, West Cork remains as unspoiled and welcoming as ever. The fishermen fish, and the farmers farm and complain as always. In this hamlet of three hundred souls with its toes in the sea and old woods behind, our sons grew tall like the trees that were saplings when we first came. Far-flung now, in the business of life, they return at every opportunity, bringing their children with them.

Meanwhile, the view over the bay changes day to day, hour to hour, romantic in the mist, shining in the rain, bright with gorse or reddened with bracken, and, sometimes, if very rarely, whited out by snow. It seems appropriate that I should write the first few lines of this new book while looking out on a white world. *A Place Near Heaven*, my account of our first ten years here, also began with snow.

These winter nights, the sky is crystal clear and the stars are sharp, glittering cut-outs against the deep blue of space. One night, some years ago, a very young granddaughter and I looked up at the sky and we wondered if the stars were holes in a black tent above us, beyond which there was a huge, blinding light. We thought of making a two-person spaceship and travelling through one of the holes. 'Great idea, Matilda,' I said. 'But for now, West Cork is good enough for me.'

January

In January, the sea and the storms bring surprises,
and one absconds to sunnier climes at the risk
of missing some of the most outstanding
natural history dramas of the year.
Every January I have spent in West Cork has been
worth the weather; it can be very warm in the
sun, and we do get sunny days.
Sunny mornings after storms are especially lovely.
The beach is swept clean, the mudflats shine like silver,
the air is washed and, after all the night's buffeting
and knockabout, the day breaks on a glittering,
unwalked world.

~

A grey adolescent seal and a pair of pure white adult spoonbills in front of Timoleague Abbey in the falling light of a mid-January Sunday were only two of the delights of West Cork this winter. As I stood watching them, I was glad I hadn't opted for the sun. On damp, wintry days with skeins of ragged-looking rooks flying over the ploughed fields, rain clouds lowering like sodden eiderdowns overhead, my boots stuck in mud and the dog as mucky as a Vietnamese pot-bellied pig in a wallow, I wonder what I'm doing in dear old Ireland; is it patriotism, masochism or an early sign of lunacy? Sometimes I think how nice it would be walking the sunny paths and watching the bloom mats bloom on the dry deserts of the Canaries or Morocco, but as Sir Boyle Roche, the 18th-century MP, so wisely told the Irish parliament, 'Gentlemen, I am not a bird: I cannot be in two places at one time.'

A few hours earlier on that Sunday, I had walked the strand at Courtmacsherry and seen, literally, thousands of sea potatoes drifting on the sea's surface or washed ashore, their near-globular, air-light shells lying in drifts where they had been blown across the beach. It was a brilliant morning, bright sunlight gilding the wet sand and the sandy, viscous sea. The tide was far out and I could venture beyond the usual limits. I found cockles galore, stranded and at the mercy of any oystercatcher, grey crow, gull or forager like myself that found them. The ready availability was too seductive to forego and, so, I came home with a bag of fat cockles and suggested to the *chef de cuisine* that we might have seafood spaghetti instead of Sunday chicken. Happily, she agreed.

We had been living on the harvest of the bay. That evening, *spaghetti volgone*; the previous day, herrings from our fishermen friends, the O'Donovans, the day before that, razorfish both raw and flashed in a pan of oil and garlic for thirty seconds. It's no wonder razorfish are a highly prized delicacy and almost unaffordable in the best restaurants in France and everywhere good seafood is appreciated, but living on The Fortunate Coast I enjoy them at no cost at all.

Walking the beach after the storms, I found them in their hundreds, lying in their fractured shells above the tide line or, more often, washed clear of their shells altogether. Glistening white strips, for all the world like fillets of raw squid but much more tender, they lay on the dark sand and, harvesting them as I went, I occasionally snacked on these five-inch long, toothsome shellfish-fingers as one might snack on sticks of celery.

Razorfish spend their lives in vertical burrows at or below the low-water mark, poking their twin siphons above the sand as the tides come in, filtering nutrients from the sea. The body is a tube, tender and vulnerable inside the long, thin, scabbard-like shell. Sometimes, sand grains in the tube have to be washed out before one eats them, but these, de-shelled and scoured by the storm, were ready-to-eat digits of *al dente* seafood, sharp with the taste of the sea.

Wondrous, indeed, are the creatures delivered by the ocean. The sea potatoes, *Echinocardium cordatum*, traditionally called Virgin Mary shells in West Cork (the dotted outline of a V and M are a feature of the carapace), do not, unfortunately, provide another free seashore meal — it is in the nature of the shells washed up that they are always, in my experience, empty. They might well be worth trying, were they to arrive full of meat — other sea urchins, the spiny urchin, for instance, are consumed in Mediterranean countries and are quite delicious, spooned out of their shells as one might spoon an egg. However, the sea potato we find is an empty, if interesting, shell, so fragile that the slightest pressure will break it; yet the creature lives by burrowing through the wet sand, using its spines for leverage. Thousands lay on the shores of Courtmacsherry Bay on that mid-January weekend.

The spoonbills, taller than our now-resident Little egrets and with spatula-tipped beaks, were a phenomenon to be noted: the last spoonbills I saw were in Morocco but there is a colony in Holland. Meanwhile, the grey seal (a pup, born in autumn and, after the usual brief three weeks of mothering, left to fend for itself) had spent the day within easy view of the road. When I saw it, it was lying on its back on the bare mudflat and curling up its tail, possibly to scratch its nose — it looked like a hoop or a discarded truck tyre in the winter twilight. The tide was creeping in and, just then, the lights came on to illuminate the beautiful edifice that Timoleague Abbey, built so long ago — and despite the zealous efforts of Cromwellians to destroy it — still remains.

On this enlightening, surprising and temperate Sunday, I was glad indeed that I hadn't gone chasing the sun. I should never have even contemplated it. Who would miss the January wildlife displays in West Cork? Last year, we had a sixty-six foot long fin whale in the bay.

～

The first news of the whale that beached itself opposite the village one grey January morning in 2009 reached my phone in a message left at 8.00am. I read it two hours later. I had been up half the night, trawling through archives for mentions I'd made of Little egrets and their colonisation of the south coast, this to help out some earnest pupils at a local primary school who were doing a project on waders. I found I could trace egret history in the bay from 1990 when I had mentioned a lone bird, then a rarity, to the establishment of their now annual nesting colony in Cillmanistir wood, opposite Timoleague Abbey. There, in early May, their chicks stand perched in the swaying treetops like cotton wool balls on spindles a hundred feet above one's head. When I woke late and played the answering machine, I recognised the salty tones of local fisherman Brian O'Donovan, phoning me from his mobile, out at sea. Three other messages also alerted me to the stranding. I swallowed a half cup of tea and set off walking; my wife had taken the car to work.

In June 2001, by the time the news of two killer whales cruising the river Lee in the middle of Cork city reached me, they had already gone back to sea. Would the same thing happen with the Courtmacsherry whale? Unfortunately, no; this whale was going nowhere. On the village pier, a small crowd stood looking at a sandbank a quarter of a mile away on which a large, dark object lay. A fin whale, sixty-six foot long, the second largest whale on earth, it looked like a collapsed, grey barrage-balloon or a giant bin-bag blown onto the sand. How could even the tides shift a creature so enormous? I later learned that its weight equalled that of eighteen Land Rovers.

Some of those amongst the watchers had witnessed the creature's last throes. At first, they thought it had strayed into the bay and would return to the open ocean. Not so: it had apparently deliberately navigated into our estuary to die. As the tide fell, and it was stranded, it had stirred at first — and even blown — and then ceased to stir. Onlookers watched, from near and far, as its life force ebbed like the tide, slowly drawing back to expose its hugeness. The O'Donovan brothers, in their small trawler, had been the first to see it; my other phone calls had come from an early-morning farmer and a lorry driver who had watched the unfortunate animal in dismay. Our friends Peter and Fran Wolstenholme had spotted the huge shape as they were getting up and then viewed it through binoculars from their bedroom window;

their house, like all the Courtmacsherry village houses, faces the sea. On the pier, little was said. It was all over; there was nothing worthwhile to add.

A neighbour gave me a lift around the bay to where the corpse could be accessed from the road. We parked amongst a long line of cars. Four hundred yards out, the great, dead animal lay silhouetted against a grey sea, small waves breaking against its flanks. A man in a wet suit stood a distance away; he had paddled out to reach it. Surfboard under arm, he stood alone, in almost classic pose, staring at the ocean.

As the tide dropped, the first intrepid onlookers began to wade towards the sand bar across cold, knee-deep water, some in wellingtons, some bare-footed. They stood around the body in the chill, grainy light. I watched through a telescope from shore, then set off for home to write about what I had seen. I would return when the tide had ebbed further and the crowds had thinned. Later, when the experts had investigated, I would hear the data, the length, weight and condition of the creature, what had likely led to its demise and what could now be done with the enormous body. I had seen enough to appreciate the extent of the tragedy, to see the huge bulk of the beast dwarfing the humans who stood around it, to gauge the size of the broad tail, to catch the gleam of the winter sun on the steel-grey skin and the sickle-shaped fin on the vast back, and the grooves of light and shadow on the pleated throat.

How sad it was to see such a magnificent animal beached and lifeless. Looking out at the sandbank, with the wind-blown sea breaking in hazy white caps beyond, I was reminded of Shelley's bleak and lonely lines, 'Round the decay/ Of that colossal wreck, boundless and bare/ The lone and level sands stretch far away.' But the whale, unlike King Ozymandias, was innocent of pride, a true master of its element and awesome still, even in death.

~

At about that time — mid-January — as we stood in the cold wind (and considered it worth it), the first primroses were already in bloom on a patch of rough ground in front of the ruined 12th-century Cistercian monastery at Abbeymahon on the opposite shore. On this Gulf Stream coast, we have much weather but little climate, and we can have days in winter when, in sheltered corners, the sun is as warm as on midsummer's day. To see primroses in flower in December is like meeting spring before Christmas; in 2004, they were open on December 12th. Entirely wild, perhaps they seeded themselves after the abbey was suppressed and its gardens abandoned seven hundred years ago. Are they the earliest primroses in Ireland? Are they a manifestation of global warming? So far, so good; no icebergs have drifted into our bay, where white clouds of gulls dance and dip over the sprat shoals and, farther out, the still-living whales roll and roil, sending spouts of spume skywards like pillars of salt, as reported to me by friends walking the cliffs on the Seven Heads. Whales are a not uncommon sight off our local coast, especially the baleen whales, so big that they can be seen miles offshore. But besides the giant fin whales and huge humpbacks, there are minke and killer whales, white-sided, Risso's and common dolphins (the latter in their thousands), and troops of harbour porpoises leap the waves off holiday beaches in summer.

On bright days, Abbeymahon, reduced to a stump and a few walls, is a great place to sit and enjoy the winter sun. I have more than once whiled away an hour in the warmth of its sheltering walls, scanning the slob and the birds. In their eight hundred years on the shores of Courtmacsherry Bay, how often have the stones I sat on soaked in the warmth of winter sunlight and lost it again to a December snowfall? How often have the earth-mortared walls split in the fierce heat of bygone summers? The walls crumble but the stones abide. So, too, the low, stubby headstones that mark the graves of long-dead monks and parishioners buried beneath the soil around me. If ever they bore names, they are long obliterated but I doubt they ever did; they are no more than shards of unhewn rock stood upright, grown with grey lichen. The peals of the angelus ring distantly from Timoleague. How many angelus bells have these stones heard? The primroses have been flowering in this holy ground for centuries. I have been recording their flowering for a dozen years or so, scarcely a footnote in their history.

Passing in front of Abbeymahon, on the sea side of the road, is the paved walkway created in 2001, a laudable tourist initiative, much used by visitors and locals alike. The three-mile-long pathway makes new use of the grassy verge between road and sea upon which the Timoleague and Courtmacsherry Extension Light Railway once ran. The first trains, linking with the countrywide network, steamed down the bayside in 1891 and, as the commemorative plaque says, 'opened a golden age for Courtmacsherry and the Barryroe Peninsula', bringing trains full of holidaymakers from Cork and beyond in summer and, in winter, carrying away large quantities of sugar beet, grown by Barryroe's 'strong' farmers. It closed in January 1962, a most regrettable error: it would be a novelty sure to attract tourists today. However, the walkway is a great success. Rarely is it without clients, weekdays and weekends, in clement and inclement weather, and even at night I see office workers and the walking-women-of-Ireland swinging along in bright reflective jackets, flaying their arms with such enthusiasm that I fear they might detach and fly into the bay. Wooden benches invite the walker to sit and savour the views and the bird-action, for there may be as many as 20,000 migrant birds to observe on a winter day. Wayside plaques, twelve-inch-square glazed tiles set in concrete mullions, depict the species in full colour, with attendant information, these made by Wolstenholme, the potter-who-watched-the-whale-from-his-window, expert bird-watcher, skilled artist and master ceramicist.

But it is the birds themselves that elevate the walk from a mechanical perambulation into a heart-stopping spectacle. I never cease to marvel at their displays. A tight formation of dunlin rockets down the channel towards me, turns and disappears into thin air. Five seconds later and fifty yards away, they reappear as a sudden blink of light before turning and disappearing again. Now you see them, now you don't — nature is the master illusionist. The winter plumage of dunlin is brownish-grey on the back and head. Their camouflage disrupts the normal effects of light and shade. Flying low, at high speed, in a compact mass, they are 'lost' against the background of mud and water. When they turn, their white bellies catch the light and they are then, momentarily, a mass of blinding spangles before they turn and 'disappear' once more.

Speed or deceit are the best defence against predators but sometimes it seems to me that they are simply celebrating the sheer joy of flight. Of the shore birds, the dunlin, barely bigger than house sparrows, are especially spectacular. Over the muddy channels of the bay, they rise and fall like phrases in a symphony, slow now as they ascend, fast as they fall, swooping and sweeping in undulations, suddenly rising from horizontal to vertical, a pillar of birds spreading and contracting like a concertina or one of those expanding Christmas decorations we take out each year.

In pennants and *banderas* they fly, and the rush of their wings is a loud whisper as they pass fifty yards away from where I stand at Cillmanistir wood beside the water. Backwards and forwards they hurtle, now towards the abbey at the bay head, now towards the bay mouth and the sea. Their numbers swell as they sweep down the channel edge, plucking companions off the mud banks. I stand enthralled; they take my breath away.

The manoeuvres of bird flocks are one of the most thrilling sights in nature and in winter one may best see them. When light falls on an object, its shape is emphasised by brightening the upper surface and darkening the lower: light above, shadow below. The plumage of many birds reverses this effect: the upper parts — the head and back — are dark and the belly is pale. Thus it is with dunlin, as with other birds of bare, open terrain like estuaries and seashores. Less than one hundred pairs of dunlin breed in Ireland but some 150,000 individuals arrive from Russia and Scandinavia in winter. How fortunate we are that they come!

~

But new sights — new birds, new people — can also be marvellously diverting. As T.S. Eliot had his countess Marie say, 'I read, much of the

night, and go south in the winter.' Yes, my wife, Marie, and I do read
— it is cosy in front of the open fire on winter nights — and we do
sometimes go south in winter. We find we have new eyes when we come
home.

Often, we visit the small and unspoiled island of La Gomera, in the
Canary Islands. We spent many summers there in the 1980s when the
children were young. The Valle Gran Rey — the great, green, terraced
Valley of The Great King — became almost a second home, Marie
teaching at the local college and our youngest son, Fintan, attending the
local school.

I am immensely fortunate in that I can write my weekly column as
I travel. In India, riding the trains for fifty hours at a time, I could
scribble notes as I sat with one son or the other in the open door at the
end of the carriage, watching the lines of women in their brilliant saris
in the rice-fields, the men in their ox-carts, the small boys on their
huge water buffaloes, the kids playing makeshift cricket in the dust
outside villages in the evening, the girls with brass pots shining like
ingots on their heads as they walked home after fetching water from the
jheels.

In Cuba, we fell in love with Baracoa, a town far from Havana in
Oriente province in the far south-east. My brother Gerry said in an
email, 'I hope you've found the Cuba you hoped to find.' From the
moment I set foot on the long empty beach that starts at the town, and
saw the tall palms and coconut groves in the distance beyond the Boca
de Rio de Miel (the Mouth of the River of Honey), and then saw the
clear, sparkling waters of the river with blue herons fishing the shallows,
I knew I'd found the Cuba I'd hoped for.

One winter, perversely, we migrated south to the snow and rented a
two-room, comfortable cabin in the Alpujarras, on the upper slopes of
the Sierra Nevada in Spain. To be perched on a terrace below the highest
peak in Spain, snow all around us, was a unique experience. Sometimes
entirely cut off from the village ten minutes above us and the village ten
minutes below, we did, indeed, read much of the night. An abiding
memory is of the marvellous wood stove that heated the cabin toast-

warm and would keep going until morning on a single log of olive wood, burning it to a handful of ash, all its energy consumed to keep us and the water warm in that snowbound hut.

These days, in Ireland, in these iced-up economic times, old husbandry returns and I find men cutting up fine ash trees that have fallen onto a West Cork beach from the woods above. As one of them said, with a back boiler on the fire, the trunk of a single tree would save oil bills for a twelve month, and another said that when you cut your own timber, you get warm twice. However, for the past decade or much longer, nobody bothered to harvest these fallen trees, although many locals knew the wood was there and free for the taking. If I had had a chainsaw and a four-wheel drive with a trailer, I'd have enlisted the sons — or, indeed, the entire complement of sons, daughters, grandsons and granddaughters that visit us here in summer and, between us, we could almost have carried away the trees without ever cutting them up. Beach salvage; when it is fine timber such as this, it is doing nature a favour to remove it. Instead of becoming a hazard to shipping when it sooner or later floats out to sea, it provides comfort and warmth without depleting our last, pitiful stocks of fossil fuels.

Now, with the children grown into independence, if we stay at home in winter it is by choice. In fact, even with the recent cost-of-living 'readjustments', it is cheaper to spend the winter elsewhere. But West Cork is hard to beat in winter or summer, with the kaleidoscope of weather, and the constant changes in nature that weather brings. We have the migrant birds of the bay, the whales and herrings in the ocean, and the society of neighbours and friends, West Cork literati and tax-exempt artists, and West Cork locals, who are as literate (but no longer, unfortunately, as tax-exempt) as any one could find.

On weekend nights we share a meal with friends or go to listen to music in the pub down the road. It is always live music and always lively; and in nearby Clonakilty, population 4,000, there are seven or eight different pubs with live music on a Saturday night. On weekdays we get out for a walk alone, and with friends on Sundays. The walking hereabouts is great; unfailingly, there are wonders to be seen. In

Gomera, we walk the mountains *senderos* and the forest tracks, where the groves of tall Canarian pines are like cathedrals. In the Sierra Nevada mountains, we walked the old paths from village to village, including to Trevelez, the highest village in Spain, where they cure the hams of the lowlands into *serrano* in the crisp, dry air. We walked jungle trails in Guantánamo, the province in which Baracoa lies, and bathed in the sparkling streams. We saw the *guajiras Guantánamera*, as the song goes, the olive-skinned peasant girls walking along the dusty roads with baskets of coco pods on their heads, and we admired how very beautiful they were.

But walking in Ireland is hard to better. For beauty and diversity, the landscapes and seascapes rival anywhere on earth and the same route will never be the same twice in any season. Winter or summer, all and any weather may be encountered, changing by the hour. The other Sunday, as we walked along Cloheen Marsh, near Clonakilty, the sun broke through and lit up the bogland, sere and brown, over which horses grazed. It glanced off the flanks of horses half a mile off, and those nearer, between us and the sun, were bathed in a nimbus of light, piebalds and skewbalds, long-haired horses untrimmed for winter, bright in their colours, beautiful to watch in their groups and communities, grazing the marsh. The glow of the land, the misty distances, the horses fetlock-deep in the sward, the ponds shining like silver ingots might have been painted by Millet, might have been a scene from the Camargue or the plains of Hungary. The scattered ponds were hosts to teal and widgeon, black silhouettes against the water, and ranks of black-tailed godwit, long-beaked, long-legged waders, roosted in orderly rows along the edges, waiting for the night.

While the marsh was sheltered, on the opposite side of the causeway, the tide was full in, and the water choppy; it was not a warm day, but dry and sharp, with a fresh north wind blowing. There, rafts of shelduck, their white, black and chestnut plumage dramatic against the pastel green sea, and widgeon, in their hundreds, bobbed on the wavelets, facing into the wind. Nature is not only romantic in its beauty, but in its resilience too.

~

Besides the migrant waders, every winter, huge flocks of thrushes, mainly redwings, but also fieldfares, song thrushes and blackbirds, arrive from the Baltic states and near-Russia to fill their empty bellies with the haws on the West Cork hedges and invertebrates in the Irish fields where the grass, in the mild winters, continues to grow. In 2010, weather conditions in northern Europe drove them here in their hundreds of thousands, but for many it was a tragic journey. I remember a mid-January Sunday when the talk in the pub was all about the birds, and everybody, the hard chaws, nature watchers and shooters alike, expressed their sympathy for the redwings. Arriving on our then frozen shores, they were almost as legion as the painted lady butterflies that arrived in their millions from Morocco in the halcyon days of June. Small, brightly coloured thrushes, with the profiles of robin redbreasts — and not much bigger — they had flown over Sweden, Norway and the North Sea only to find the fields of Britain as snowbound as Scandinavia, and so they pressed on. By the time they made a landfall on the south-west coast of Ireland, many were so depleted that they literally couldn't rise from the roads and died under the wheels of cars. Those that survived stalked the still-green fields in voracious ranks, scratching for sustenance. But, then, came the snow . . . .

In the pub, Kevin Hanly told us how his cat had brought in six redwings and one fieldfare that morning; it was a stray cat he'd saved from starvation, and he was almost sorry now. 'Hobble her for the duration!' was one citizen's advice. Belling would never do — a half-dead thrush would never hear the bell nor have the energy to escape the cat; those that did fly, flew low, never rising more than a few feet above the ground. The citizen said he'd seen his cat catch one in mid-air. Cats killed hundreds.

On that Sunday, Michael O'Clery, illustrator of *The Complete Guide to Ireland's Birds* and *Finding Birds in Ireland*, reported that at Bolus Head in Kerry in the morning sunshine, he watched 'thousands of redwings flying in low over the sea and dropping onto the first field they came to, while others arrived high and fast, and flew on inland. Fieldfares, song thrushes and blackbirds were in every acre, along with lapwings, some golden plover and woodcock. Flocks of snipe were arriving too, and some were feeding on the road verges, oblivious to traffic. Virtually every field toward Ballinskelligs and Waterville had redwing, fieldfare and snipe. Watchers at Bolus estimated the day's totals at 15,000–20,000 redwing, 5,000–6,000 fieldfare, 1,000–2,000 blackbirds and song thrushes, 1,200 snipe, 22 woodcock, 200 lapwing, 2 jack snipe and 1 water rail. At Galley Head, in West Cork, 30,000 thrushes were counted in the course of three hours. Many birds were exhausted and just sat on the ditches looking stunned. Even on the summit of the Magillicuddy Reeks large numbers of redwings and some fieldfares were seen. Corpses of redwing and song thrush lay along the West Cork and Kerry roads.' They were foraging in town streets in Killorglin, and Michael O'Clery picked up several emaciated birds during a short walk. He said, 'With snow now falling, conditions for these unfortunate birds is worsening, and I'm sure many thousands will succumb in the next 24 hours.'

And succumb they did. The saddest sight I saw was a photo of a redwing which, after its long and perilous passage, had at last reached our saviour coast but was so weak that it had drowned in a rock pool on the shore. Its fires — the rust-red plumage beneath the wings and the cadmium yellow under-beak — were still bright, but the corpse was wet and bedraggled, like something thrown away.

A week later, the snow melted and soft weather followed. The redwings had somehow made shrift and for the thousands that died, thousands survived. In that hard week, everybody we knew put out bread; a widower pal of mine told me that he bought two loaves of brown sliced pan for the birds every day. 'Soft weather' is far more common than snow in West Cork; we have seen snow only four times in twenty years and on only three of these occasions did it last longer than a few hours. The weekend after the thaw, the weather was so soft and warm that after ten minutes walking one shed one's jacket, and after twenty minutes, one's sweater, and ended up carrying half one's wardrobe for three-quarters of the walk.

~

Our route that day was the untrodden paths of the Seven Heads, with the sea breaking on black rocks below us and mounting in great, oceanic swells. The tracks we walked were made by foxes or hares; there are no cattle in this terrain, the sheer drops from the cliffs too dangerous for them and the land eroding more every year so that our friend who owns a few acres of it must annually lose a small percentage of his store to the water coming down from the land above, or the sea sweeping in below, or the wind taking it away during storms. The sun broke through the clouds towards sunset and it reflected on the only glazed window left in a lonely ruin on the cliffs, making it glow with a golden flame as if a candle was burning inside. Was the ruin re-inhabited, we asked ourselves, or had the ghosts of those who once lived there lit a candle to guide wanderers? The same light must often have caught that window when people lived there and they, too, might have seen it on winter evenings as they walked home from the small fields, past the ruins of older dwellings, stones upon stones returning to the earth.

As we passed a deep cleft in the cliff, cries sounded below and a troop of choughs swooped up like a fistful of black, silk handkerchiefs thrown aloft by a conjurer, and they flew above us, ghostly against the cobalt light. Edging closer, I saw the scoops where they sheltered under the roots of sea thrift on a ledge above the sea. This will be their nesting place in spring, I thought; no four-legged predator could reach them there, only a peregrine or a black-backed gull. I would pass by in March or April, and investigate discreetly. Meanwhile, my companions had marched on and I had to rush to catch up with them, the dark coming swiftly down as we crossed fields in the near pitch-black, stumbling over whin bushes and sheep. What is that glow in the distance? I asked, panting as I rejoined them. That, said our friend, the veterinarian, is Butlerstown. That is our beacon.

At the pub in Butlerstown, there was a blazing fire, friends met by arrangement, with our teenage teetotal drivers standing by to ferry us home. A few pints downed, a few airs aired, the squeezebox squeezed, the *bodhrán* drummed, the fiddles fiddled. There was bonhomie abroad, with Jim, the vet, in great voice, and the family of a local emigrant celebrating his return from Australia.

On our way home, a fine fox springs from a ditch and in two bounds crosses the road and leaps like a race horse at full stretch onto the ditch opposite. The courage of nature is awesome. We pass houses on the roadside bright with Christmas lights. I think of the candle in the window of the ruin. Times have changed so quickly. However, as I write this book at the end of the first decade of the new millennium, fewer fairy-light Santas gallop across the roofs of country bungalows with their teams of reindeer. Paint is chipping on the once-elaborate House for Sale signs standing beside proud driveways that now lead to estates never to be lived in and, in some cases, the very houses themselves are beginning to show signs of distress. On country back roads and alongside marshes, we pass ghost-estates where only madness abroad could have conceived their location ever to be right for family homes.

In our village of Courtmacsherry, however, little has changed. A few of the houses in the Georgian terrace facing the sea have been expensively renovated and are much the better for it. In the estates built at the village fringes, the houses are large and tasteful; many were bought as holiday homes; a small number are rented long-term. I'm told that a few commuters' cars pass down the village street at the crack of dawn each morning but I'm never up at that time. A handful of IT home workers, with young families, have moved in; they are great additions to the community and a few swell the weekly Texas Hold 'Em poker game at the pub. In the boom, those who could afford it built themselves environmentally sound homes to high standards of comfort and design, as indeed we did ourselves, and this is good to see. Some local authority housing of exceptional quality was also built. The new-built private houses that remain unsold are on small, expensive estates. They are well maintained, as they wait for the world to get rich again and out-of-town buyers to arrive. There are few opportunities for employment in the village; its attraction is the mild climate, the scenery and the quality of life.

The millennium boom left many scars in midland Ireland as the young, aspirant and hard-working raced to get a foot on 'the housing ladder'. Large estates of starter homes were raised in the middle of nowhere, with promises of infrastructure to come. Now we hear stories of half-finished commuter estates where only one house was bought before the bubble burst. While the unsold stock hurts only the developers and the banks, in some cases the single bought-house visits untold grief upon its buyers.

In the winter floods of 2010, the downstairs floors of many new estates stood thigh-deep in water and buyers discovered that their properties stood on a flood plain. They discovered that they would never again get house insurance, that they were burdened with mortgage repayments on a property not only halved in value by national economic mismanagement but, as a result of location, having no sell-on value because nobody would ever buy it again. These unfortunate buyers and their children woke to find themselves looking across a quagmire edged by windowless houses standing in shallow ponds with nothing but the darkness of the countryside all around them. They might as well have bought a leaking boat marooned on a rock in the sea.

How could they have known? The culture they bought into was endorsed by the great and the good. Nobody demurred. The government rubber-stamped the local councils, the local councillors rubber-stamped the land for development, the state-employed engineers gave planning permission, the developers raced one another to build, the auctioneers talked up the scheme and the need to buy before prices rose further, the churchmen said nothing — and, finally, the banks, pillars of fiscal responsibility, further reassured punters by effectively pushing money at them to buy. These unfortunate people never doubted but that they were buying into a real world, not a virtual one, that the house would be theirs and their children's to live in and enjoy as they gave two-thirds of their lives paying for it. Instead, they find that they might as well have bought cardboard boxes: the lifestyle, the schools, shops and bus services they were promised, the permanent jobs, were all an illusion. In fact, nobody from the top down stood to lose but them.

For a mad decade, we had Cathleen Ní Houlihan, one of our mythical embodiments of Ireland, riding a Celtic Tiger; then, the inevitable happened and she fell off. My father used to recite us a rhyme when we were young: 'There was a young lady from Niger/Who smiled as she rode on a tiger./They returned from the ride with the lady inside/And a smile on the face of the tiger.' Perhaps we'll get sense now that high-riding Cathleen has landed befuddled on her sunbed-toasted derrière and is back, as Yeats so pithily put it, in the 'foul rag-and-bone shop of the heart'. Maybe Patrick Kavanagh's 'true gods of sound and stone' will save us. The music and runic verse, the ogham stones and stone crosses are still part of the landscape and deeply etched in the imagination, a portal to another perspective, as obdurate as the stone.

This other-world sustained the Irish through hard times and engendered a character and a national literature that is the envy of the world. In the depth of the winter solstice, the sun still strikes the back of the inner chamber 62 feet (19 metres) deep in the Neolithic mound at Newgrange, as it strikes the axial stone at Drombeg in West Cork. Darkness gives way to light. Darkness does not prevail, and paradise is not lost because an eleven-year wonder has dissipated. The majority of our neighbours were settled here long before the bubble landscape, in homes and farms family-owned for generations. They are an adaptable people. Cows are still wealth, firewood still warms and the soil still sustains. Together, we live in communities where there is song in the pubs on Saturday nights, funerals are hugely attended and we don't have to worry too much about locking up our cars, or even our front doors. When Marie and I brought the family to West Cork from London twenty years ago, I knew we would never get rich here and we haven't, but our surroundings and the community we live in has delivered a way of life beyond all riches, and I would not exchange it for a banker's pension and penthouse apartments in London, Paris *and* New York.

~

It is a measure of the local tranquillity that a heron fishes nightly under a light only yards away from the village street. At ten at night, for three-quarters of the year, one can walk the entire length of the village and not meet a soul or a car passing, and absolute silence reigns. The same goes for ten in the morning or three in the afternoon. The only moving object, the old collie that used to lie halfway across the road and occasionally rise to scratch its fleas, is long dead, and I'm sure he wasn't run over.

A solitary, lissom figure often seen around the village, where she spent her entire long life, is also gone, and missed. Peggy Whelton was a daughter of Courtmacsherry and owned one of the houses in the long terrace of two-storey Georgian dwellings facing the sea. Her garden was across the road, on the sea side, and she lavished her love on it, bringing seaweed or sand in a bucket, or water from the house during dry weather, for she never would spend the money on a hose. She was a fit, athletic woman, a fine figure even in her eighties, slim and breezy with white hair and an upright posture; indeed, she always reminded me of the film star Katharine Hepburn, in one of her outdoor roles. One would see her striding the road in any and all weathers.

A spinster, Peggy was said to have been the belle of the village in her youth but she never married; there is some tale of unrequited love. She was an intelligent woman — we passed on the broadsheet newspapers when we'd read them because she wouldn't buy them herself — with a great interest in nature and wild plants. Indeed, there is a book on my shelves, John Akeroyd's *The Encyclopaedia of Wild Flowers*, which Peggy gave me. When the Courtmacsherry post office closed, she would cycle three miles to the office in Timoleague on pension day, come high winds or high water which, until recently curbed, often spilled across the road when spring tides and onshore gales conjoined. Once, we met her on the road near Bandon, twelve miles from Courtmac, when she was over seventy years old; she'd pushed the High

Nellie bike up Scardoon Hill, a formidable climb even on foot. How she'd head down it, with a drop of one in ten in places, was beyond us. We offered to throw the bike into the back of the car and give her a spin home but she wouldn't have it. She had a mischievous smile when she talked; one could see that she must, indeed, have been a beauty when she was young. I have never heard a bad word spoken about her. In the summer, when the holiday-making children would drop crisp packets in the street, she'd pick them up.

The heron that fishes under the streetlight often stands sentinel at the end of an old pier, Tanner's Pier, now reduced to a scattering of wrack-grown rocks opposite what was once the Earl of Shannon's summerhouse, now the elegant Courtmacsherry Hotel. On summer disco nights, powerful strobes, beamed from the hotel, roam the sky over the bay like the anti-aircraft beams that crisscrossed the night skies over London during the Blitz. The tall bird, sometimes called Johnny-the-Bog or Judy-the-Bog, stands a few hundred yards away at the pier end, shoulders hunched, silhouetted against the gleaming water. In due course, it takes flight and flaps on its capacious wings to the bottom of the slipway across the street from the Anchor Bar. There, in the glow thrown by a streetlight on the water and within earshot of the music from the Anchor on Saturday nights, it fishes for a late supper, the clever bird.

I say 'clever' because it has learned that fish are attracted to the light — but even cleverer is its understanding of refraction, how water distorts the position of submerged objects, so that they appear to be where they are not. What is more, the fish, its prey, is moving. Yet, it can hunt successfully even when the surface is as calm and reflective as a mirror, or riffled by a breeze or broken into wavelets, or stippled with raindrops, or so thick with sand that it seems a miracle that the bird can detect any movement at all. Nevertheless, with unerring accuracy it snatches anything from a slippery eel to a half-pound mullet, tossing its head back the better to gulp it down.

Later, it rises in its own time and flies to the head of the new pier and stands stock still under the big arc light, as if for viewing. The sea below may be swarming with sprat, but it can't reach them, so it isn't fishing. What is it doing there? Posing? Why isn't it at the roost? Is it an insomniac? Does it like the strains of the music from the bar? Sometimes, one of the pier otters, or their kits, appears and scampers around it, or noses the nearby air but doesn't come too close. Billy Fleming, at the Anchor Bar, swears he's seen it launch itself from the pierhead and swoop low over the water — and might it not be picking up fish on the way? He'd never actually seen it catch a fish, he said, only that it was possible. And I agreed.

There is great entertainment in watching a heron fish. The bird moves along the shallow edges. It treads delicately, the water sometimes no higher than its feet, sometimes up to its belly. It finds a spot where it overlooks the surface: the sun, or the street light, will not be behind it, casting its shadow. It then stands motionless, and waits. When the prey arrives, it lowers its head and neck, slowly and smoothly, crouching until its dagger beak is near the target. Older birds sometimes move their heads from side to side, the better to calculate the degree of refraction and the distance. Then, zap!, and end of fish — or, if it is a miss, a shake of the head and it straightens again and resumes its statue-stillness.

The new-come Little egrets have, in the last ten years, moved into the traditional heronries. Although more numerous, they do not appear to be in competition with their larger cousins; for a start, the herons, being taller, can fish in deeper water. The egrets and the spoonbills, the pure white Johnny-come-latelys, are beautiful, but it is old Johnny-the-Bog, standing hunched on the weed-grown pier on a misty January evening, that most conjures up Ireland for me.

February

The transformation of winter to spring is almost secretive, as if nature, like a cautious settler, is reluctant to be seen for fear his incursions might be nipped in the bud. Deep in the briars, amongst the tatters of last summer's leaves, the woodbines begin to green, the buds unfolding, darkening, beginning to gain strength. Woodbine climbs everywhere in our local woods, green stars in the darkness. On woodland margins, French gorse is already in flower, although it doesn't yet have the heady, coconut scent it exudes on hot, mid-summer days. It seems it has to cook in the sun before it releases that particular unguent magic.

~

The old year slides into the new. Winter is over and February, according to the old Irish calendar, is the first month of spring. It's extraordinary how a few warm February days can put a spring in the step, bring the hedgerows to life and put a buzz in the air.

As we eat breakfast, we look out over a field silver with dew. The leaves of the holly shine like small mirrors in the sun. I am off for a walk: *Carpe diem*, as Horace, the Roman, so sensibly said — Seize the day! In compensation for my indulgence, I will work this evening until dinner-time when the sun is long set: meanwhile, let me not miss the *taispe* in the air, for it will not be there for ever. Who knows what our Atlantic weather will bring tomorrow, hail, rain or shine. One of the great joys of West Cork is that no two days are ever the same, but the weather is rarely unkind. We have summer in winter, and winter in summer. All transitory, changing not simply by season but hour to hour.

As I walk the lanes in my shirtsleeves, the morning is so warm that it seems foolish to be carrying my jacket, so I stash it under a bush. Below me, the bay is as flat as mirror glass, the painted boats set in it like toys. Big sand bars divide the channels, acres of sand as white as tropical atolls. Far away, on one of these sand peninsulas, a man walks with his dog. He reaches the tip where the tide breaks and, for a minute, I think that he'd better beat a quick retreat before he gets the water in his boots. But it is alright — he turns and strolls landward: he has time to spare.

Out beyond the tip of the sand spit and the shelter of the woods and headland, the sea piles into the bay in long, low waves, one behind the other, with hardly an interval between. It is symmetrical art in motion. As the tide begins to change, the boats in the channel swing slowly around on their moorings and point seaward. Out on the flat ocean, white water breaks silently over The Barrels and Horse Rock, the distant redoubts of seals. Beyond them, the sea stretches blue to the horizon, under a sky without a cloud.

By early February, although the growing season has barely begun, the spiky twigs of the blackthorns are white with flowers. On the blackthorn, it's always flowers before leaves; on its near relation and, usually, close neighbour, the whitethorn, it's the other way around. After a good summer, the blackthorn branches are weighed down with sloes, big and black and flawless as dessert grapes, while the whitethorn bushes are heavy with fat haws, red islands shining in the September sun.

Now, in this springtime sunlight, glittering hoverflies hang over the buds of the Alexanders, tall, celery-like plants with heads like umbrellas of small flowers. 'Umbelli-fers', such plants are called — not 'umbrella-fers'. There are dozens thus constructed, from hog-weed to pignut, from wild carrot to fennel and angelica. Along with wild parsnip, chervil and lovage, they are the progenitors of many of our garden vegetables and their wild ancestors were eaten long before they were tamed. But caution: deadly hemlock is an umbellifer too.

As I walk, song thrushes flute from roadside trees, tentative notes, more piccolo than oboe, rehearsals for courtship. I am reminded of a spring afternoon when I came indoors and said that a robin was singing its head off in the garden. Dara, our elder son, then twelve years old, feigned great interest and asked me to show him the headless robin in the tree.

Walking along a clifftop path, I watch half-a-dozen fulmar riding the wind, and they watch me. Small sea birds, relatives of the albatross, with beaks like miniature Derringer pistols (one nostril above the other), they seem to exult in the very air that supports them. Stiff-winged, they glide out over the sea and, without a feather-flap or tail-twitch, come planing back at breakneck speed, disappearing from view under the cliff and then suddenly popping up like so many jack-in-the-boxes to sail horizontally beside me, watching me out of the corner of an eye. The first time it happened, it made me jump. Feeling some presence close by, I turned to see a bird suddenly appear, cruising over the abyss no more than ten feet away from my shoulder.

That these fulmar were celebrating the joy of flight, there could be no doubt. Back and forth they glided, diving and floating, rising and falling, requiring not a single wing-beat to stay aloft, letting the air do it all. If we humans could ride the wind as effortlessly as skaters on ice, how thrilling it would be!

~

Some in this parish call the grey heron by the title of Curly-the-Bogs. This is probably because the tip of his topknot dances when the wind blows, and choosing a unisex title, rather than Johnny- or Judy-the-Bog, is simply a parochial tradition and has nothing to do with political correctness. The sexes are, in fact, identical in appearance and both incubate the eggs. In any case, long live localisms and parochialisms! They are the root-stock of language and, in this case, all three of the vernacular names better describe the bird — its solitary habits, its habitat and plumage — than does the name 'heron', a word of long-lost Indo-European origin said to derive from his call. On February nights, the village is still and silent, as it is on most nights of the year and, as usual, old Johnny-the-Bog is to be seen standing, stooped like an ancient Scrooge, on the farthest rocks of Tanner's Pier. In fact, he fishes there at every season and is absent only when darkness and high tides coincide.

It is no wonder that nothing attracts a heron as much as a well-stocked garden pond where finding breakfast, dinner and tea is, as they say, as easy as shooting fish in a barrel. In fact, in the final strike the beak moves as fast as a harpoon from a gun. It doesn't spear the fish but snatches it, lifts it wriggling out of the water, and swallows it in a gulp or gulps. It seems that there is little a grey heron likes better than a fat, gleaming koi, not because it is worth its weight in gold for its decorative markings but because it is easier than spending hours standing in freezing water up to its knees.

However, ornamental fish ponds are rare in rural Ireland and old Johnny, Judy or Curly must live by stealth and expertise. It is satisfying to watch him fish. If one can match one's patience with his, the hunt has all the elements of a drama. Patience and perseverance are of the essence because, in natural surroundings, many attempts will fail: fish are smart, too. So he awaits a second chance and then, stab, and this time an eel is lifted high and wriggling as it disappears down the gullet. Good-bye, eel. As Ted Hughes, the great nature poet, said of thrushes hunting on a lawn, 'No sighs or head scratchings. Nothing but bounce and stab/ And a ravening second . . . .'

~

While one cannot begrudge the heron its eel, eels are now in dangerous decline throughout Europe. When a celebrity chef recently cooked one on TV, there was outrage. 'He might as well be making a panda sandwich!' the eel-lovers cried.

Until recently eels were a staple in the diet of herons and a wonderful diversion for small boys and, sometimes, their smaller sisters. As schoolboys wading the rivers in short trousers, my brother and I would find an eel under every flat stone. In Tipperary, my friend Jim

Moore, with a patched rear end to his pants, used to fish sizeable specimens out of the slow-moving, deep-brown river Suir, using a line tied to a hazel pole and with a bottle cork, a scrap of roofing lead and a hook and worm attached to the business end. One evening, in County Mayo, I met a silver eel — as they are called when they migrate — slithering over grass in a dew-wet field a half mile from the lakes. It was, perhaps, crossing from Lough Mask to Lough Corrib. From there it would find its way into the Atlantic and swim 3,000 miles to the wide Sargasso Sea where it would spawn.

Remembering how much we loved catching the young 'bootlace eels' in those short-pants days, as an adult I often took my children eel-hunting. It is a challenging sport with spills and thrills, and the hunters often slip and fall on their behinds in the water. The eels are quick and almost impossible to trap in a jam jar; the only way to catch them is with one's hands. During a long day on the beach, the pursuit of eels made a perfect change from the surf and the sand castles. Ankle-deep in a freshwater stream running across the sand, we'd lift the flat rocks and the elvers would wriggle away and drift downstream to the next rock, and we'd lift that one and they'd do the same again, and we'd enlist the younger brothers and sisters to form a cordon of bare feet but, more often than not, the eel would slip through their toes.

What wonderful dark and sinuous creatures they seemed, when we eventually captured one and put it in a jam jar and it swam up and down! We would let it go, of course; we had no reason to harm it and it was far too small to eat. But many a summer day on the beach was part-spent in eel and sand dab-chasing in the clean little rivers that flowed to the sea across the sand.

Not long ago, I found a twelve-inch long yellow eel in our garden stream and we decided we'd call the house Abhainn na hEascainne, Eel River, as if the little watercourse contained legions of black-and-golden eels, although, in fact, I've only ever seen one.

Once, when I was in Holland, I joined Dutchmen in throwing back my head and ingesting smoked eel inch by inch like a sword swallower swallowing a sword. Deeply do I regret it! These days, I wouldn't eat eel even if it came to me raw in an *unagi* sushi. I have a warm spot for eels. They have provided mankind with small mountains of nourishment over the millennia, this evidenced by the fact that eel bones are found in the prehistoric shellfish middens, often identified as isolated hillocks, which are a feature of the West Cork coast. At Barryshall, near Timoleague, a few miles from our home, one such midden was found deep below ground by a farmer digging a drain. Although half a mile inland, the site was originally on the edge of the sea.

While the face of the ocean seems like a template for eternity, there is nothing eternal about the coasts that hem it in. The sea relentlessly reclaims the land, sand bars shift, estuaries widen, huge bays and beaches are raised by the clash of tectonic plates. Courtmacsherry Bay, once deep enough to allow wine ships to sail all the way to its apex at 13th-century Timoleague Abbey, was lifted by the Lisbon earthquake of 1755 and has ever since been of great interest to scientists but unnavigable to all except small boats.

The first humans to arrive in Ireland settled along the coast, and the shellfish mounds and seams are their legacy. In West Cork, they no doubt found the climate kind, the shore replete with fish and molluscs, and the living considerably easier than in the dense forests inland. Nevertheless, they had to be a tough bunch, one would imagine, these small groups of hunter-gatherers. It is well for us to romanticise the curtains of soft rain as seen through the double-glazing of the 21st century; our progenitors had enough to do trying to stay warm and dry in their rude huts or caves.

~

On a February morning of bright sunlight one can easily forget the days when the great watering can in the sky sweeps in off the sea, towing rain clouds like colanders behind it. The squall arrives and rain flings itself at windows and peppers the roof slates like bird-shot hitting corrugated iron. Myles na gCopaleen's famous 'nocturnal downpours' extend into the day and we have diurnal downpours too. Torrents pour down side-roads to reach the bay. They excavate gullies along the verges and deposit silt like river beaches, then carve it up into millstreams, meanders and oxbow lakes.

Sometimes at night, in an interval between the deluges, we jump up from the fire and hurry out for a walk and a bit of air. The fire is a habit, not a necessity; it is 11 degrees centigrade out of doors. Staying on the road — we would need webbed feet or snowshoes to cross the fields — we set off up a hill and find one could surfboard down it. A river an inch-deep rushes along the pavement, gurgling merrily as it goes. Higher up, under some trees, the road is misty in the half-light, like a cool-temperate jungle. Head-high waterfalls issue from the bank, scouring it of the dark mosses, maidenhair ferns and toadflax that colonise it in summer. These cascades are plunging spouts of white water, noisy, splashing, unceasing; one could irrigate a desert with their flow. But away it all goes, all the water, back into the Atlantic whence it came.

In weather like this, it is no wonder our unfortunate forebears suffered from pulmonary ailments. Never mind the first colonisers in their caves — the dampness of the 19th-century *bothán*, with its turf roof and unmortared stone walls, was lethal. It is a testament to the resilience of our ancestors that they didn't all go to early graves. Until recent times, interior walls that did not weep in winter were unachievable in Ireland, yet we find much older structures where, even during the most persistent downpours, the earth floor remains dry, and weeping walls are nowhere in evidence.

Such a place is the Gallarus Oratory on the Dingle Peninsula, the work of a master craftsman thirteen centuries ago. A prayer-house for the Kerry saints, it still survives, just a couple of hours' drive over the Cork-and-Kerry mountains as enshrined in song.

The design is inspired; perhaps a saint designed it. Nothing was used but stones and a few planks of wood for the door. It is now as it was then — or, at least, as it was after its first decade of life, when the lichens and wall rue had begun to colonise its stones. Unlike the white bungalows that dot the Dingle landscape, it is 'of' the place; it is organic. Simplicity and durability are its outstanding features. It is modest. It is functional. The form could not be bettered for the clean lines of its aesthetics. The shape is of an upturned boat, the sides curving gracefully upward to the roof ridge of the keel. Clearly, the early saints understood and appreciated the beauty of simplicity. Light pours through a single-shafted window in the gable; the proportions of this window make it a work of art. Meanwhile, outside, it wears and weathers like the stones of the walls and the fields; it grows gardens of mosses; it shelters minute life. It is a testament not only to the durability of materials and design but to the resilience of the faith that raised it. For thirteen hundred years it has stood; not an alteration has been made to the stonework; not a stone has been stolen. Time has colluded with the stones; only the wooden door that originally sealed the entrance has succumbed and been replaced.

When storms sweep in over Smerwick and The Three Sisters, the air inside the cell hardly moves, a candle doesn't flicker, the buffeting of the wind cannot be heard. In summer, motes of dust hang in the shaft of light from the window; the passage of the sun is tracked on the dust floor. This quality of beauty and durability was achieved in the 8th century, with no tools but a mallet and a stone chisel. Would that the white boxes that litter the landscape all turned grey overnight and were as self-effacing and dignified as this humble cashel. Behind it, the green and golden hills climb skywards with their stone-walled fields, and farm-houses scattered here and there on the lower levels. On typical Atlantic days, the sun pierces the clouds like a giant searchlight sweeping across them. Dark at one moment, they are dazzling at the next. Ballydavid village basks in sunlight, and the blue waves dance beyond.

One September, we saw a swallow feeding its young in a nest high on the wall of the Gallarus Oratory, under the vaulting roof. Swallows know a good nest site when they find one, and return generation after generation. Perhaps, as the old saint prayed, he watched their ancestors take first flight through the shaft of the window into the vault of the sky outside. One cannot but admire the Spartan comforts of Gallarus.

At least the saint was dry and, by all accounts, he was a holy man, an example to the Kerry people and those stalwart Irish monks who went forth to bring light and education to Europe in the Dark Ages.

Gallarus was a Kerry saint, like the famous St Brendan the Navigator, but there have been famous West Cork saints too. It is said that St Patrick, the Welshman or Breton credited with converting the Irish, never went west of Skibbereen. Saint Cíaran, born on Oileán Chléire, Clear Island in Roaringwater Bay, was the first Irish-born saint and was preaching Christianity thirty years before Patrick set foot on Irish soil. According to the Annals of Innisfallen, he was born in 352 AD of royal blood, and the inhabitants of Corca Laidhe, West Cork, were the first 'to believe in Christianity in Ireland'. Cíaran was consecrated a bishop in Rome and preached in France, Cornwall and Scotland: he was one of the four Irish saints to greet Patrick when he arrived. Then, as now, West Cork was replete with holy men, and holy women. St Gobnait (pronounced Gob-net) is pre-eminent amongst the sanctified females and, indeed, a convocation of Irish bishops raised her to the status of a national saint. In the bitter winter of 1602, Donal Cam O'Sullivan Beare, leading his doomed followers on their ghost-march to County Leitrim, camped by Gobnait's well to pray. More about that tragic march later.

In the early 6th century, Gobnait founded a women's community in Ballyvourney, an inland village where — as in Cape Clear Island — Irish is still spoken. The community was dedicated to healing the sick, and Gobnait was a strong believer in the curative powers of honey. Fourteen centuries later, despite all our science, we return to such natural medicines; honey has become a staple of naturopathic healers and is now ubiquitous in health food shops.

On 11 February, on the saint's feast day, streams of pilgrims walk the path to St Gobnait's well. There is a sense of the ancient and other-worldly about the scene. The well itself, the shaded path, the fields around, seem imbued with the sense of arrested time that one feels at the prehistoric stone circle at Drombeg and at isolated pillar-stones or wedge tombs that have survived millennia in lonely fields and bogs all over this county, for Cork holds more prehistoric artefacts than any other county in Ireland. Here, as at the lake island site of St Finbarr's oratory at Gougane Barra, there is the sense that one is walking on 'holy ground', a place where pilgrims, down the ages, have come to worship their gods and be transported beyond time present into time eternal.

In Ireland, the veneration of wells is an old habit, going back to pagan times. Water is, of course, eternal — its flow may be arrested but never halted, it vapourises and becomes clouds, it descends as rain, an eternal cycle. Springs have always burst forth from the earth and brought life. Indeed, some of the rituals of St Gobnait's Well — such as the tradition of doing the round of the site in a clockwise direction, just as the earth makes its round of the sun — argues that Christianity adopted and adapted the customs of the pagan worshippers rather than subsumed them. A tree stands beside the well, and throughout the year pilgrims attach ribbons, rags or scraps of personal belongings to it, so that its bare branches are bedecked with mementoes, including holy pictures, petitions, mass cards, medals and rosary beads. The believers carry away bottles of water to bless their homes and to bathe their aches.

While attendance at Sunday mass has fallen in many parishes, Polish men, workers at a meat-processing factory in Timoleague, help fill the pews vacated by the Irish, disaffected by priestly scandals after centuries of unquestioning faith. The factory is owned by the Barryroe farmers cooperative and it processes their pigs. It is a rare rural enterprise employing 120 staff, the majority of whom are Poles. They came here during the Celtic Tiger building boom but, happily, found other employment, that grandiose edifice having collapsed like a fairground castle that had sprung a leak.

Our unconditional welcome of fellow citizens from the new European Union states argues that, in general, the Irish haven't forgotten that our ancestors were economic migrants for centuries, indeed up to the 1950s and 1960s when the economy was in the doldrums here. Meanwhile, these newcomers to Timoleague and our local towns work every hour God sends them. Although some hold degrees from old and respected universities, they are prepared to stack supermarket shelves, something Irish people with options prefer not to do. Marie, in a private initiative, gave free English language classes to Poles, Czechs, Latvians and Lithuanians in Clonakilty — only to find, after six months, that the Vocational Education Committe had taken cognizance of the classes and directed her to a fund from which she was later paid for her work. Fortuitous was this income too, given that the tuition fees for Dara, studying 3-dimensional design and furniture-making, had been a drain on our funds. It couldn't have come at a better time.

~

Mid-February evenings can be like those of autumn — soft and romantic — and the mornings so misty that the wooded shores of the bay might be the Newfoundland coast, with fog drifting in off the Grand Banks. When I think of Newfoundland, I'm reminded of that wonderful line of John Donne, the later-to-be holy man, enraptured by the sight of his mistress undressing for bed. 'Oh, my America, my Newfoundland!' he cries, as he embarks on a voyage of exploration around and about his paramour. America — discovered only a century before — promised all the exotic charms of a new-found land. Later, having eloped and married her, and been imprisoned for his cheek, he wrote, 'John Donne, Anne Donne, Un-done'. Later still, age and vocation drove the good Donne to God and scholarship. Abandoning the seminal hyperbole, he went on to become Dean of St Paul's.

On this romantic theme, I recall that, over our twenty years in West Cork, the weather on Saint Valentine's Day has often been delightful and in 2010 it was one of the most all-round perfect February days for years. In our corner of the world, the sun shone from dawn to dusk and, it being a Sunday, almost everybody was at leisure to enjoy it. We walked, most of the afternoon, and as we returned to the car and drove home 'tired but happy' (often the final sentence in our primary school essays) the sun was a great red ball in the sky, descending dramatically on Courtmacsherry Bay and painting it all the colours of the spectrum. The peace in the air and the uplifting effect of the light, passing via the retina into the pleasure centres of the brain, induced a benign euphoria. All along the way, we saw folk gazing out at the sea, some with cameras, some with children, some of them lovers with hands entwined. It was like the final scene in a Hollywood Technicolor film, the world standing in thrall at the end of a perfect day.

Earlier that afternoon, from the ramparts of James Fort, we had looked across the water at the glittering power boats and fine houses of Kinsale. The sea was azure, upon which white-sailed and red-sailed yachts, yawls and windblown craft of various kinds manoeuvred slowly, sails barely filling, for there was little breeze. They were lovely to watch, moving in slow minuets around one another.

Old James Fort, restored somewhat in recent decades, stood in fields of green, with furze bushes in flower. Leaving it, we crossed a small beach called Jarry's Cove. As we picnicked in the sun, we watched children dig sandcastles, a dog chase a ball into the sea and young men pucking a *sliotar* back and forth between them. There is no finer instrument than a hurley stick for exercise and diversion on a strand. On the big beaches, the hurlers, male or female, can stand a hundred yards apart and lob high balls one to the other, hitting them into — or snatching them out of — the sun. For the onlookers, the sound of the puck is pleasant to hear, and the graceful swing of the *camán* and the flight of the *sliotar* pleasant to watch. Hurlers-in-the-ditch often criticise the performance of their teams at big matches, but you will hear little criticism from hurlers-on-the-sand.

Earlier a group of enthusiastic young Italians had asked us directions to Ringarone Castle, one single gable only of which still stands. They had already been to James Fort and Charles Fort and, even after all that walking, were clearly ready for more. While we sat on the beach, young men speaking a foreign language passed us, one carrying a portable barbecue, another a bag of charcoal and a five-litre bottle of water. They were followed by a number of women, perhaps their wives and teenage daughters, all bearing bowls, dishes or young children. One wore a hijab, the Muslim head scarf. Doctor, baker or candlestick-maker, she was clearly at home in Ireland, this new Ireland, on a glorious day that we shared with half-a-dozen nationalities, or so it seemed from the voices that we heard.

At four o'clock, there were perhaps thirty people still on the beach, a constant coming and going, with the yellowing sun still strong in a clear sky. As we left, two newly arrived families passed me on the path, small children with sand buckets as if it was high summer, their eyes big with excitement as they beheld the white sand, the glistening sea and the hurlers and beach people all touched with gold: 'O brave new world, That has such people in't!'

A small girl, no more than four years old, wearing a pink jacket, smiled at me as if she could barely contain her joy. I love my grown-up children just as I did when they were small, but I sometimes miss the wonderment that the world held for them and which they shared with me — and that their being there helped me not forget it.

~

In the hamlets and towns of West Cork — none of which have a population exceeding 5,000 — there is no light pollution, and in dry February weather the nights are very clear and the sky full of stars. All the star-shaped lights are, as we know, spheres that are reflecting the light from our sun. It is hard to conceive that beyond our sun is another sun with its millions of planets, and beyond that, another, all floating serenely in space, one behind the next, to infinity.

~

Before February ends we are sure to have storms. One February Saturday, as gales swept in off the Atlantic, and this coast was another country, a woman rang me to say there was a small black-and-white bird hiding under her car and that, as far as she could see, it was a Little auk.

Little auks do not turn up every day in West Cork; they are normally seen only when blown ashore by storms. The last auk reported hereabouts was in 2001, so I hopped into the car and drove over to take a look. On the way, I stopped to tell a friend, Jeremy Smith, that there was a solitary Little auk under a car in Ballinspittle. 'What kind of car?' he asked. I said I had no idea. 'Well,' he said, 'if it's alone it might be looking for an Escort . . . .'

The woman turned out to be quite right; a Little auk it was, indeed. She said that when she had first spotted it, it was sitting in a chilly puddle under the car. We thought that it was perhaps missing the wide Atlantic, where Little auks frequent the edge of the pack ice and delight in glacial seas because the plankton, on which they feed, thrive in icy waters. Black-and-white, and plump, almost as broad as they are long, they tend to stand erect like tiny penguins. Sometimes called the 'penguins of the Arctic', they were, in fact, called penguins before penguins as we know them were so called.

Little auks are, indeed, tiny. It is extraordinary to think that a bird no bigger than a magpie without a tail should spend all winter far from land in the Bering and Chuckchi Seas; their range circles the globe. What was a small, High Arctic bird doing a mile inland on the Irish Riviera in West Cork?

When I arrived, the auk was ensconced in a large cardboard box, with a schoolgirl called Celia, who was clearly fascinated by nature, busily photographing it on her mobile phone. I volunteered to release it on my way home but found the surf running onto the storm beach at Garretstown so rough that I decided to bring it home to Courtmacsherry and release it in our sheltered bay when the tide turned and would carry it out to sea. Meanwhile, having collected a drum of salt water, I decanted it into a blow-up paddling pool once used by the children and popped the auk in. It swam about, apparently very contented; it did not attempt to fly away, although its wings worked efficiently, as witnessed by the lady who had found it when it had skimmed across her yard.

I released it after dark, when the tide had turned. I saw it swim off, a dark speck in the beam of the harbour light reflected on the black water. It was heading down the estuary, towards the sea. It would have to swim a long way before it met companions. How awesome it was to think of that tiny bird, hardly bigger than one's fist, swimming alone on an infinity of ocean, through storms and blizzards, past glaciers and icebergs. Perhaps it would skim the wave tops, its stubby wings whirring as if it were a wound-up toy. Auks are gregarious birds. With luck, it would find an escort but, this time, with feathers like its own. It had seemed quite unworried by human beings, probably because it had never seen one before.

~

Mute swans are resident on our bay, nesting in the salt marshes, and beautiful they are as they cruise the dark waters of the river Argideen in families or in pairs. The swans that come to Ireland from afar are whoopers from Iceland and northern Europe, and Bewick's swans from Siberia and Russia. Bewick's swans are smaller and more delicate than the whoopers, which were, probably, the birds Yeats describes in 'The Wild Swans at Coole'. He says, 'The trees are in their autumn beauty', and the swans scatter on 'clamorous wings'. Both species make a mighty racket, especially when they first touch down in Ireland — Hoop-a, hoop-a, hoop-a, a triumphant, trumpeting call.

March

Were there ever lines that better capture the delights of March than Shakespeare's 'When daffodils begin to peer,/ With heigh! the doxy over the dale,/ Why, then comes in the sweet o' the year;/ For the red blood reigns in the winter's pale . . .' How beautiful is the image of the doxy (the beggar's wench) crossing the dale 'in the sweet o' the year', with youth and joy abounding! Or should we read it in the voice of the beggarman himself who cries 'Heigh!' and sets off with his 'doxy' o'er the dale, the red blood of his passion pounding?

~

March is a transforming month for all living things — beggars, doxies and ourselves. When we go west towards Marie's home place, we see lambs gambolling in lush green fields below hills where golden gorse and purple heather have replaced the umber carpet of the month before. As I stand at the sink washing the breakfast dishes, I watch rabbits chasing one another around the field beyond the small stream and the big beech trees that border our yard.

In recent years, I've taken to doing the breakfast washing-up and I enjoy it. Maybe it's a sign of maturity; my father used to do the same from the time he retired, and continued it into his ninety-first year. Perhaps he found the exercise contemplative, as I do. Standing there, sponging the dishes in the warm, amniotic fluid of soapy, eco-friendly water, I watch the come-and-go of sunlight, birds and breeze, and the antics of the testosterone-fuelled buck rabbits chasing their lady does around the field. Adrift in this Wordsworthian idyll, I dream fifteen minutes of my life away, eyes glazed, hands dipping and rinsing automatically. No wonder women are so calm and far-seeing, given that many enjoy such simple therapy three times a day!

After rain, the view is magical in the sense that we associate the magical with the sparkling, and when the sun comes out after rain the world is full of light. After an overnight downpour, the morning sky is blue, and raindrops cling to the twigs of the bare trees. The sun filters through the naked branches and hits an old holly bush which becomes a thousand mirrors reflecting white light. Around it, the air is smoky. On the branches of the trees there are not only the usual diamonds, but small orange fires like sapphires, emeralds and opals. A white star flashes low down in the undergrowth, like a semaphore — intermittent, regular flashes of intense light. Some of the raindrops are as garish as tiny Christmas tree baubles, red, purple and gold. In the darkness of the under-storey, a blackbird forages in the leaf litter. Blackbirds are very handsome birds, especially the glossy-black males, with golden beaks and orange eye-rings. Glimpsed in woodland darkness, the black plumage and golden bill lend the blackbird the aura of an interloper. When disturbed, it utters a hair-raising shriek and dives into the undergrowth like a villain fleeing a crime. Austin Clarke made it the subject of his poem 'The Blackbird of Derrycairn', presenting it as a symbol of pre-Christian Ireland, its song calling upon the monks in their dark cloisters to leave 'God's own shadow in the cup now' and come out under the pagan sun. The verses were, it seems, a translation of an early Irish poem in which Oisín, bard of the Fianna, debates with St Patrick the merits of paganism over Christianity.

Perhaps it was to bring the pagan bird into the embrace of the church that a 7th-century story told how St Kevin of Glendalough was praying with hands outstretched when a blackbird flew down and laid its eggs in his palm. The good saint kept his arm outstretched until the eggs were hatched and the brood had flown. Seamus Heaney wrote a poem about this story of the imagination, putting the reader in

Kevin's place, feeling the ache in his arm, his knees numb and his fingers sleeping — or, in his fortitude, transported into 'the shut-eyed blank of underearth . . . Alone and mirrored clear in love's deep river'.

While blackbirds' nests are generally hidden in saints' hands or dense shrubbery — and not yet built in March — a close relation, the mistle thrush, builds on the limbs of big trees long before the leaves appear, making no attempt at concealment. 'Missile thrushes' one might call them, for the rate at which they wing across our yard to the high beeches where they nest every year. It is easy to mistake one for a sparrowhawk come to snatch an unlucky diner from the bird table.

Paler and larger than a song thrush, the mistle thrush characteristically forages in open fields. When hunting, it stands very upright, listening for the movement of invertebrates in the grass. It is with us all year, and is one of the earliest breeders: in March, there are already eggs in its big, untidy nest. It enjoys the romantic name of 'Stormcock' for its habit of singing loudly from the topmost branches of tall trees even on the wildest March days, perhaps serenading its mate sitting on the eggs below it.

Each year, a pair nests in one of the mature beeches opposite the upstairs windows of our upside-down house. Having our daytime living space — the dining room, sitting room and kitchen — on the first floor, with French windows leading to a broad wooden balcony outside, has its advantages. While not quite at tree-top level, we have a panoramic view of the jumping-and-humping rabbits and the passing foxes and pheasants in the field opposite, of a patch of the bay below, and of the branch of the particular beech tree upon which, as fortune would have it, the mistle thrushes build every March.

We may glance up from breakfast or lunch (or the kitchen sink) to watch the progress of nest-building and clutch-rearing at eye level in the tree some fifty yards away, across the gravelled yard (the 'courtyard', if one wants to be fancy) and the 'eel river'.

The nest is a rough-and-ready affair, and it sits in a slight depression on a limb as broad as one's thigh. An overhead branch offers some shelter from the rain. There are no shoots or suckers on which the nest may be anchored, like the nests of most tree-nesting birds. One year it was blown off in a gale. But generally the pair are successful in their prominent location, and raise two broods. They fight off predators — more of this later — and we enjoy the 'nature watch', getting close-up views through the telescope permanently focused on the nest through the dining-room window.

The cliff-dwelling ravens that I watch every year often have their chicks hatched by mid-March. They refurbish the old nest annually, and comfortable it looks, indeed, its deep cup lined with horsehair. In February, I see them tumbling, nose-diving and even flying upside down in courtship displays over the sea. They have paired for life and are, so to speak, renewing their 'marriage vows'. The nest rebuilding follows. In early March, there are pale blue eggs, then bald chicks, squirming pinkly in the cup. As walkers pass, the female rises from the nest and both parents stand guard on fence posts above the cliff, resplendent in their glossy, black 'courting' feathers. With raucous croaks, they berate passers-by invading their privacy, raising their crown and throat feathers as they scold.

They feed the chicks, at least in part, on shellfish captured on the sandbanks of the bay. These they carry aloft and drop onto rock surfaces, to split them. They may also occasionally take a very small rabbit, or a bird.

In history, ravens were the symbolic birds of death and carrion. A legend relates that it was only when a raven alighted on the shoulder of the mortally wounded Cuchulainn, the mythical Irish warrior, that his enemies dared approach him. He had tied himself to a pillar so that he might face his adversaries, even in death. A bronze statue commemorating the 1916 Rising and exhibited at the GPO, Dublin, depicts this scene.

The Vikings carried banners bearing the images of ravens into battle to remind the foe of their impending fate. I recently came across some lines of runic poetry referring to ravens, Icelandic sagas relating the victories of Viking warriors in the 10th century. 'We fought with swords on the Irish plains. The bodies of the warriors lay intermingled.

The hawk rejoiced at the play of swords. The Irish king did not act the part of the eagle. King Marstan was killed in the bay: he was given as prey to the hungry ravens . . . .' And, elsewhere, 'In the shower of arms, Rogvaldur fell: I lost my son. His lofty crest was dyed with gore. The birds of prey bewailed his fall: they lost him that prepared them banquets.' Bloody stuff! The Vikings rejoiced in combat and killing. Each verse begins with 'We fought with swords . . .' and there is much account of bodies delivered up as carrion.

In Ireland, uniquely in western Europe, the power of the Danes was brought under control when, at the battle of Clontarf on Good Friday 1014, the army of Brian Boru, High King of Ireland, beat the invaders and their Norwegian allies back into the sea which, to paraphrase 'Dark Rosaleen' by James Clarence Mangan, ran 'red with redundance of blood . . .' A one-eyed Viking fleeing the battle found the ancient Brian, then blind, praying in his tent and split his skull with a battle-axe.

Those who know their mushrooms will tell one that the Vikings ate fly agaric — *Amanita muscaria*, the classic red toadstool with white spots, common in Ireland — before going into battle. They then went 'berserk' — which actually means naked — and charged into the fray wearing only reindeer-skin sporrans or nothing at all. For those who like to experiment with 'magic' mushrooms, Viking behaviour — what with pillaging, raping, and carrying off Irish women to Iceland — is hardly to be emulated. Besides, the amount of toxins in fly agaric varies from cap to cap. While some might simply induce a minor foaming at the mouth and a desire to split Brian Boru's skull, others, apparently, are so powerful as to fell the mightiest warrior even before he gets his kit off and his horned helmet on.

Historically, my family, the Enrights — in Irish, the Mac Innreachtaighs — were indigents (emphasis on the 'gents') of both banks of the Shannon estuary, and a sub-sept of the O'Briens, the clan of the famous Boru. My revered ancestors would have been in the ranks at Clontarf on that fatal day. McLysaght and other genealogical luminaries say that Mac Innreachtaigh means 'party organiser'; we were, no doubt, the organisers of knees-ups for the royal O'Brien line. In

1014, the Enrights may well have arranged the wake and the hooley for poor dead Brian at Clontarf before we all headed back to Clare, having put manners on the Vikings.

While the ravens nest on the cliff at Coomalacha, at Bird Island, a bare rock forty or fifty yards off the western tip of Dunworley Point, cormorants and shags are, by now, carrying tatters of seaweed to the rough platforms on which they will lay. It is easy to tell the shags from the cormorants — they are smaller, more shiny-feathered, and their curly topknots are clearly silhouetted against the sparkling sea. They stand remote from the cormorants (although they are cousins) which look drab by comparison, apart from the bright white breeding patches on their thighs. Herring and lesser blackback gulls have staked out their territory on the higher parts of the rock. They are egg-thieves or chick-thieves, ever-watchful for an opportunity, but the cormorants and shags are vigilant, one of the pair always on guard while the other hunts in the sea, returning with a gullet full of warm fish chowder on which to feed the sitting partner and the young.

Often, of a warm March day, we watch the courtships and the nest-making, the bickering and the attempted robberies from a perch on the cliff above. A sloping rock, south-facing amongst the low gorse and heather, affords a fine platform on which to lie back and enjoy the sun, or sit upright and watch the come-and-go on the island and the light twinkling on the empty ocean. Choughs often pass overhead, their jet-black plumage glossy and bright in the sun and the feathers at their wing tips like a handful of fingers outstretched. They look for all the world like oversized blackbirds, but with curving red beaks and red legs. When they see us, they call a warning to each other, wild and piercing cries, in tune with the loneliness of the place.

~

When we lived in London, I saw nature only at weekends or in hurried glances as I cycled through Primrose Hill, Regent's Park or Hyde Park on my way to deliver lessons to my private pupils while, each day, myself learning more about the texts that I taught.

While such glimpses whetted my appetite for summer and our trips to West Cork, as a family we were very privileged, living, as we did, on the edge of Hampstead Heath, one of the finest of London's green spaces, with its modicum of wilderness wherein grew briars and tares and two bathing ponds were situated, one for men, one for women, both with brown, muddy water inhabited by fish and frogs — and indeed Marie claimed that the children and I always smelled like amphibians after our dip. There were nuthatches and jays in its trees, the former entirely absent from Ireland, the latter less often seen. Swifts arrived in early May and flew past the balconies of our red-brick Victorian apartment-block in screaming squadrons, providing evenings 'full of swifts' wings' and great excitement for us tenants who would sit outside and watch them swoop and dive until the light went from the sky. Such sights are now no more; the over-landlords had the roof renovated and all the nesting niches were blocked up. It spelled the end for our tribe of swifts, perhaps five hundred strong, which came every year from Africa.

At weekends, we visited the woods at Virginia Water in Surrey, where nightingales might be heard, or the reservoirs near Rickmansworth, where reed warblers and sedge warblers nested, and we could hope — fond hope! — to spot a bearded tit, a species rare everywhere and quite absent from Ireland, or a water vole, ditto. We never saw these tits or voles, but I loved those walks, usually accompanied by various of my children and my children's children, foraging walks for forest mushrooms or exploratory reconnaissances of the river Chess where we waded in bare feet, and crayfish and stone loaches could be found.

In my childhood, I lived in small towns in the widely scattered counties of Kerry, Cork, Tipperary, Mayo, Donegal and Kilkenny, the family moving home as my father rose through the ranks of the Munster and Leinster Bank, now the Allied Irish Banks, the recent antics of which would make the poor man turn in his grave, being, as he was, a person of unwavering probity who continued, unto his final, ninety-first, year to say his prayers nightly on his knees beside his bed.

By the time I returned to Ireland with Marie and our two sons in 1989, he had retired and had built a house in the midland city of Kilkenny. When we decided to make the break with London, our destination was West Cork, 'wild', unspoiled and far from cities; and I had fallen in love with it more each time we came on holidays. To me, of all the places in Ireland — and I knew the geography of Ireland well — it seemed to offer the most in terms of a vibrant tradition, welcoming people and a sensible pace of life. It was by the sea, it had world-class scenery and it had a society whose values would serve our children well.

We came with little money and found Lisheen, a fine house going for a song. It meant a huge mortgage, a cause of concern to my father, the ex-bank manager but, typically, I believed we would manage somehow and Marie joined me in my optimism. The optimism proved unfounded. Marie, a qualified teacher, could get no work; vacancies rarely arose in country schools. I secured eight hours a week of night classes, driving to towns twenty miles away in all weathers to teach Spanish to beginners. But, as good fortune would have it, buying Lisheen turned out well. After a year, as repayments became unaffordable, we were approached by a buyer willing to pay us a huge premium on our purchase price. Following the sale, a friend offered us a quaint, wooden bungalow with a tar-paper roof at a peppercorn rent, a lovely little place where we were free of debt and immensely happy and where, shortly afterwards, I was visited with a blessing that I never expected and which, for over twenty years, has given me pleasure beyond compare.

I was offered a weekly column in the *Cork Examiner*, now the *Irish Examiner*. It happened by chance; again, good fortune came to the rescue. One weekend, my father, then aged eighty-five, drove down from Kilkenny, with my mother, to visit us. He brought us a sack of potatoes, she, a basket of home-made soda bread and apple tarts. On the Saturday afternoon, I drove the family to the head of the bay at Timoleague to show my father a fine plate-glass window — since removed — with the legend 'Munster and Leinster Bank' inscribed in gold leaf. It must have been one of the last such windows surviving in Ireland, for the M&L had long since become the AIB. I suggested that he stood in front of it for a photo, and he did, a tall, dignified-looking gent wearing, as always, a suit with waistcoat, collar and tie, and a soft hat. He stood, leaning on his walking stick as I took the shot.

On the way home, I mentioned that I thought I had once, as a small boy, accompanied him from the M&L office in Clonakilty, six miles away, to the Timoleague sub-office which he, as the accountant in Clonakilty, opened for business one day a week. I was right: he remembered taking me there with him and — his memory still razor-sharp — recalled that it was fifty years almost to the day since he had first stepped across its portals. Much taken with the story, I knocked it out on my old Grundig typewriter as soon as I got home and, a few days later, without telling him, sent it to the *Examiner* along with the photograph, no fee requested or expected. I hoped it would be published simply to give a bit of pleasure to an old man.

On the following Monday morning, I received a phone call from an *Examiner* editor, the poet and journalist Seán Dunne. Seán told me he would be publishing the piece, along with the photo, without changing a word. I was very pleased; it would be a great surprise for my father, who was proud of his years of service with the bank. Had I written for any other papers? Seán then asked. Well, yes, I told him, but few and far between were the pieces I had ever submitted or ever had published: they were in *The Times of India* and *The English Journal* in Japan. Well, said Seán, would I like to try a few pieces for the paper. 'On what?' I asked. 'On anything that interests you,' he said. I was looking out at the mudflats of Courtmacsherry Bay as we spoke and the birds in serried ranks picking across them. 'Would a thousand words on an Irish slob interest you?' I asked him. 'Send them in and we'll see,' he replied. And thus arrived the opportunity to do what I had always wanted to do, but had never found the time or the openings to make happen. Now, home once more in Ireland, I had, thanks to Seán, secured the privilege of recording the natural history and the history of our family and of the village every week in written words. Age has not dimmed this pleasure, nor custom staled. . . . The calendar of nature constantly intrigues me and I am blessed that it is part of my livelihood to observe and record it. Seán, to whom I am forever grateful for that opportunity, passed away in 1995, aged 39, perhaps a casualty of the cruel axiom 'Those whom the gods love, die young'. He was certainly loved by those who knew him.

~

In March, at the Old Head of Kinsale, kittiwakes, small, elegant gulls, and guillemots and razorbills — not unlike penguins as they stand upright on the rocky ledges — busy themselves staking out nesting niches on the cliffs and sea stacks. An expedition to the car park outside the massive gates of the famous — or infamous — Old Head golf course, is well worthwhile. Between the surface of the sea, three hundred feet below, and where one stands, the air is full of birds, the sea stacks crowded with nesters, every ledge and fissure occupied. As the fulmars and kittiwakes drift by at eye-level, riding the updrafts above the sea, one could almost reach out and touch them — but, 'Children!' we warn our offspring, 'do not try!' Cliffs are dangerous places and the view of the nesting colonies is not improved by shuffling a few feet closer to the edge.

The Old Head golf course, begun in 1993 and launched in 1996/97, is an outstanding example of the riches-to-rags saga of post-Celtic Tiger Ireland. During the boom in the world economy, overseas golfers, largely American, flew into Cork Airport and were transferred by helicopter to the course. Then, around 2006, things began to change. Offshore 'big hitters' no longer arrived, and as the decade marched on, our Irish 'big hitters' conspicuously distanced themselves from extravagance, even if they could still afford it. As I write, green fees are a fifth of what they were, this in order to attract local golfers, once considered the lower end of the market. Rumour has it that the Old Head course is for sale, with no takers. *Sic transit gloria* golfers.

For decades, the long finger of land above steep-sided cliffs near Garretstown, albeit privately owned, had been a public amenity. In good weather, as many as five hundred visitors might be seen walking its paths at weekends, enjoying the dramatic scenery and bracing air. It was the haunt of birdwatchers, whale-watchers, anglers and abseilers. Initially the outrage focused on the transformation of this spectacularly wild area, only forty minutes from Cork city, into fairways for the few and the inevitable demise of the indigenous wildlife.

As land-clearance and building commenced, the public was prevented from going farther than a public car park at the landward end. Huge gates were erected by the new owners, two Irish brothers who had made their fortune as builders in England. Razor-wire topped the ancient walls, and the traditional access, via the ruins of the 13th-century De Courcy castle, was closed off. When I interviewed one of the brothers, John O'Connor, for a television documentary on Rights of Way which I wrote and presented for RTÉ, he was frank: ordinary members of the public were not welcome within the gates; the Old Head was to be the exclusive preserve of its members or green-fee subscribers from then on.

As the bulldozers swept all before them, I penned various laments for the loss, sometimes tongue-in-cheek, as in my *Examiner* column of 8 June 1993 when I wrote: 'The chough, the rare bird to be found on the Old Head of Kinsale, is, of course, pronounced "chuff", as in "Stuff the chuff — let's have another golf course"!'

In the *Examiner* on 12 April 1994, I noted: 'My wife, son and I, watching kittiwakes from the cliffs, saw two otters swimming below the Old Head of Kinsale, in a storm-lashed sea. They swam to a jagged sea stack, where they scrambled ashore. Then, one following the other, they cantered off across the rocks. A minute later, they had disappeared into the cold and darkening evening, survivors in an element of which we could never be part. If a visitor to Ireland had seen them, he would have remembered it as the highlight of his holiday experience. A visit to the Old Head alone would have been a highlight. Why wasn't it made into a National Park?'

And, on 2 December 1995, still voicing my objections, I wrote: 'Last Sunday, in the dying light of the November evening, two prime puck goats guarded the locked gates at the Old Head of Kinsale Golf Course Development. Like bearded ancients from our shaggy past, they seemed to dare anyone, public or developer, to pass. Huge-horned and yellow-eyed, they were of another time, reminding visitors of the wildness they had come to see but could no longer find.'

Objections proliferated from 1992 onwards; the gates were picketed and, at one stage, the wall-tops were breached and 'Free the Old Head' picnics were held. A major cause of public resentment was the provision that Life Membership, priced at £IR10,000, would not be open to Irish citizens, while requirements for International Membership disbarred all but non-resident Irish from that Second Kingdom of Golfer's Heaven, otherwise accessible to persons from all corners of the earth at £IR2,000 a year. Under the provisions of 'Irish Corporate Membership', two Irish company members could pass through the pearly gates: an annual payment of £IR5,000 would give access to the blessed two. Other Irish golfers could play at £IR1,000 per four-ball, green-fees which were beyond the means of all but a few.

It seemed that a unique peninsula of Ireland was to be effectively closed to the natives. Irish citizens would have no voice whatsoever in its future; the locals could be caddies, but not members, in their own land. The Old Head, enshrined in Irish lore and history, could be sold to non-nationals who could keep the imposing gates closed to all but their friends. Russian oligarchs or American gangsters could effectively own a section of Ireland in perpetuity.

In the years that followed, the golf course did come to pass and a very fine course it was, aesthetically landscaped and even with standing stones, à la prehistoric artefacts, installed for the degustation of golfers from New Jersey or Novosibirsk. At various stages, compromises were offered, such as charging a fee for walking which, while accepted by uninformed visitors, further enraged the 'dispossessed' locals. However, 'dispossessed' they remained, and the golf course developers triumphed.

Not so, however, in the case of a course mooted for 'development' on Cloheen Marsh, near Clonakilty. To paraphrase the famous line in the Nazi play, 'When I hear the word "development" applied to land in its natural state, I reach for my gun . . .' As Barry Lopez, one of the finest nature writers of our time, said, '. . . nowhere is the land empty or underdeveloped. It cannot be improved upon with technological assistance. The land, an animal that contains all other animals, is vigorous and alive.' Meanwhile, the owners of the Old Head course, perhaps sensible to the harsh realities of today's economic climate, now graciously allow walkers through the gates at no fee.

~

Sometimes, in March, sitting on the balcony, we see a heron fly overhead with a twig in its beak, heading for the woods alongside the bay. Solitary at other times, herons are 'sociable' in the nesting season. However, they are notorious for quarrelling at nest sites. Up on the tall tree-tops, they thieve and bicker, constantly improving their homes at the expense of their neighbours as soon as their backs are turned. A twig here, a wisp of horsehair there. A 'bicker' of herons would well describe a heronry, as their nesting colonies are called.

One day, crossing the fields from the school bus, Fintan found a heron's egg under a tall tree in the old Kincragie estate which lies across our stream. Light blue and as big as a hen's egg, it was broken, the bright yellow yolk seeping out. Perhaps the parents' bickering was the reason it had come to grief.

Year after year, the same nests are used, the old lining thrown out, a new one added. New twigs replace the old, and the whole commodious structure is spruced up and restored. After years of addition and reinforcement, the nests are so large one could almost set up house in one. I can't but think that there is some old story about a king or a bard on the run finding refuge in a heron's nest. Charles II of England, obviously an agile king, spent a day hiding in an oak tree when pursued by Roundheads; perhaps he made himself comfortable in a squirrel's drey or in a heron's nest.

Now, egrets, very rare in Ireland until fifteen years ago, nest in the heronry in Cillmanistir wood, near Timoleague. Looking up into the canopy in June, one can see the newly fledged chicks standing beside the nest on their long legs, like balls of fluff, perched precariously. However, they are a hundred feet above and it is a neck-cricking exercise. One might lie on one's back and watch them through binoculars, but droppings spatter the ground as densely as paint blobs on a Jackson Pollock canvas, all in pink and cream. Perhaps they have been feeding on the opossum shrimps that cloud the shallows of the Argideen river above Timoleague House.

Walking home from Timoleague in the darkening light of a March evening, one may see two or three thousand rooks standing in long, shadowy lines in a field across the bay. Whether Cillmanistir, 'the wood of the monastery', was planted by the Cistercian monks of 12th-century Abbeymahon, just down the bay, or by the Franciscan monks at 13th-century Timoleague Abbey, across the bridge from it, I don't know. Perhaps St Molaga, the 7th-century holy man who founded Timoleague — Tigh Molaga, the house of Molaga — planted it. It's a very old wood anyway and its tall sweet chestnuts provide shelter and nesting sites for thousands of rooks, a dozen or so egrets and at least four pairs of Johnny- and Judy-the-Bogs. Parasol mushrooms grow there in the half-darkness, and families of badgers have dug extensive setts everywhere.

When the last rook stragglers have flown in across the darkening sky, the first regiments take wing, sweeping across the bay towards the wood, airborne carpets of rooks, furling and unfurling, climbing and falling. Reaching the trees, they swing again, all in unison, towards the field and climb higher as another regiment, newly launched, swirls out over the water below them. Soon, all the thousands are aloft, flying hither and thither on planes of air, black patterns against the sky, breathtaking in their complexity. As they fly, they raise their voices in a metallic clamour, a sort of massed triumphal cry that somehow seems as old as the wood and the abbey by the water.

It is somehow appropriate that the black crows should fly at night. They have the sky to themselves, this army. In the mornings, the pale breasts of the dunlin flash in the sunlight; in the evening the silhouettes of rooks deepen the dark.

After the evening convocation, the flock settles in the wood, and the parliament briefly and raucously debates. Then, abruptly, all bickering stops. The wood falls silent, and one would never guess that it houses more than 2,000 sleeping birds. Marie, remarkable woman that she is, says she can smell rooks if we pass under them on the telegraph wires when we are out walking. They smell musty, she says.

Ours is a kind coast, indeed; we enjoy some of the mildest weather in Ireland. Oftentimes, when we watch the weather maps on TV on winter nights, we notice that a sort of band divides the south-west coast from the chilly Ireland to the north of us. But sometimes, too, we see the symbols for rain clouds, like black jellyfish with dripping tentacles, suspended over West Cork. However, as regards the temperature, our values are almost always in a sunny orange circle, while other Irish counties have theirs in frosty blue.

~

'March comes in like a lion and goes out like a lamb', so they say, and as I walk through the forest towards Wood Point at the head of the bay, the wind roars in the canopy above me and sends me scuttling for open space before something falls on my head. Above me, tall ash trees and pines lash and sway, putting the heart across me when I hear a loud crack, and a branch hangs skinned and broken while the wind plays with it like a cat with a piece of string. But then, for all the tumult, a wren bursts into song — so loud a voice for so small a bird! In late March, wood anemones already dot the ground under the trees, and acres of the forest floor are covered by the spear-like leaves of ransoms, a few flowers already open. Elsewhere, bluebells are in leaf but not yet in bloom. It is impossible to walk off the path without standing on some living thing.

Dylan Thomas once wrote, 'my sky blue trades'. In March, the wild sky is often china blue and the sun so bright that, as I near the headland, I have to narrow my eyes to look at the sea. Far beyond, the wide and empty ocean flashes like mirrors; close in, it is white-maned and fierce, roaring and leaping onto the rocks like carnivores onto prey. Nature has its cycles and recycles. It bites chunks out of the land and returns them to the depths whence they came.

Sunny mornings after a storm are a delight, the world a clean, washed place, the sky a thoroughfare of small white clouds, very high, or with no clouds at all. What a joy to walk the beach in such weather, the wind buffeting one's ears and sand devils racing past as if cavorting for joy in a world of zephyrs! Beyond, white horses leap on the low waves of the incoming sea, their manes blown back in the blast. At low tide, the village strand is two hundred yards wide and half a mile long, laid out between the woods above and the channel alongside. During my two-mile circuit of beach, woods and cliffs, I often see not another soul. On the cliffs at the head of the bay, I stop to look out at the churned sea and watch the cormorants, shags and great northern divers breast the choppy waves as to the manner born.

In the same weather, farther up the bay, the gulls sweep and soar, their cries lost on the wind. In the channel opposite the village houses, merganser ducks float in small flotillas close to shore. Godwits, curlews, redshank and greenshank take to the fields. The little dunlin hunch their shoulders and hunker down in the salt marsh grasses. Philibíns, as we call the lapwings, stand amidst comrades in tight-knit bunches, their topknots dancing in the blast.

In various of the West Cork bays, sprat spectaculars continue into March, the shoals up to a mile long, as evidenced by the birds that ride the sea above them or descend upon them from the sky. The sea is teeming with sprat; they can be smelled in the streets of Kinsale.

It is thrilling to watch the shoals from the cliffs above, the gannets rocketing in formation into the sea — pow-pow-pow! — throwing up spray like trails of shells exploding, the kittiwakes dancing over the surface, the razorbills, guillemots, divers and mergansers dipping and diving and surfacing with beaks full of fish, gulped down before they dive again. Big grey seals are there, too, a thrill for my grandchildren from the English midlands, where seals are seen only in zoos. Fat bulls raise their flat heads and roly-poly necks to look at us; the heads of the smaller females glint like lacquered netballs in the sun.

How the gannets avoid spearing a seal, or pinioning a merganser, amazes me. They spin at the last minute before hitting the water; there cannot be more than a square yard of vacant surface into which to dive. To be hit by a gannet, diving at fifty miles an hour, with a six-inch dagger beak, a body a yard across and weighing as much as a goose, would surely be life-threatening for the victim. But they are experts in the air and I have never heard of one impaling a bird or mammal, hitting only the target fish.

The winter sprats are much larger than the summer whitebait that appear on London restaurant menus, often served straight from the freezer. A mixture of baby herring, sprat, sand eels and other juvenile fish, they are sometimes driven ashore by shoals of voracious mackerel.

One night, perhaps three years after we had set up home in Ireland and the boys were still young, I stepped out of our house and noticed that the low waves were bright with phosphorescence and seemed to roll unusually slowly and viscously onto the rocks. The phosphorescence was the scales of a million whitebait and the rocks were coated with stranded fish, the rock pools filled with them. I called the family out to view the silver shore. It was enchanting. Together, in the moonlight, we harvested basins of the bounty from the rock pools. I still have the photographs of the fish: unfortunately I didn't have the technology to photograph the silver coast.

Flash-fried or deep-fried whitebait are immensely filling fish. Alfred Lord Tennyson's brother, Frederick, a less successful poet, wrote a couple of lapidary lines after a bout of whitebait-overindulgence: 'I had a vision very late/ After a dinner of whitebait ...' Thomas Love Peacock, the 19th-century satirist and noted gourmand, also recalled a memorable fish-fest, noting that: 'Perch, mullet, eels and salmon, all were there/ And whitebait, daintiest of our fishy fare ....' However, in

Ireland, or at least in West Cork, whitebait seems to be little eaten.

A sprat lays as many as thirty thousand eggs (herrings lay eighty thousand). On winter nights, the shoals come up the bay, attracted to the pier lights, and are easily gaffed with hook and line. They are as delicious as fresh Spanish sardines, and so rich in oil that one can rarely manage more than a dozen. The best way to cook them is to fry them crisply after first tossing them about in a bag of flour laced with chili powder.

Local fishermen tell me that there is no market for sprats and they would rather not catch them at all than have to dump the harvest back in the sea. Irish fishermen are increasingly aware that the sea's bounty cannot be pillaged without consequences; the sprat feed the herrings and many other commercial fish. When the sprat shoals move on, good-sized pollock, whiting and hake are trawled close inshore.

~

As the month ends, the weather is, indeed, often 'lamb-like' but can change on a whim. On a March Sunday, we drove west in blinding sunlight to walk the Sheep's Head peninsula, a high ridge between Bantry Bay and Dunmanus Bay, now a way-marked route and one of the finest scenic walks in Ireland. By the time we arrived, the weather had turned around, and as we walked, the horizons were no longer distant but claustrophobic, grainy with rain, the mist and sea uniting out beyond the dark rocks where white waves broke soundlessly, as if in slow motion. Beyond them, nothing: a grey veil. No wonder we are famous for our fairytales. As the sky darkened, the bare bushes, bent by the wind, seem like shawled hags, a regiment of them, retreating. Waves of mist, Poor Marys of the Mountain, swirled away below us, weaving down the wet, green hill.

Later, when we emerged from the village pub after a drink with our walking companions, it was already dark and the clouds were like swirls of ink in water crossing a half-moon as pale as the segment of a lemon. We were all in good form, as we bade each other au revoir, our veterinarian friends who sing and play their guitars, the businessman who plays the box, the pretty farmer from Tipperary who wrings sweet sounds from her tiny concertina. Good companions — we have, perhaps, found equal, but never better, wherever we have been in the world.

April

Any day now, the flocks of martins will be arriving in Ireland, followed by swallows, then swifts. Having crossed the Sahara, they pause in the reed beds of the Coto Doñana in Spain and the Camargue in France, waiting for the south-east winds to carry them to their familiar Irish eaves and barns. They will have flown five thousand miles; let us hope the weather is warm and the upper reaches of the air thick with insects to welcome them. God speed the swallows!

~

In April, the rhododendron that towers above the small gate lodge at the entrance to an old estate at Kincragie bursts into glorious flower. Bedecked with crimson blossoms larger than the palm of one's hand, it is a dramatic sight as one takes the dog-leg turn and suddenly sees it, soaring resplendent against the sky, particularly when the sky is blue.

One can hardly see the dark-green leaves for the blossom. Rhododendron is a curse in many old forests and wild areas of Ireland, and eradication programmes, with volunteer students and others, have limited success in its control in Killarney National Park, Glengarriff Woods, the Vee in County Tipperary and elsewhere. But when it blooms on a tree thirty-foot tall, it is spectacular.

Approaching it, one walks up the hill from the sea, passing the quaint Church of Ireland chapel with its laurels and shrubberies, and is immediately submerged in the shade of the tall trees that grow over the road above and below and cut out the light at any time of day. On one's right, a sort of mini-cliff face of shaly rock rises twelve feet above the road, colonised with maidenhair and hart's tongue ferns, mosses of all kinds and tresses of toadflax with small blue flowers. If there has been rain, springs spill from the crevices and fall into the roadside drain, splashing merrily down to the sea. The air is slightly damp, almost misty. Tennyson, author of atmospheric bitter-sweet lines such as 'The woods decay, the woods decay and fall,/ The vapours weep their burthen to the ground . . . .' would have loved it here. It is the quintessential West Cork woodland, like Parknasilla, like Glengarriff — old woods, deep-green laurel forests and water. And then one turns the dog-leg in the road, coming out into light with the little gate lodge and the resplendent rhododendron rising high above it and the dark driveway stretching away into mystery beneath the shade of giant redwood trees.

How lucky we are to have old Kincragie House and estate as part of the village: and what a pity the village has never managed to acquire it as an amenity. Once the residence of the Earl of Shannon, who, like rich and idle landlords everywhere in these islands, maintained exemplary gardens and planted exotic trees on his estate, it changed hands upon his death, finally being bought by a German family in the 1950s; but they soon left and, as the story goes — and there are many different stories — the ownership passed into the hands of various German banks, no single one of which, over the decades, has been able to establish clear title, and thus this outstanding property has lain abandoned for some sixty years.

During these years, the caretakers, the first appointed by the German owners — who removed, apparently, to America, then to South America — and the second taking the job upon himself after his uncle, the first caretaker, died, couldn't hope to protect the walled orchards, gardens and woods and Kincragie House itself from decay. The original caretaker was paid and lived in the gate lodge; then his pay stopped arriving, it seems. After his death, his nephew occupied the lodge every second weekend, lighting a fire within. Meanwhile, the walled orchards, the pathways and the grand house fell into dereliction.

When we first saw it, twenty years ago, it remained salvageable, with the roof still on and the outbuildings and orchard walls intact. Briars had not yet blocked the pathways around the house, and Japanese knotweed, the most destructive of alien invaders, hadn't yet burgeoned to subsume more than an acre of meadow as it does now, spreading each year. The field across the stream from our yard puts up a large number of early purple orchids in May and, as the spring and summer progress, becomes a haze of yellow bartsia, self-heal, meadow buttercups, fleabane, daisies, knapweed, meadow vetchling and other vetches, trefoils and clovers. Horses from the riding stables graze there and a lovely sight they make when we look out our windows, horses white, black and roan, with rabbits hopping, grooming or basking all around them. Quite regularly we see a fox pass, or a fine cock pheasant, glorious in full breeding colours, strut across the sward as if he owned it.

In summer, stands of thistles provide a food source for the spiky black caterpillars of painted lady butterflies, and ragwort — a not entirely welcome weed — is host to the black-and-amber striped caterpillars of the glossy, daylight-flying cinnabar moths. Flag irises grow in a damp corner and, on the briars around the edges, blackberries burgeon in good years. Butterflies in their dozens flit over the grass, meadow browns, ringlets and common blues, while small tortoiseshells, red admirals and the various whites haunt the briar flowers, and spotted woods spiral and scud in the shady boundary of the beeches and on the hedges of blackthorn, whitethorn and ash. The woods and meadows of 'Cragie remain a delight for locals and visitors, who walk or exercise their dogs there.

The driveway to the house, albeit mossy and unused, is extant and bordered by magnificent trees, including Monterey cypresses of enormous girth and giant redwoods that soar to 120 feet (40 metres) tall. Myrtles are abundant, and holm oaks and sweet chestnuts plentiful in these woods. One of the finest of all the Earl's arboreal legacies is the huge cork oak standing in front of the Courtmacsherry Hotel, once his summer home. It is said to be one of only two cork oaks in Ireland. When, on summer or festival weekends, Billy Adams at the hotel sends strobe beams into the night sky, the rough, fissured bark, the convoluted branches and the millions of small, evergreen leaves look stunningly beautiful as the beams move across them.

~

It was on an April day in 2007 that our beloved dog, Nicky, disappeared. Nicky had replaced Sally, our previous springer spaniel, after her death from diabetes in 1995. I often mentioned Sally in *A Place Near Heaven*, my previous book on West Cork. Therein, I noted that, on the morning after she had passed away, a certain small boy, now grown to manhood, told us that he had sobbed himself to sleep and had used up an entire box of tissues with his tears. Nicky, another liver-and-white springer, came to replace Sally, and after a decent interval her affectionate nature, loyalty and enthusiasm began to fill the gap in our household and our hearts. She had foxy-red flashes on either side of her muzzle, a feature inherited from some golden cocker or red setter that had featured in her genetic mix.

Like Sally, she sometimes transgressed through pure enthusiasm or affection. She howled when Marie went out. She would follow her about our rambling house — all the houses, bar the cottage, were rambling — and I could locate my wife by first locating the dog. When Marie went out to teach, Nicky would sit by the door and emit howls, eerie noises and, eventually, high-pitched yelps as she awaited her return, often a vigil of many hours.

I didn't always take kindly to fair Nicky's cacophony: it isn't easy to catch the rhythm of a sentence when a howling hound is filling the air with plaintive moans. I would order her to silence, and this would work, temporarily. She would lie on her belly, abashed, ashamed, and wagging her tail while looking at me with contrite eyes. But before long she would start up again. The only time these mournful arias didn't happen

— and this will stretch my reader's credulity — was when Marie remembered to tell her in a confiding but firm tone that she had to go out but that she would be back later without fail. Then Nicky would relax. When I announced my intention to go for a walk, she would leap, as only springers can leap — all four legs leaving the ground — and bark in excitement. Off we would go, Nicky running ahead, rushing into every briar brake, dyke and bog hole, running along the edge of cliff-top ditches and scaring the life out of me. And it was on one such day, when Marie was abroad on a short holiday, that Nicky vanished into thin air.

In the column I wrote that week, I said: 'Our beloved old dog disappeared the other day: I believe she was dog-napped. Either that, or she dematerialised, and I don't believe that can happen to dogs. A spaceship might have beamed her up, but I don't believe that either. The circumstances were mysterious. I'll explain what happened, and you tell me . . .'

At this time, Nicky was twelve years old, and while her hearing and sight were not as finely tuned as of yore, she was by no means deaf, blind or senile. When I last saw her, she was bouncing through a field of long grass, springing almost as high as she used to when she was a three-year-old. She had a smile on her face. I don't subscribe to anthropomorphism, but her eyes were shining and she was clearly as happy as could be.

At the bottom of the field, I took out binoculars to see how the young ravens were doing in their nest on the side of a rocky cove over the sea. There were three large fledglings inside, shiny black and ready to fly any day. I watched them for five minutes, then turned to continue along the cliffs. There wasn't a soul to be seen, in any direction. Nicky the Dog wasn't around either, so I assumed she was snuffling about in the nearby ditch, following her nose.

I whistled for her as I walked off and then, thirty yards farther on, sat down in the sun at a favourite spot and looked out at the Old Head of Kinsale, seven miles away. When Nicky still hadn't joined me after five minutes, I concluded that she'd become bored while I was watching the ravens and had walked home alone. Home was only ten minutes away via paths she had walked a thousand times before. Such behaviour on her part wouldn't have been unusual. She sometimes took the notion to return alone — perhaps she thought Marie might be back from holidays. I was sure that she'd be there, waiting, at the front door, when I returned.

Thinking no more of it, I followed our usual circuit through the woods full of white ramsons and bluebells and down onto the beach, and home from there. I dawdled, enjoying the sights en route; I investigated the rock pools and so on. When I got home, Nicky wasn't there. An hour later, she still hadn't returned.

I walked back to the cliffs and scanned the walls of the cove with binoculars. The tide was out now, so the boulders below were exposed. Risking life and limb, I climbed down the steep sides and searched behind and under any boulders large enough to conceal her. I could find no trace. The slope above me wasn't entirely perpendicular — although almost so — and was covered in light vegetation. Had she fallen, she would hardly have been killed outright and would have barked in distress.

As I walked home, I met a woman who told me there'd been some people picnicking farther along the path, in a cove by the woods. Although Nicky would never have gone with strangers, I thought she might have stopped if they'd offered her a titbit from their hamper, and perhaps she was still there. But these people weren't to be found.

By chance, Dara and Fintan were both home at the time. We searched widely, the boys and I, on that day and on the day that followed, returning again and again to the cove and the cliffs and ditches all around. Nicky had disappeared in, literally, a matter of minutes in an open field, twenty feet from an overgrown cliff face protected by a ditch of furze and blackthorn. And there hadn't been a human soul around.

I couldn't imagine anyone stealing an old dog deliberately. She was friendly and, I suppose, had she taken that (longer) route home, she might have been tempted by a sweet biscuit from the picnickers: she, like her predecessor, Sally — and, apparently, many springers — was diabetic and we never gave her sweet things. It is conceivable that they thought she was lost — although she had a collar — and decided to take her home.

She had been with us from the first year of her life, and the house felt strangely empty without her. The children may have been away from home for periods of time, or my wife, or myself, but she was always there, always in her bed below the stairs when one came down in the morning, always following one to the fireside at night, always leaving the sitting room and trotting off to bed when one stood up from the armchair to turn out the lights.

My sons had to leave the day after her disappearance. Alone in the house, I missed her company. Poor dog, I thought, that this should happen to her in old age! I kept believing that she would turn up outside the front door, barking to be let in.

I posted 'Lost Dog' notices on telegraph poles, in the shop in Courtmacsherry and in the filling station and post office in Timoleague. The following week I wrote: 'Following the publication of my column about the mystery of our missing dog, fourteen readers were good enough to phone the *Examiner* or to email me to offer advice or help. Their concern says a lot about the kindness still abroad in the Ireland we live in. The warmth of their response gladdened the heart while, in the event, the reality saddened it.' Regrettably, I had bad news for them. The unfortunate dog had been found, dead. How it happened compounds the enigma of her disappearance. I cannot believe it is sinister. But there is one niggling thing.

The first and only sighting was reported in a telephone call three days after she had vanished. Dara, who had come home again, took the call. The male caller had seen one of the 'Lost Dog' notices. His description sounded ominously like our much-loved Nicky. When he'd been out walking in the half-dark that evening, he had come upon a good-looking dog, a springer, he thought, lying dead above the tide line on Howe Strand, two miles across Courtmacsherry Bay from the cove at Coomalacha where I'd last seen her. It was after ten at night when he called, and the tide was coming in fast. If she was still there in the morning, he would check the details and call us back.

He did call us and from his, now clearer, description, we drew our sad conclusions. I drove to the beach and found that, sure enough, it was Nicky. Dara had brought a spade and he buried her twenty yards above the high tide mark, where the sea wouldn't reach her.

At home, the house continued to be strange without her: it continued to be strange for many days afterwards. My wife, who was in Spain, was told. She was, of course, affected. She, more than anyone, had looked after the dog.

It is still a mystery how Nicky died. As I said, she was bouncing through the long grass beside me as we walked down the field and I stood above the cove, watching ravens in the nest. If she had fallen down the cliff and was injured, she would have barked, and I'd have heard. There was almost total silence, no waves crashing in, only the background hum of nature of an April morning. Also when, an hour afterwards, I returned and scanned the steeply sloping cliff face, I saw no track of her fall through the vegetation. When I climbed down into the cove, I found no trace of her amongst the rocks.

The tide had been only half out at the time she disappeared. If she had fallen, and survived the fall, she would have found herself in shallow water with rock platforms nearby, onto which she could have clawed herself to safety; springers are adept swimmers. Alternatively, if she had been killed in the fall, I would have found her body on the shore when I climbed down.

It is possible that she *was* killed in the fall and washed out by the falling tide before I returned to search for her. But minutes after she had gone missing, I had been scanning the sea's surface with binoculars and I had seen nothing unusual. Her coat was 70 per cent white, very white; even in death, it was still vivid. Being an old dog, she could, I suppose, have had a heart attack as she lost her footing on the ditch above the ravine, and fallen straight into the sea and been washed away. There is also the possibility that she was hurt in the fall and couldn't swim but I dismiss this, because she would surely have barked for a short while at least, and I would have heard her.

We will never know. Strangest of all is the fact that, as her body lay there on the lonely strand as lissom as in life, *rigor mortis* long past, one thing was missing. Her collar was gone. How it could have opened or come over her head will forever be a mystery.

We now had to accept that this four-legged family member had met a fate beyond our ken. We were offered a nice pup to replace her but weren't sure if we wanted to take on another dog just then, or ever. I well remembered the mongrel that was my inseparable companion when I was a boy, just as my sons and daughters – now grown up – would, no doubt, always remember Nicky.

Looking out our first floor windows on misty spring mornings, the rabbits thumping and humping in the field would remind us of how Nicky loved to have a go at chasing them. But springers aren't built for speed and the rabbits loped away, unhurried. We wondered if they were playing tricks on her, but she had seemed to enjoy it.

~

On April days that are as warm as midsummer, as they often are, shield bugs, hover flies, bumblebees and butterflies are all on the wing. Swallows and martins again split the skies, skimming the earth or spiralling into the blue, spinning and diving, crisscrossing their comrades in the upper air. Newly awakened from hibernation, the peacock and small tortoiseshell butterflies are in vivid colour. Sometimes one comes upon the desiccated remains of small tortoiseshells behind curtains or cupboards, wrecks of great beauty, the bodies of those that sought refuge in our homes in winter but didn't survive to fly again in the new spring. The dry wings are like scraps of vivid tapestry. Peacocks can live for almost a year. They feed on sally blossom when they wake in spring and sometimes migrate as far as Iceland.

Give me Ireland on a sunny day, when things are green and a light breeze blows. I would not exchange it for any Mediterranean shore where the sun rules and there's not a whisper of air to ease the heat.

Below the cliffs at Coolim, the sea lies like a great pool of blue enamel bordered by black headlands, with slopes of yellow gorse pouring down to brown cliffs potholed with caves and indented with white coves and beaches. To the east, the long finger of the Old Head of Kinsale extends far out into the ocean, its ruined towers and gleaming lighthouse silhouetted against small puffs of distant cloud. As I watch, two terns pass back and forth in the distance, white specks above the ocean: sandwich terns, with black caps and scarlet beaks, quartering the enormous breadth of water as they search the surface for small fish. Once spotted, they rocket down to seize them, every bit as spectacularly as gannets. There isn't a boat on the sea, or any evidence of my fellow humans other than the ruins, the lighthouse and a few faraway farm houses across the bay. The nearest habitation is Coolmaine Castle, two miles distant, set in the new lawns and woodland created when it was bought in the early 1990s by Roy Disney, grand-nephew of the cartoonist and film producer, whose antecedents were Irish, I'm told.

By April, the sea pinks on the cliff sides are showing, and the scurvy grass is covered in white flowers. How convenient that it grew close to the sea, this important source of vitamin C for old-time sailors facing long voyages and the curse of scurvy which, at best, rotted their gums, and at worst, took their lives. At Coolim and the Old Head, herring gulls and kittiwakes sit on their nesting ledges below the pink splashes of sea pinks, and fulmar, guillemots and razorbills colonise every cranny. In shallow water, opossum shrimps and their various crustacean cousins cruise in clouds: they will provide the growing fuel for the baby pollock, herring and mixed sprat soon to follow. Gobies and shannies return to the rock pools as the inshore sea temperature rises. Sea lettuce, too, unfortunately, returns to the mudflats and sandbanks. Various schemes are mooted to remove it, even to harvest it. But at the time of writing, little funding for public works is available and little seed money for private enterprise, this thanks to the mismanagement of our economy by our government and bankers during the Paper Tiger years.

On the cliff, too, where a heaving pie of black-and-blue gooseflesh and pin-feathers filled the cup of the ravens' nest a month ago, there now sit four enormous, glossy birds. Only the pink edges of their gapes betray that they are fledglings. They are an essay in patience. Day by day, they sit, adult-size, waiting for the moment to come when they have put on that last ounce of bodyweight which will give their wings the strength to fly. They had better get it right — the sea is thirty feet directly below; they will either glide and rise, or fall and drown. I'm sure there will be no tragedies. They are already robust birds and one wonders how the parents manage to find the sheer volume of food necessary to feed them. One adult stands guard on a fence post on the cliff above the nest; as I approach, it takes flight to drive off a chough that had entered its air space. Its mate is, presumably, off foraging. While tender fledglings are already in the nests of many wild birds, they are less threatened by ravens than by marauding cats. We see them even at night, skulking in the lanes far from any human habitation: they range far and wide. Unfortunately, badgers and foxes, consumed by the urge to find mates, throw caution to the wind. They lie prone and bloody on the verges, casualties of road-kill, a feature of almost any rural journey we make at this time of year.

Homeward-bound from the sea, I pass along a narrow avenue of fuchsia in new leaf, and speckled wood butterflies pirouette around my knees when I pause to admire it. French gorse in the hedge is at its most glorious now; the goat willows are covered in pastel-green catkins and the sycamores in young, red leaves. Bluebells are filling up the woods, vying with the onion-smelling white ramsons and delicate wood anemones for space. They are so dense, one must stay on the path or risk trampling them. Now, day by day as April ends and May comes in, the woodland floor blues over with bluebells growing denser and denser like pixels until at last all is a purple haze, saturated in a deep, unbroken blue. Robert Frost memorably wrote about stopping one winter evening to watch the 'woods fill up with snow'. On those late spring evenings you could, if you had the patience, watch the Irish woods fill up with blue.

∼

For some years now, we have had a pair of wood pigeons that come to bathe in the stream that runs between the pebbles in the courtyard. I think it is the pair that annually nests in our sycamore, or their progeny. The local killer cat has given up trying to stalk them. To sneak up on a pigeon is nigh impossible — it seems to have eyes in the back of its head. In fact, pigeons have a visual range of 340 degrees, leaving little or no blind spot, especially when the bird is bopping along, head dipping and rising like one of those toy dogs in the back windows of cars.

Meanwhile, the woodcock, a strange-looking bird indeed, can literally see what's going on behind it. In the course of evolution, its eyes have moved to a position high on its head and far to the sides, giving a visual field of a full 360 degrees. Thus, it can see in all directions at once. Even with its beak buried up to its nostrils as it probes for food, it can still keep a look-out for predators approaching from any point of the compass. It is no wonder that this miracle of nature looks bizarre. Its ears are below its eyes to the front of its skull. This is because there was no other place to put them but, as any shooter will tell you, in the deep, dark forests where woodcock roam, these ears serve them well. Birds have been around a whole lot longer than humans. Fossils of the first creatures with feathers indistinguishable from those of modern birds have been found in slate deposits in Germany and dated at 150 million years old. Bones from herons, vultures and kingfisher were found in London clay laid down 38 to 54 million years ago. We are but johnny-come-latelys here.

While the wood pigeons coo dementedly, as wood pigeons do, a song thrush sings each evening from the flowering cherry in the garden. With its mate, it forages in the field, along with pairs of blackbirds, chaffinches, grey crows and magpies. A reader of my column telephoned me to ask how he might keep magpies from stealing the eggs of thrushes in his garden, as happened last year. I didn't know what to advise. Some would say shoot the magpies — but they are such elegant birds. As I write, one is sitting on the bird table outside my window, its black wings intermittently turquoise or gold as it catches the evening sun. As long as there have been song birds, there have been magpies. Nature, as we know, has its checks and balances, and perhaps it's best we don't interfere. We have done enough harm already to Mother Earth, damaged its water and polluted its air. Since the exploitation of fossil fuel and the industrial revolution, human enterprise has taken a huge toll on our planet's resources and its biological diversity. Under stones and in the bark of trees, in the soil itself and on the sea floor, humble things protect our future from unknown disasters. None are superfluous: they have kept us going until now. Microscopic nematode worms, ten million to the square metre of topsoil, control and destroy the many pests that would otherwise devastate our crops. We kill them when we use artificial fertiliser. When we annihilate an organism, we simultaneously murder an unknown soldier upon whom our survival may depend. As the crisis facing the planet worsens, we begin to understand that to keep this huge living organism alive and healthy, we must treasure and nurture it, rather than poison its essential parts.

Our future is challenged by burgeoning population growth. Global development versus global destruction becomes the issue. We must arrive at self-sustaining systems before we reach the point of no return and, like the Easter Islanders, perish through ignorance, competitiveness and the worship of false gods. The challenge is to evolve systems that will keep the land, seas and air of this planet alive and guarantee the future of the entire human family.

The economist demands that we exploit every natural resource, and champions GM seeds and chemical fertiliser; the environmentalist champions conservation. The one threatens the atmosphere and the land, the other locks the Third World poor into inefficient agricultural methods incapable of feeding their increasing populations. As we allow the forests to be felled and the oceans' great resources to be fished to desolation, every thinking person knows that enlightened global governance of natural resources is the only solution. But how can this be achieved? Globalism and world governance are rife with dangers. What can we individuals do? As Patrick Kavanagh, the poet, said, 'To know fully even one field or one land is a lifetime's experience.' Our only recourse is to raise our voices in protest and in demand. Change happens when the voice of the majority demanding it drowns out all others. Every change that has been effected in those aspects of nature within human control started with the voice or actions of an individual; an individual started NGOs which have, for example, put an end to wide-scale whaling.

We are all of us, naturally, absorbed in the personal and the local. It is natural that some of my neighbours get hot under the collar about the decimation of salmon by cormorants in the river Bandon or of sea-trout in the Argideen by mink. These 'sport' fish are ours, not theirs, to harry! Visiting anglers bring income to local providers of accommodation, food and services, who, naturally, resent such predations. Feeding cormorants and mink is not their priority.

Similarly, our local fishermen would hardly have been as enthusiastic as the small crowd that gathered on Courtmacsherry Bay one April afternoon to see a young grey seal released after convalescence at the Seal Sanctuary in Dublin. In Dublin, it was fed on herrings; it would now begin to feed on the fisherman's fish. Defying nature and nurturing seals that would otherwise not survive will, they fear, create a 'cormorant situation', cormorants having greatly increased in number, courtesy of anglers who have stocked the rivers with salmon parr, a readily available food source for the birds.

Although we are absorbed in the personal and the local, turning a blind eye to issues affecting the fate of the world is no longer an option now that human activity threatens natural cycles. Human behaviour can save the world or destroy it.

~

In April there are, traditionally, showers. April showers are enshrined in song and in weather lore. Ireland wouldn't be Ireland without some rain. As we look out on Kincragie field from our dining room, rain curtains the view while night begins to fall. Nevertheless, the horses graze on, the magpies continue to build their big domed nest in a tall tree against the grey sky, the rabbits hop, oblivious of the weather, their white scuts bouncing through the grass, and the cock pheasant walks elegantly and unconcerned into the drizzle. Rain doesn't faze nature a bit.

One evening, Marie drove a friend whose car had broken down to a special rehearsal of the Butlerstown Variety Group. Like the hundred-plus members of the group, she faithfully attends rehearsals for months on end after which we, their neighbours, are treated to a marvellous show. Farmers, fishermen, shopkeepers, laid-off builders — sometimes two or three members of the same family — contribute their time and talent to making it a success. The hall, seating 250 people, is filled to bursting every night for seven nights and, in recent years, extra performances have to be put on to cater for enthusiasts who arrive from far and wide. The atmosphere is wonderful and there is not a dull moment or flat note from start to finish.

There is no question of West Cork being a boring place where rustication transforms previously cosmopolitan persons into the living dead. Far from it. Other rural locations may be mind-numbing, but not the towns or villages of the south-west. Artists and film actors, film producers and writers settle here: some continue working part-time in the world from which they have fled, making whistle-stop visits or brief tours abroad. Meanwhile, locally there is plenty to keep the mind occupied, with music of all kinds, poetry readings, literary festivals, book launches, gallery openings and theatre. Furthermore, we are not far from Cork city and the Opera House, cinemas and theatres there.

Alexander Pope wrote a witty ditty entitled 'Epistle to Miss Blount, On Her Leaving the Town, After the Coronation' in which he laments the fate of the lady who '. . . went from Opera, park, assembly, play/ To morning walks, and prayers three hours a day [. . .] Up to her godly garret after seven/ There starve and pray, for that's the way to heaven.' I think he would not find such a lady hereabouts. Those I know seem to enjoy parties and gatherings; they may well pray, but are certainly not at a loss for entertainment.

While the Butlerstown show is biannual, every year there is the Rossmore Drama Festival in which amateur and semi-professional companies from all over Ireland put on internationally acclaimed plays at the village hall in Rossmore. The companies participating are all prize-winners in a national competition; and nationally we are no slouches in the realm of acting or writing. We are, indeed, a theatrical people — not histrionic, in the manner of the Mediterraneans, but measured, dramatic storytellers with a verbal tradition millennia old. The quality of the plays staged at Rossmore would satisfy even the most exacting dramaturge and are simply highly enjoyable for theatrical innocents like myself.

Chamber musicians come to entertain us once or twice a year in the glorious setting of Bantry House, one of the finest stately homes in Ireland. Also at Bantry, there is the annual West Cork Literary Festival with internationally esteemed writers, talking, signing books and 'What-ever-you're-having-yourself . . .' The natural friendliness of West Cork disarms even the most shy or stand-offish, and it is not at all unusual to see prominent literary figures engaged in conversation with locals at the bar — and why wouldn't they be? The Irish are amongst the best retailers of stories in the world, and the oral tradition is as robust as ever in these parts.

At Courtmacsherry, we have a story-telling festival in late summer when yarn-spinners from all over Ireland weave their spell to sell-out audiences at the Courtmacsherry Hotel. Across the bay, there is annual opera at Burren House with soloists from Covent Garden, Scottish Opera and the English National Opera.

Folk music and fiddle festivals abound. In local pubs one may find oneself only a few feet away from performers one has previously seen only as specks in one's opera glasses at the Albert Hall. West Cork is infinitely relaxed and human. Affectation or posturing would be risible in the ambience of the venues where many fine musicians play.

Every weekend night in the pubs in our village and others one can enjoy the lively and competent backbone of hard-working local musicians with, sometimes, internationally known blow-ins playing alongside them. In Clonakilty, there may be seven pubs with live music on a Saturday night, from honky-tonk, through country, to trad, jazz and techno. There are also *seisiúns* of Irish music, where all are welcome to join in, and a mixed dozen or more of fiddlers, banjo-players, squeeze-box artists, *bodhrán* players, guitarists, *uilleann* pipers, country singers, *sean-nós* singers and tin-whistle maestros provide wholesome, wild and skirling music, to be enjoyed by an enthusiastic audience at no cost at all. This tradition hasn't changed during our twenty years in this kind climate. The only hindrance to it has been the drink-drive laws which have cut a swathe through inter-village rambling since we first came. However, there is always the device of the designated driver who drinks only fruit juice and gets the celebrants safely home.

Before passing on to May, I must record a fascinating drama witnessed by one of Fintan's pals on the village pier last April. When he told me 'a group of hawks' had arrived, I feared it was a flight of fancy: he made it sound as 'everyday' as a flock of sparrows. Hawks rarely travel in groups, except on migration. Kestrels hover alone; sparrowhawks rocket through forest glades like solitary grim reapers; peregrines are most often seen as a lone speck in the sky. But, no, he insisted: a group of four had suddenly arrived at the pier, pursued by clouds of screaming gulls, chattering jackdaws and heckling rooks.

They circled, despite the harassment, stocky, brownish birds, with broad-based wings, pointed at the tip. Then a wood-pigeon flew out of a tree on the village street, heading out over the bay. And now the picture fell into place. One hawk spotted it and flew fast and straight as an arrow in pursuit, striking it in mid-air as the others followed close behind. The unfortunate pigeon exploded into a cloud of feathers — a 'fright moult', so called — and was then carried for a hundred yards or so until it was dropped into the sea, where it struggled to swim for a moment before sinking. All the time, the other three hawks had kept close company with the killer, despite the tumult of outraged birds all around.

It was, clearly, a family of peregrines, and the parents were teaching their offspring how to hunt. The family was apparently well fed; they didn't need the food source in this case. I have heard of similar behaviour, of an adult peregrine catching a pigeon, carrying it aloft and then dropping it repeatedly and giving a fledgling an opportunity to try its skill at recapturing the disorientated bird.

The fledgling failed. As the pigeon winged desperately for freedom, an adult would again descend upon it at, perhaps, one hundred miles per hour and snatch it in the air to carry it a distance and release it again. Nature is intensely cruel. But, at least, unlike the cat playing with the mouse, this was a tutorial. Killing is the peregrine's sustenance and trade. It does not have a dish of high-protein KittyBitz to resort to.

May

The evenings grow long again. There's a *Gray's-Elegy-in-a-Country-Churchyard* feeling in the air. Across the bay, a herd of Friesians winds slowly up the hill on the way home for milking. One can faintly hear them lowing as they follow one another in single file.

On the green patch at the end of the village, children are playing, big ones and small ones together, their calls and squeals carrying on the still air. It's good to see them abroad at this time of the evening — summer isn't far off now. When I pass again twenty minutes later, the light is almost gone and their mothers stand at their front doors, calling them in. Like Gray's ploughman, but reluctant rather than tired, the children homeward plod their weary way, 'and leave the world to darkness and to me'.

~

We have a song thrush that sings its heart out at any old time of day and always in the evenings. It mustn't have much to do. It sings from a branch high up in a beech tree with the sky blue behind it and a gentle breeze stirring the new green leaves, shining and trembling in the sun.

Lovelier weather, a lovelier song, a lovelier setting I could not imagine. Beneath the beeches are bloom mats of flowers, primroses along the stream bank, bluebells and violets, wild garlic, meadow buttercups and red campion, sanicle and stitchwort and every kind of weed one could imagine, sorrel and docks, tutsan and ferns. The hart's tongue, male ferns and lady ferns are all unfurling, their tips like baubles or hairy molly caterpillars or ammonite fossil shells.

In May, there is of course the dawn chorus to wake us with an unscored avian cacophony, and the demented cooing of wood pigeons to keep us awake when we try to go back to sleep. During the day, robins, wrens, tits and chaffinches pipe seemingly spontaneously. But the song of the song thrush surpasses all the others.

Besides intermittent afternoon concerts, our beech-tree thrush gives a sustained performance every evening from seven until half-past nine. I ask myself what is his partner doing while he sings chorus after chorus to the sunset, trying out new warbles, throaty chuckles and thrills? Sitting in her nest, listening as I am? Admiring the cadenzas, the grace notes and thinking what a fine fellow I've got here?

Perhaps she is lulled to sleep, feeling comfortable and secure, with the warmth of the eggs deep in the down of her breast. She will know that it is 'himself' who is singing; no other thrush species in these islands has the characteristic of repeating its loud, clear phrase, twice over in each burst of song. By listening for this repetition, one can tell the outpourings of the song thrush from those of the mistle thrush or blackbird. But our garden blackbird continues his fluting song long after the thrush has finished; it's dark before he stops.

In contrast to the song thrush's warblings, the utterances of birds contrast dramatically. The 'yackety-yackety-yack!' of the magpie's machine-gun staccato outside the window might send a visitor from Baghdad or Beirut diving for the floor. Magpies are certainly no danger to us humans, but for a few months each year they do pose a threat to garden birds. Otherwise, however, they are useful citizens of nature's kingdom, feeding on insects, clearing up the road kills and disposing of corpses in the wild. How often does one find a dead bird, wood mouse, vole, rat, stoat, hedgehog, badger or fox? These creatures, too, die of natural causes and they don't all go underground to do so or obligingly bury themselves as their last act on earth.

Magpies spend three-quarters of their lives foraging on the ground. If we witness magpie murders in the garden, it may be partly our own fault. When gardens are neatly trimmed, the owners can find birds' nests easily and the magpies can too. It isn't surprising that some householders are deeply shocked after seeing a synchronised magpie raid on the family of the friendly robins or blue tits that they've watched build their nests and industriously feed their offspring. Now, they suddenly hear the tommy-gun chatter of a magpie onslaught and the panic-stricken cries of small birds. They rush out to see pink chicks carried off like meat on butchers' hooks, only the hooks are the shining black bills of a magpie pair, ferrying them to their young.

The magpies kill for only a short season and largely only to feed their chicks. But the cat stalking in the brambles kills gratuitously and as often as it can, not for food but for sport. Its victims are not only nestlings but fledglings hiding in the undergrowth, still reliant on their parents for food. For those who enjoy birds in the hedges, now is the time of year to bell the cat.

~

According to the old calendar, the feast of Bealtaine, occurring in the month of May, begins the Irish summer. May, with its rough winds, clears away the debris, throws down the last dead leaves, cleans the world for the new. Then, everything grows, wildflowers burst from the earth and the trees put on leaves in millions. Horst, my German friend in Kerry, sends me, in the post, a handful of chanterelle mushrooms, newly born.

The tonnage of vegetation that springs from the earth is surely an annual miracle revealed before our eyes. I say 'miracle' because for all our science and explanations, we still do not know from where, as Dylan Thomas put it, comes the force that 'through the green fuse drives the flower'. Science explains it is a matter of light, of nutrients, of the urge for reproduction. And science deserves respect for the great work it has done. But the planet must first turn to the light, must continue to spin in the cycle that brings heat and rain, makes soil anew, and feeds the creatures that inhabit and improve it, that puts up flowers which bees will pollinate, and moves the winds to move the seeds to colonise new pastures. And all this seems a miracle to me.

At times, one can almost hear the growing and dying of the vegetable world which, if we let it, would colonise every human artefact in a few short years. My son brought back photos he'd taken of Angkor Wat in Cambodia, once the seat of a king of kings, its mist-capped towers and sumptuous palaces all now colonised by vines and creepers, nature triumphant and outliving man.

Our staff and our sustenance is, of course, the greenery that regenerates year upon year. It's as well we humans cannot consume most of it — the leaves on the trees, the gorse on the hillsides. Otherwise we'd surely eat ourselves into starvation, devouring the homes and sustenance of the very life forms that sustain us, upon whose unpaid work we rely. These thankless creatures aerate the earth, pollinate the crops, reseed degraded land and seed remote islands. It's no wonder Gandhi would not step on an ant.

~

Nowadays, in May, the weather is more often beautiful than not. In our twenty years here, we've seen the climate patterns shift so that late spring and early summer are the best months and it is a brave man who, following tradition, takes his summer holidays in the latterly uncertain climates of July or August, and risks incarcerating himself and his wife in a rented chalet with fractious children while the skies bucket down outside.

It is not always so: there have been good Julys and Augusts but, increasingly, the weather in these months is a bagatelle. Certainly, over the last decade, April, May and June have been far lovelier months than those that followed and these are now the months during which we urge our friends and family to come and visit. One can't swim, of course, unless one is hardy, although sometimes we have found sea temperatures in late June to be better than tolerable. In June 2010, we were flopping about in the shallow water off the beach at Broadstrand for twenty minutes at a time and the lengthening evenings saw men, just back from work, taking the children for a post-prandial, pre-bedtime dip.

May is delightful for its brightness and freshness, the birds in new feathers, the migrants arriving, the trees in new foliage and the long acres of the verges lighting up with buttercups that shine as if they were sprinkled with gold powder and then varnished. Primroses, violets, herb Robert, vetch, fumitory, daisies and dandelions, wild garlic and bluebells, all flower in gay profusion along the roadsides, regardless of whether they're noticed or not. It's extraordinary how many plants can cram themselves into a few yards of West Cork ditch — and that is your common or unpretentious ditch: there are exotic and specialised ditches too, which sprout cuckoo flowers, wood sorrel, wild currant and the like. There's nothing like a swathe of wild flowers to slow down the perambulating artist, amateur botanist or hedge scholar. And there's the music too, the sonorous hum of the bees — the bumbles, carders, honey and cuckoo bees, bees of all hues and tonal registers going about their leisurely business, buzzing from flower to flower, their lacquered wings catching the light.

In 'the merry month of May', there can be few more delightful ways of whiling away the time than stopping by ditches on a sunny afternoon. It was Thomas Dekker who first employed the aforesaid skipping alliteration in a poem written in 1600, while a contemporary composer called Byrd wrote a song with the same title. In Dekker's verse, the poet tells his girl, 'Sweet Peg, thou shalt be my Summer's Queen.' While this suggests that May was equally summery back in the 17th century, we have no less an authority than William Shakespeare, country-born and a man fine-tuned to the seasons, telling his lady or gentleman friend that 'Rough winds do shake the darling buds of May/ And summer's lease hath all too short a date . . .' — and who would argue with him?

However, in May, sometimes a sort of breath-held stillness overtakes the world which, if one were religious, one might call 'holy'. At the other end of summer, in September, there are such evenings too, with the heavy stillness one feels in half-dark churches when there are few worshippers or none, and time hangs suspended in the steady air. Light filtered through stained-glass windows has a density unlike the light outside. It induces a sort of over-awed silence. In the silence, whispers carry, as do the half-heard murmurs in confessional boxes and the exchanges of slippered sacristans arranging flowers.

But out of doors, when we walk the cliffs on May days, Shakespeare's world prevails. It is, indeed, a bud-shaking and hair-raising world for those who have hair to raise, a hat-lifting world for those who wear unsecured hats. On weekend walks on the Seven Heads we are treated to a rough, invigorating mixture of brilliant sunshine and powerful blasts from the north-west. Where there are fields — usually somewhat inland, a distance from the cliff brow — the dark-green, silage-grass prairies shimmer as they bend in the blast. The sea below us is as blue as the sky above but choppy with white horses, a churning, watchable sea with the waves running away from, not towards, the land, and long, green swells sweeping west to America. Sometimes, the gale catches the wave tops and a veil of fine spray pirouettes for a hundred yards over the surface like a dancer in a gossamer gown. It's wild to be out: the wind could drive one distracted; one could see things that aren't there.

Heads down, we keep going and plug up and down most of the headlands of the Seven. My cap blows off, rises twenty feet and sails two hundred yards onto the black rocks below. 'Leave it!' says the good wife. 'It's gone into the sea . . . .' But it is a cap I like and so I scramble down over the knife-sharp rocks splashed in yellow lichens and white sea ivory and find it, indeed only yards from the water. It's the climb up again that nearly does for me. It's worth it for the old cap but I'm looking forward to a sit-down at Mary O'Neill's in Butlerstown, and maybe she'll sing a rousing 'Rathlin Island' as she pulls pints behind the bar.

~

As I said in the book that inspired this book — *A Place Near Heaven: A Year in West Cork*, published in 2004 — it was skipping a stone on Courtmacsherry Bay of a tranquil summer evening that made me think of coming back to Ireland after thirty-two years living abroad, often in very beautiful or interesting places, exciting cities and out-of-the-way, unspoiled islands.

I always knew that, if I ever came home, I would make sure to live by the sea and, indeed, it was the sea that seduced me, the light on the water, the profound world beneath. The Atlantic was my love, more than the Mediterranean or the Pacific or the Indian Ocean: it was my own sea. I was born on its shores, my cradle literally looking out on Valentia Island and the 'western ocean', as Tomás Ó Crohan, author of *The Islandman*, the lapidary book of the Blasket Islands, called the Atlantic. Sea breezes would have shaken the hood of my pram.

We were not mistaken in our choice of place when we chose to set up home in Ireland. Courtmacsherry has proved, down the years, to be as full of interest as any Irish village of a few hundred souls could hope to be: and the comings and goings on the sea have made it all the more interesting. 'The shrimp boats are a-comin', and there'll be dancin' tonight', the Mississippi bayou song goes, and shrimp boats come into Courtmacsherry too and there's dancing in the Anchor Bar of Saturday nights.

Of 'human interest' were the various shipwrecked mariners that were delivered to our door when we briefly owned a guesthouse in the village, amongst them a small wiry man of well over sixty who had sailed a wooden boat — twenty-two-foot long with a free-board of just two feet above the waterline — from America, accompanied by a young Icelandic girl who had answered his advertisement for crew on the internet. They had been shipwrecked three times in the passage, and each time survived. Once he was washed overboard in a storm and, but for the fact that he was roped to the mast and the gunwales were all but under water, would not have been able to scramble back on deck. After midnight, somewhere off the Old Head of Kinsale, they had lost their mast in a gale and were towed into Courtmac by the lifeboat. They arrived at our door, cold and bedraggled but, next morning, were chipper and bright, and going about repairing their craft so as to sail on.

Another exotic arrival in the bay was *The Karma of the East*, a yacht that had left Kinsale with some local worthies aboard, sailed to Morocco, loaded up with hashish and headed home, hoping to coincide with and join the many small boats from West Cork ports that would accompany the flotilla of Tall Ships scheduled to make a gala entrance to Cork Harbour that year. Arriving off the coast too late to join the flotilla and to enjoy the cover it would provide, they lingered off the Seven Heads where their galley caught fire, this conveniently necessitating their being towed in to the quiet, unpoliced harbour of Courtmacsherry. Unfortunately for the crew, Customs and Excise officers had been expecting them, and had arranged a reception committee on the pier. Perhaps the name of the boat did them a disservice: it might have been better named for Saint Jude, the patron saint of hopeless causes.

Meanwhile, the sea continues to deliver more salubrious bounty. We get fresh fish from the boats, and the ocean that gives up the fish welcomes back our leavings — food for the crabs — on the tide. Nothing is wasted; shrimp pick over the discarded morsels and congers or dogfish chew on the bones.

The village too, being a seaside place, has a frisson one will not find in mere inland villages. In summer, we have a certain glamour here, suntanned folk promenading the street (there is only one) in their summery get-outs, and yatchies coming ashore from their sleek craft, moored alongside the small pontoon, a new addition to the pier. Even on the worst weekend of winter, there are a few visitors from Cork who have holiday homes, some of them passed down through generations. Billy Fleming, at the Anchor Bar, faithfully hires good musicians to entertain on Saturday nights, although it is hard to imagine that he makes much profit except in the 'holiday season' which, in any case, lasts no more than ten weeks. It is more a tradition than a commercial venture: the Anchor has belonged to the Flemings for two generations. Like many long-term village residents, they do not have the pressure of a large mortgage, as do some of the families who bought into the village during the Tiger boom, the husbands, and sometimes the wives also, commuting to Cork for work, fifty-five minutes away. One new resident commutes to London weekly. Her tireless travel is a testimony to the quality of life she enjoys at weekends.

As for ourselves, how lucky we were to ride the swells and ebbs of the boom time and not sink, or have a financial weight around our necks curtailing our lives. It was the benevolence of fortune; there was no clever master plan, no 'investment portfolio'. One might say some guardian angel looked after us, or that it was our parents' prayers, if such prayers are heard. We moved houses five times in our twenty years here, not to climb any property ladder, but because circumstances dictated. By chance, we were on the cusp of change — property rose in value from 1991 and in the late 1990s spiralled until, in 2006, it plummeted almost overnight, in contradiction to the 'soft landing' the errant bankers, developers and government ministers had promised.

But, back in 1992, we had our second stroke of luck. A year after selling Lisheen, the friend who had rented us the small house at a peppercorn rent explained that his sister and family were returning from Britain and would like to move in as soon as we could find other accommodation. Fortuitously, almost the next day, the lady who had bought Lisheen phoned us from Australia, saying that she could not occupy the house in the foreseeable future and asking if we could help her find tenants. Realising that the rent would be far beyond our means, I gave her the phone numbers of some local house agents. However, she had no luck in finding a tenant and, some weeks later, phoned to ask if we would be interested in renting Lisheen ourselves. I explained that we could barely afford the token rent we were paying to our friend. To my surprise, she said that that rent would be acceptable because she wanted someone living in the house and, since we knew it already, we would be ideal. Thus, we moved back in, hung our pictures back on the same spaces on the walls and stood our furniture in the 'footprints' in the carpets where it had previously stood. Sally, the dog, took up her usual bed in the back kitchen and so we came to live three more years in Lisheen, before the owner sold it on to another buyer.

In early 1995, we moved to Courtmacsherry, to a large bungalow which we would rent until the family met that same summer to agree its sale. In the event, they couldn't agree and we continued renting until, in July 1996, we brought my mother, then aged eighty-five, to live with us. My father had died only weeks before and she was now alone and, owing to a stroke, unable to care for herself at home. My brother Gerry and his family lived in Spain; it would have been impossible for her to adapt to life there. Neither, for reasons of circumstance, could my sister offer her a home. Courtmacsherry, we knew, would suit her, with its quiet way of life and our family around her. Marie, whose parents had passed away many years previously, was the first to suggest that we should take her into our care.

However, as summer changed to winter, it became apparent that our beautifully located, but old-fashioned, rented bungalow was not exactly conducive to the well-being and health of someone so frail; therefore, when my parents' house was sold, we used our share of the proceeds to buy a property that would be more suitable. We wanted to stay in the village. I loved the bay and the birdlife, Marie loved the woodland walks and the proximity of an old and valued friend, Anne, and the boys loved the sea for surfing and swimming and they had made friends here too. As a family, we had developed a great *grá* for the place and so, although the only property for sale in the village was a noted Georgian guesthouse and restaurant and we knew nothing about keeping or feeding guests (and had never ambitioned to do so), we bought it. It had a comfortable private apartment accessible by wheelchair and perfect for my mother.

How we would manage the guesthouse, we had no idea. We would have to keep the business turning over because when my mother died we would sell it. Marie was a teacher, I was a writer: we would hope to return to our old lives after my mother had passed on. A house with nine en suite guest bedrooms, a huge, stainless-steel restaurant-kitchen with ten-ring gas stoves and fridges big enough for an Eskimo to cool off in, plus a dining room seating thirty diners would not make for an ideal family home. However, in the meantime, we had to cater for guests. We did contrive, somehow, to manage. We were happy there, at Travara Lodge; and when my mother died a year and a half later, we put it on the market. Fortuitously, it didn't sell. It did, the following year, at an enormous premium. This was Tiger time and we were amazed at the price the estate agent suggested and which we subsequently got.

Meantime, caring for my mother while running a language school and a guesthouse, and writing weekly columns and feature articles, would have been all but impossible without help. Theresa Hunt, then a young village girl, now the mother of four children, came in every day to be a companion and helpmate for my mother. If there is a heaven after life, I believe Theresa will go there and, I hope, meet my mother whom I'm sure will thank her for the love and care she gave her in that last year. If she had been her daughter, she could not have done more. Mary, Theresa's sister, meanwhile, knew the arcane secrets of preparing rooms for guests, of tidying and cleaning and changing linen — she had learned it as a teenager, working at the hotel. The Hunts, a large family, always contributed greatly, in one way or another, to the well-being of the village and the community. The local district nurse, Mary Kearney, went far beyond the call of duty in seeing to my mother's welfare. That is the nature of the community we live in: that is the kindness of this place.

~

In 1995, a year before the sad events that befell my parents, Marie and I had the idea of buying the Old Courthouse in Timoleague and creating an English language school for foreign students on the ground floor. Later, we would install a living space upstairs with fine views from the back windows over Timoleague Abbey and Courtmacsherry Bay.

From soon after our arrival in Ireland, Marie had been operating Language Holidays Ireland from our home in Lisheen, teaching the few students we got as a result of an excellent review in the influential *Gio* tourist guide, written by a Japanese journalist to whom I had given a lift in my car and who turned out to be researching Ireland for the magazine. Having journalism in common, we struck up a conversation and I invited her home to lunch. We became friends and things developed from there. To make LHI a business that would help support us, we needed premises. Some friends thought we were mad to even consider renovating a building almost three centuries old with no services of any kind. In truth, we weren't sure of our own sanity. That it would cost a lot of money was the only certainty, but if we got it right, it would be money well spent. For one thing, we could design a small quality-before-quantity school to Department of Education specifications. Into the shell, with its sound walls, we could fit airy classrooms, WCs, a kitchen and social space, and a Resource Room for library and audio facilities. Moreover, the building would have real dignity, backed by history, and be as impressive as any Dublin or Cork city school.

The Courthouse, built *circa* 1700, had history. Daniel O'Connell, the great champion of Irish Emancipation, had 'appeared' there to defend — and secure the release of — two Irishmen arrested for murder following a tithe-riot in 1821, but nobody local seemed to care much about that. It had been, in turn, a market house, with an Assizes court upstairs, then a grain store, then a garage with a petrol pump in one of its gracious arches. It had been used as times and fashions saw fit, the stone facade pebble-dashed over and the elegant arches bricked up and turned into blind eyes. There were no mains services. The concrete floor was shattered, showing bare earth. Most recently used as a car-repair garage, the ground floor was a huge space, 820 sq. feet (76 sq. metres), with a stout tree trunk at the centre on top of which, running from wall to wall and helping to support the upper floor, was a length of track salvaged from the old Cork-Courtmacsherry railway.

Downstairs was cobwebbed, dark and dingy — but not dank or damp. The ceiling was fourteen feet above the floor, beamed with strong, dry pine. The railway track support had been installed only because huge weights of grain had once been stored above.

Upstairs was like a small cathedral. Three fine, many-paned Georgian windows looked out onto the street, all still glazed and in salvageable repair. Again, there were cobwebs but no damp patches anywhere, and the wide, old floorboards were 60 per cent recoverable. There was a partition at one end, with a 'ticket office' window, perhaps where grain chits were issued and tallies paid. High up in the roof, the huge supporting beams were still in perfect condition. The rafters and roof beam, twenty-five feet above the floor, showed no signs of dry rot or damp.

Putting the upstairs work 'on the long finger', we hurried to begin development in April 1995, hoping to open the school on 1 June. A Kinsale friend recommended a builder and he turned up, a small, stocky, fifty-year-old man wearing sharp-toed cowboy boots and jeans and driving a shiny Jaguar saloon. I liked him; he was no-nonsense. He immediately reminded me of the diminutive Italian-American tough-guy actor Joe Pesci, famous for his Cosa Nostra roles. This association was no doubt reinforced when he told me that his companion — who was to do the house-painting — was a part-time opera singer. Our architect, Ross Cathal O'Brien, son of the man who owned the local MacCarthy Reagh castle at Kilbrittain, had his shoes tied with household string, one arm of his spectacles sellotaped to the frame, and the buttons on his sports jacket affixed to the wrong holes. However, Ross was reputed to be touched by genius and, indeed, he proposed an excellent plan.

Access to the lower floor would continue via the centre arch; in its market-house days, horse-carts would have been driven through this arch to deliver produce. Now it would be gated, opening on to a small, cobble-stoned, glass-paned entrance courtyard, the curve of the gate-top being an obverse of the stone arch above it. Steel-frame windows, made on site, would fill the adjoining arches, these windows to be set on the inside of the three-foot thick street-facing walls, giving the frontage a three-dimensional perspective. Cobblestones paved the recesses of these arches, with a bollard in each. Light, softened by muslin curtains, flooded into the new classrooms through the big windows, and the paint colours were bright. The whole building, inside and out, was now very beautiful.

Most wonderful of all, for us, was the exterior stonework, revealed when the pebble-dash was chipped off. Having originally been constructed for a municipal role — to tax the Irish downstairs and hang them upstairs — the building was designed to be monolithic and awe-inspiring. It is unlikely that anybody alive then had ever seen the

Old Courthouse other than in its pebble-dashed condition. When we began to remove the plaster, villager after villager stopped to admire it and to tell us that we must, at all costs, keep the lovely stonework revealed. In doing this, there was much labour for our builders. Cleaning nearly a thousand square feet of raw stone was a formidable task, and repointing it impeccably even more so. Standing there in the middle of the village, covered in scaffolding and draped with nets, we really had no idea how lovely the finished product would look. Then, one day, we drove around the corner to see it revealed in its glory, with the window ledges painted wine-red by the opera singer.

We recorded the date when the Courthouse was first built, 1700, in a limestone plaque above the central arch, and affixed a brass plaque to the wall noting the visit of Daniel O'Connell. I imagined O'Connell, 'The Liberator', riding in out of the dawn, direct from Kerry, his cloak flying behind him, to dismount and rush upstairs to the Assizes court. Tithe-riots were the response of the Irish to an English law decreeing that Catholics should pay a tenth of their annual income to the support of the Protestant clergy, a preposterous injustice. Charlie Madden, the owner of the pub across the street, a somewhat larger-than-life personality, as pub owners often are, has said that The Liberator never came within a bull's roar of Timoleague or its courthouse. Charlie is a respected arbiter on matters of the Gaelic Athletic Association and on republican history, but I have the word of a man of God, the late Fr James Coombes, local historian and parish priest, on the subject of O'Connell's visit, and on that authority I rest my case.

Thus, the courthouse renovations were completed in record time under Joe Pesci's offices, and classes began on schedule. The people of Timoleague, one and all, were generous in their praise, without a begrudger anywhere. We were pleased to have restored what was already there, to have returned magisterial dignity to the village centre — and to have given The Old Courthouse, as headquarters of Language Holidays Ireland, a new freehold on life.

~

In May, as the days warm up and the rain of the winter stops, we begin to see what Marie calls The Timoleague Outdoor Social Club, a small group of not-so-young men in caps and hats, sitting in the sun on the new, brightly painted benches beside the Abbey, with a pleasant view of the bridge and the waters of the lovely Argideen. If they choose to walk a hundred yards farther, they can enjoy a view up the river to Timoleague House, so perfect on its left bank, with gardens around it and dark trees in which up to twenty egrets roost like cranes in Chinese paintings, only they are white. The egrets that forage on the nearby mud banks, reflected in the brown water when the tide is low, further enhance the view.

Higher up is Inchy Bridge, whence, long ago, before the 1755 Lisbon earthquake and the raising of the bay floor, sailing ships could ride on the incoming tide. From April onward, newly arrived visitors to Ireland passing the bridge at midnight could be forgiven for drawing the wrong conclusions upon seeing a huddle of men in Polaroid glasses standing about, hands deep in pockets or leaning on the parapet looking into the water below. A family of Timoleague Mafia sending an associate to 'sleep with the fishes'? Surely such things could not happen in amicable West Cork!

The shadowy figures are, in fact, a companionable society of dedicated sea-trout anglers, no more threatening than the Timoleague Outdoor Social Club, unless you happen to be a fish. Nightly, from early March, they leave the comfort of their firesides and set off into the dark, there to try, by subtle wrist-flicking and lure-dangling, to seduce clever fish into taking their bait and joining them on the bank.

Sea-trout are shy, so anglers must fish for them at night, casting flies by the light of the moon or, on moonless nights, in total darkness but for the river's silvery glow. Daubenton's bats, the 'water bats', roost beneath Inchy bridge and hunt over its waters. Sometimes, as an angler casts his line, a bat takes the fly in mid-air and then has to be unhooked and released. Happily, it happens rarely. These fishermen like the bats: they keep the midges down. Besides, they know and admire nature and

I've heard many a story from them of otters and owls observed during their night watch.

Those of us who live by the sea tend to forget the sweet tranquillity of inland waters. This was brought home to me when the potter Peter Wolstenholme led us along the Argideen banks above Timoleague one sunny afternoon. He has fished the river by day and night for twenty years.

In the lower reaches, dense shoals of large mullet faced into the brown current, healthy and shining, singularly unlike the slow, grey mullet one sees cruising limpidly in the murky waters of the Lee below Morrison's Island in Cork city.

It was a superb afternoon and, continuing upstream on paths dappled in sun and shade, we stopped now and then beside a pool or gravel bed to see what we could see. Damselflies and dragonflies hawked over the water, their wings shimmering in the sun. I had no idea that the river held so many fish and that they could be so easily seen. With the aid of a pair of stylish Polaroid sunglasses, adult sea-trout could be observed in the deep pools, lying on the bottom, their dark shapes and white fins visible through the glare on the water. Closer to the surface, juvenile sea-trout swam in shoals.

The adult sea-trout go to sea in winter and the females return in May. They sit on the bottom, moving little and feeding not at all, their body fat transforming into roe so that, when the spawning time comes in November, they have pendulous bellies and hardly a pick of meat on their bones, all their substance having metamorphosed into eggs. The juveniles, with a mere teaspoonful of roe, also attempt spawning, lying between larger females whose potent and abundant eggs attract the milt of the males.

At spawning time, the sea-trout female, stimulated by the male rubbing his body against hers, digs a trench in the gravel, lies on her side and deposits her five thousand to ten thousand eggs. The male then spills his milt, or seminal fluid, over them. After thirty to one hundred days, depending on water temperature, the fertilised eggs hatch into 'elvins', like tiny tadpoles. The elvins now try to make their own way in their watery world but suffer a 95 per cent mortality rate. After two or three years in the river, those that survive move into the sea to feed. Some — the juveniles we saw — return to the Argideen after a few months, weighing about half a pound. Others, 'one-sea-winter fish', feed for longer and return weighing two to three pounds. While roughly 50 per cent of Atlantic salmon die after spawning, and 100 per cent of some Pacific salmon varieties, female sea-trout spawn year after year.

There were brown trout in the river too, and silvery minnows and salmon parr with thumb-print markings on their flanks. A kingfisher shot past us, a bolt of iridescence through the shadows. We saw a dipper's nest, but not the dipper: previously, I've seen these remarkable birds, also called water ouzels, walk along the bed of the Argideen, totally submerged. Above all, we enjoyed the cool and dappled peace, and the river's murmuring and twinkling in the sunlight.

It must be other-worldly to stand silently on the bank at night, half-hypnotised by the flow, one's mind lost in the arcane strategies of fish-luring.

~

Sometimes at lonely coves we come on bleak memorials that speak of heartbreak for the parents of children or young men lost to the sea. A summer afternoon, joy and laughter and then tragedy, and years or decades later strangers read these testaments to love and unforgetting, memorials to loved ones gone forever, young lives lost so needlessly.

In February 2006, we got the news that one of our oldest and closest friends, Bhaskar Bhattacharya, had been drowned just south of Madras in India and, in late May, we set off for London to attend an obituary party held in his memory. He had just finished making a TV film for Channel 4, and was to fly home to his wife and son in New Delhi the following day. In the early morning, he and the director and producer of the film decided to have a last dip in the Indian Ocean. Knowing that that coast is notoriously dangerous for bathing, they ventured no farther than waist deep. However, that was enough. An undertow suddenly caught them and the sand they stood on washed away from under their feet. The other two, a young man and a young Irishwoman, managed to struggle ashore; my friend, not so young and a twenty-a-day smoker, was submerged and, within seconds, drowned.

I have swum on the opposite coast of India, in the far south-west in Kerala and on the west coast south of Goa. There is always a sort-of 'longshore drift', if that is the correct term. Waist-deep, one can sit and float in the water, and be carried for hundreds of yards parallel to the shore at the same speed as a child might run along the sand. Happily, in these places, one isn't carried out to sea.

June

How dreary to be somebody!
How public, like a frog
To tell your name the livelong day
To an admiring bog!

Emily Dickinson

~

In June, for the past five or six years, frogs might indeed seek bogs in which to cool off and trumpet their names to the unlistening. In June, more often than not we wake to skies as peerless blue as a hedge sparrow's egg. Since we have moved into the new house, I step through the French windows onto the gravel of the courtyard just to greet the day and sometimes we breakfast on the balcony above, looking at the Kincragie fields through a gap in the line of tall beeches on the other side of our boundary stream.

As if placed there by some great film-set designer, two horses, one large and white, the other small and black, graze together in the ankle-deep buttercups. All around them rabbits nibble the grass, bask at full length, or keep watch. They often forage in pairs, one standing alert on its hind-legs, ears popped up, while the other basks or grazes beside it. When I look again, they have changed roles. I had never thought rabbits could be so coordinated.

At about five o'clock on the evenings of days like this, I down tools — close the book, shut down the screen — and head for the big beach at Broadstrand on the Seven Heads, a twenty-minute walk away from the house. The air temperature may well be around 22 degrees centigrade, so plunging into the sea is painless and one can comfortably wallow about for half an hour. On the entire half-mile long beach, there may be ten families or small groups, some well kitted-out with buckets and spades, rubber rings and mini-surfboards. There is rarely heavy surf. A light breeze takes the edge off the heat most pleasantly.

Later, at about six-thirty, I drive down to the pier and get a half-dozen mackerel from the angling boats. 'Take more, take more!' the skipper's young sons urge me, and I take a couple of big pollock as well, one for the following day and one for the freezer — although freezing fish seems unnecessary when, almost every day, except in stormy weather, we can get fish freshly caught from the pier. We greatly appreciate the generosity of the skippers. I try to buy them a pint when I see them in the pub.

Mackerel barbecued over beechwood embers are much tastier than those cooked over charcoal bought at the shop. Marie boils our first early potatoes (in 2009, they were our first ever potatoes) and makes a salad of rocket, lettuce and oak-leaf lettuce, dressed with olive oil and balsamic vinegar. Now, in the garden of the new house, small vegetable plots have been created and Marie has taken to horticulture. I watch, fascinated, as she spades back the soil and reveals potatoes nestling together like families, small and clean and white, exposed to the light for the first time, as if newly born. It is wonderful how tubers displace the nourishing earth, and the earth yields.

On warm June evenings, it is comfortable to eat on the balcony. At nine o'clock, the pair of great tits nesting in the sycamore are still bringing scraps to their chicks, the rabbits are still grazing in their field of gold, and the setting sun is burning a hole in the sky over the bay.

On one such evening, we ate with friends in their garden high above the village at Barreragh, with the panorama of the ebbed bay laid out below us all the way from Timoleague Abbey to Wood Point. It was an awesome spectacle, with the countless channels dividing the dark sandbanks and mudflats, all picked out in gold. A pair of blue tits were feeding their young in a hole in an old stone wall only feet away from us and we marvelled at their industry, flying back and forth to a hawthorn tree fifty yards away and delivering caterpillars in a constant three-minute cycle. They would have been doing this since break of day, and they were still at it at ten o'clock at night. How many caterpillars were in that tree? It must have been as easy to pick up a caterpillar as to pick up a burger at a take-away. And how many young had they, that they should have to work so hard? Blue tits often have a dozen chicks in the nest, and as many as eighteen is sometimes recorded. Like wrens, their numbers are greatly reduced in hard winters; hence, perhaps survival of the species demands large broods. In fact, only about 10 per cent of the hatchlings will survive to breed in the following spring.

An ancient book on my shelves, *Eggs and Nests of British Birds* by Frank Finn, B.A. (Hutchinson 1910), tells me that 'a pair have been observed to keep feeding [the chicks] almost continuously for seventeen hours, during which time food was taken in four hundred and eighty-two times.' That works out at fresh deliveries every 130 seconds. Busy birds — and useful too. Another book tells me that in three weeks a pair of blue tits carried seven to eight thousand caterpillars and other insects to their nestlings. Apparently, they were not as efficient as Mr Finn's birds which, I calculate, would have seen off some 10,122 creepy-crawlies of various kinds.

Meanwhile, a few summers ago, excited holidaymakers often told me about an exotic bird they had seen in Courtmacsherry Woods. While shimmering peacocks from Timoleague House are regularly seen in the streets of Timoleague, we do not have peacocks in Courtmac. However, we do, occasionally, have a magnificent male Lady Amherst pheasant in full breeding regalia of brilliant white, blue, yellow and red, roaming free in the woods. For all the flamboyance of the Timoleague peacocks, I believe they would be outshone by our Courtmacsherry pheasants. Anyone watching them stepping delicately through the shadows of our giant laurels and rhododendrons might well think themselves to be in

South-East Asia. Two teenage girls gleefully told me that they had taken photographs on their mobiles and were going to tell their friends that they'd been on holidays to Bangkok.

~

On a June day in 2004 that brought the first rain for six weeks in that remarkable summer, I stood abroad with a half-collapsed umbrella in the mild green evening of West Cork. It was wonderful to see how rain worked its magic, wonderful to feel it patter on my head. We had asked ourselves if it would ever come.

How green the garden was now, and how suddenly! Sometimes, a light breeze blew across it and the huge leaves of the gunnera lifted and fell like the skirts of a flamenco dancer. The patio shone and the roses stood to attention, lifting their heads to the bruised-pink, life-giving sky.

The drought had lasted six weeks; for a full six weeks no more than a few drops had fallen from the skies, a weather event as rare as snow in these parts. One evening, alerted by a croaking, I had come upon three frogs cooling out companionably in a bog pool. They croaked *sotto voce*, grunts of satisfaction rather than trumpeting, it seemed.

Now, once again, there were wet umbrellas in the hall and dog's paw prints on the carpet. Outside, parched earth and parched plants drank thirstily; one could almost hear them gulp. Pools of water gathered on the steps and the brown patches on the lawn turned green. Birds sang, slugs crawled, snails came out of hiding. On the lawn, two blackbirds hopped and listened, hopped and listened, like wound-up toys, their beaks intermittently stabbing the grass as if their necks had springs in them. Worms were coming up for water, pink dinners popping out of the ground.

It was high time for the 'blessèd rain from heaven' to fall upon 'the place beneath'; it hadn't deserted us after all. During the dry six weeks, it had seemed as if the world had gone awry, the more so when Gerry, my brother, told me that one day, when driving from Málaga to Seville, he had had to pull in because the wind-driven deluges hitting the windscreen of his four-by-four were so violent that the wipers couldn't cope.

When, after an hour, our downpour stopped, the earth lay steaming in its aftermath and, in the hazy warmth, we might have thought we were adjacent to the Amazon. Such flights of fancy are forgivable when the view includes gunnera leaves as big as small cars; had the exotic pheasant appeared, we would have had to pinch ourselves back to reality. 'A green thought in a green shade' indeed — and one of the few couplets I know in Spanish poetry crossed my mind, *'Verde que te quiero verde. Verde viento. Verdes ramas'*, 'Green, how I love you, green. Green wind. Green branches', as Federico García Lorca, the poet, said.

~

On the midsummer Sunday of 2009, the sun was again melting the tar as six of us — the family, Gerry and a friend — walked the empty roads of Heir Island in Roaringwater Bay, the wildflowers on the ditches making corridors of colour between us and the shimmering sea. The wild land beyond the small fields was purple with cross-leaved heather and thyme, and the rocks bristling with stonecrop and lichens.

A lark rose from a patch of meadow, soared and sang. In the dog-day silence, the song carried and fell over the land just as, later, when we headed homeward on the ferry, the songs of the islanders carried after us over the sea. Earlier, when we had arrived off the ferry from Cunnamore, the pier in Heir had been deserted, with no hint that it would later be the venue for the island's musical celebration of mid-summer's day.

From the pier, we set off south-west and walked the length of the island, past the old schoolhouse and pump, through the hamlet of Paris to the promontory of An Dún. There we sat and watched the gulls floating on the air high above us. We ate apples and praised the beauty and the day.

To north, south and west, the islands of Roaringwater Bay rode on the sea before us, Sherkin and Cape Clear, their fields green in the sunlight, and the Calf Islands ahead, low and dark against the sun. When we arrived back at the pier three hours later, we found a small marquee set up, and a table of free drinks nearby. Half a dozen musicians were sawing their fiddles, plucking their guitars and fingering their button accordions, with a few singers already giving voice to spontaneous song.

Heir is a lovely island but it would be hard to say which of Roaringwater Bay's islands is most pleasing for the visitor. A few years earlier, at the request of a local representative of Comhdháil Oileáin na hÉireann, The Irish Islands Federation, I had written a book entitled *Walks of Seven West Cork Islands* and visited all the inhabited islands in Roaringwater and Bantry Bay many times.

Despite the recent economic ills, I count myself fortunate to live in a country with such other-worldly escapes on all sides. In the midlands there are the Galtee Mountains and the Comeraghs, and many big rivers and lakes; in Kerry, Clare and Galway there is scenery and solitude to rival anywhere on earth. Roscommon has veritable seas of inland water, Dublin and Wicklow the famous mountains, Donegal the wild coasts, and Antrim the glens. There is hardly a county in Ireland that isn't replete with vistas of great beauty, where nature offers a sanctuary from the cares of every day.

And so, we spent the midsummer Sunday enjoying our offshore assets in West Cork. We passed Paris at six o'clock — called Paris for the fact that it was the home of a fish 'pallace' in the 19th century when, for some decades, pilchards arrived in their millions on the south coast each summer and were netted and then pressed into 'train oil', which was used for leather and for lamps. At the pier, the hospitality of the Heir people demanded that we enjoyed 'a drop' and an hour of music before we took the boat back to the mainland shores.

I saw no hares on the island on that day or on any other visit. In the distant past, the island was named for an heir to the leadership of the O'Driscoll clan and it is called Inis Uí Drisceoil still. There are no

resident hares and, I'm told, no resident O'Driscolls. Someone said a
corncrake had been heard. I was not surprised. They are heard — but
not seen — on the magic south-western islands every year.

~

There can be few better ways of getting to know the prehistory, history
and natural history of an area than researching it for a walking guide.
From 1997 onward, I was part-financed by LEADER, a European Union
initiative to assist rural development, to write a series of West Cork
walking guides. These would, I hoped, encourage my perambulating
neighbours to explore new horizons, while informing visitors of the
delights awaiting them just off the tourist trail. We Irish delight in
showing off our land. In time, we might meet parties of ardent Japanese,
led by a person with a flag, or stout Austrians in lederhosen and braces
tramping along to a chorus of 'Valderi-Valdera'. While our bohreens
were unlikely to become thoroughfares, even a few visitors would be
welcome, bringing local shops, guesthouses and hostelries a much-
needed injection of income.

The idea of my penning a guide originally arose when the chairman
of the Courtmacsherry Committee (stress on the 'tee', as is traditional
in West Cork), John Young, asked me if I'd knock out a couple of pages
of typescript detailing an interesting local walk for the wives and
children of the dedicated sea anglers who spent most of the family
holiday out at sea on Mark Gannon's angling boats. Instead of another
day on the beach, the stranded families might enjoy a peregrination
through the woods and out to Wood Point, returning via the Fuchsia
Walk, once the daily itinerary of the genteel ladies of the Earl of
Shannon's retinue at Kincragie House.

I happily wrote a few pages and these were duly photocopied, stapled
together and distributed free at local pubs and guesthouses. In time, the
Barryroe farmers' cooperative and LEADER let it be known that funding
would be available to pay me for preparing a book of local walks,
provided I would write it and arrange for publication and distribution

myself. The logic was simple. An attractive little book, presenting the joys and wonders of the local area, its prehistory, history and natural history, might seduce strangers to linger longer and thus to better the local economy — and the cost of producing it wouldn't be high. The tourist season being little more than ten weeks, any delaying tactic would be welcome.

I was inspired by the idea. Rather than the few lines and dry dates in the *Baedeker* or *Lonely Planet Guide* on, say, Timoleague Abbey, I would write a brief but engaging history of the entire bay and the wine ships and the monks who did business with Spain. I would map out a walk up the nearby Argideen river, with its sea-trout and salmon, its kingfishers and birds that walk under water. I would have the guests saying to one another, 'Hey, why don't we stay another night and explore *this* place — why rush onward to Killarney and shamrocks-and-shillelaghs in the sky?' And thus, while I — and the local artists and mapmakers who would illustrate the book — garnered welcome fees for our efforts, the guesthouse would get another night's booking, the restaurant another sitting, the pubs sell a few more beers and keep music and musicians alive by paying them to provide entertainment.

Supported by local talent and goodwill, the books, published under the imprint of The Merlin Press, Timoleague, properly registered and with ISBN numbers, looked good and sold well. West Cork artists provided accomplished black-and-white illustrations of the flora, fauna and scenery, mapmakers drew up maps, and graphic designers, including my son Matthew, made a very pretty job of the layout and the covers. I had become a publisher, organising the process from perambulation to print, and onward to distribution. One man asked me could I supply waterproof editions. He never went walking but he read the books in the bath!

After the Courtmacsherry book, there was another, on Kinsale, then on Clonakilty and environs, then Skibbereen, Baltimore and Roaringwater Bay, then Schull and Ballydehob and, later, books on two County Kerry venues. It was a small thrill for me to see them, pocket-sized and sturdy, displayed in every second bookshop, newsagent, filling station, and souvenir shop I walked into, distributed thence by Maps and Charts of Schull. New books, or revisions, gave me a part-time job for more than seven years and the modest earnings helped feed the family and keep us going in this precious place we had discovered.

In the event, the walk books had more 'legs' than I'd ever imagined. One evening in the millennium year, David Bickley, an RTÉ television director, phoned me to ask if his son, Oisín, could interview me about bird life for a short film being made with the help of pupils at the boy's primary school. I was glad to oblige and, soon afterwards, to my surprise, David suggested that I should write and present three 30-minute RTÉ programmes under the title of *Enright's Way*, this being borrowed from the popular name by which the commentaries of the famous English walker A.W. Wainwright were known.

We did three programmes, all on issues that I thought should be brought to public attention — rights-of-way for walkers; protection of prehistoric artefacts against removal to facilitate property development; and the positive input of expatriates on rural Irish communities. We also collaborated on an RTÉ Townlands programme about Castletownsend, a unique West Cork enclave which, until the late 20th century, remained a 'corner of a foreign field that is for ever England'. Even today, the older residents in the 'big houses' in Castletownsend maintain British mores.

With David's direction, talking 'to camera' seemed easy to do and, amazingly, the programmes got 'Pick of the Day' ratings in the listings magazines. However, appearing on the goggle-box held no great attraction and I had no intention of spending time in Cork or Dublin pursuing TV work; I didn't return to Ireland for that.

Meanwhile the boys went to local schools. Fintan, who was only two when we arrived, learned Irish and the West Cork vernacular; Dara, who was going on twelve, less so, and was excused Irish. We had annual family reunions when the entire tribe arrived to stay. I wrote my weekly column, the walk books and articles for magazines at home and abroad. Marie taught English to her students who came from overseas and were boarded locally for the duration of their stay, or, when called upon and

available, filled in for teachers on sick leave from local schools — the
Rapid Response Unit, I called her, whizzing off upon receiving an early
morning phone call requesting her services in a school anything up to
thirty miles away and, often, in the back of beyond. With our combined
earnings, we managed to cover the bills, though we never had a lot left
over for luxuries. But who needed luxuries? we thought. Wasn't it a
luxury enough to be out of the city, out of the rat-race, with beauty,
peace and goodwill all around us? Our cars were always geriatric but
who cared — they motored! When we took a holiday, we went to
countries cheaper than Ireland and stayed in *pension*s or rented a house
or a flat. This suited us perfectly, being of the philosophy that tourist
hotels often distance one from the very culture and people that make
the holiday outing different from the day-to-day at home.

Since 1981, La Gomera, a small, unspoiled island in the Canary
Islands — largely unknown, even now — had been a second home to
us. We continue to visit regularly, although from 1989 we no longer had
our small house on the terraces of the great, green Valle Gran Rey —
the roofless ruin which, between 1981 and 1983, we renovated with
our own hands. When we opted to leave London, we sold it in order to
make the down-payment on Lisheen.

Flight-only tickets are relatively cheap on holiday charters going to
Tenerife, and then La Gomera is just an hour's boat ride away, across
the blue and shimmering sea. There, in a white house on the green
terraces, I write my weekly column as usual and fax or email it home. I
am amazed at how often Irish readers tell me that they enjoy my stories
about the banana farmers, cochineal gatherers and fishermen in that
foreign place, and about the magnificent mushrooms and wildlife in
the cloud forests and amongst the tall Canarian pines.

One way or another, we visit La Gomera most years, combining the
trip with a visit to my older children living in London or Hertfordshire.
We first found Gomera, by chance, when there were only a handful of
resident foreigners. As a result, we are familiar with almost as many
local people as in Courtmac. During the twenty years here, we've kept
up our connection with the island, spending most of a year there in

2002/03 when it was Fintan's 'transition year' at school. We thought it a good idea that he spend that year, often under-used, learning Spanish. Although fifteen years old, he became fluent very quickly — I think he learned as much out at sea, riding waves with his Gomera friends, as at school. It paid off: a module of his BA course at University College Cork was Spanish Literature and he has since progressed to Hispanic-related studies for an MA.

That year, I had received an advance from Gill & Macmillan for my book *A Place Near Heaven* and the money went much further in La Gomera than it would have at home. While I daily worked on the book — with a stroll through the banana plantations to take a dip on the black sand beach at sunset — Fintan attended school and Marie taught at the *colegio*. Dara, working in London, visited us at holidays, as did most of my other children and grandchildren. We were, indeed, blessed. It was a wonderful year but there was no question of living in La Gomera permanently. I speak for the family when I say that we would exchange nowhere on earth for West Cork.

~

Clouds of butterflies and a haze of day-flying moths rose from beneath our feet as we walked the Seven Heads on the glorious June bank holiday weekend spanning the last days of May and the first days of June 2009. I hadn't seen so many butterflies together since I was a child. Vast influxes of painted ladys were reported from all over Ireland. I spell them thus to distinguish them from the painted ladies and the gorgeous girls one can see 'flying it' on high heels in Irish country towns on Saturday nights.

Painted ladys migrate into Ireland every year but in 2009 they came in enormous numbers, along with brown-grey moths known as silver-Ys for a distinctive mark on their forewings. Painted ladys breed in North Africa and start flying north in early spring. In mid-May, a group of British birdwatchers twitching in Morocco reported waves of these butterflies streaming northwards over the Atlas Mountains; they somehow estimated that three million were passing every hour.

Shortly afterwards, gardens in Kent and orchards in Surrey were so inundated with the migrants that their owners could hardly find a square foot of naked ground. The phenomenon was not unprecedented; in 1980 painted ladys were so plentiful in Britain that numbers were incalculable. Similarly in 1952, 1966 and 1969. Some of these butterflies, along with their cousins, the red admirals and the silver-Y moths, would continue their northward journey and reach the Shetlands, Iceland and the Arctic Circle.

The amazing irruption of 2009 was the result of exceptional rain in the Moroccan desert which nurtured the butterflies' food plants. The strong south-easterly winds on and before the June bank holiday provided perfect jet streams to carry them across Biscay and the Celtic Sea to Ireland. On the shaley cliff paths above Dunworley, they glided and darted around us as we walked down tracks golden with sow thistles and hawkbit, the blue sea twinkling below them in the heat of the holiday afternoon.

Amongst the winged host were a few red admirals, carried on the same winds. Painted ladys and red admirals are powerful flyers. They skim over hedges and meadows, dodge through orchards and forests but, unfortunately do not always manage to dodge cars. By the Tuesday, the arrivals were heading inland. I saw many flying across the road as I drove to Bandon and was told of hundreds flitting over the Bandon river. Soon, they were appearing all over Ireland, and every garden had its complement, which we hoped had come to stay.

The caterpillars of painted ladys do not eat cabbages and are not pests. Eggs are laid singly on the leaves of thistles and nettles, their food plants, in early June. They hatch a week later and the tiny caterpillars spin the leaves around them and feed within. On warm mornings, the small, silvery 'purses' can be seen on the nettle tops, shining with dew. The caterpillars grow rapidly and form a chrysalis, suspended from a leaf. Two weeks later, in August, an exquisite winged creature emerges. It hauls itself out of its sheath, pauses to let its wings dry and strengthen, and then takes to the air. It will fly for a few weeks until the onset of winter claims it.

Painted ladys, red admirals, peacocks and small tortoiseshells, all members of the Vanessa family, are amongst the brightest and most resplendent of our native lepidoptera. Arriving in the garden each summer, they clamber over the flowers like scraps of Turkish carpet newly woven from freshly dyed wool. These days, I find butterflies beautiful and fascinating. However, in the comics my brother and I read as kids, nutty-looking English uncles leading troops of rosy-cheeked Enid Blyton children carrying butterfly-nets were figures of fun for Irish boys. What sissies they were! We, hardened hedge-hunters, could catch butterflies if we wanted to — and who didn't? — by simply throwing our coats over them, poor things. We caught baby rabbits, the same way, chasing them around the field until we got close enough to launch the jacket like a stealth bomber or an airborne manta ray and then throwing ourselves prostrate to pin it down. We didn't want to injure the butterflies and we didn't harm the rabbits, but bringing the rabbits home to 'tame them' certainly threatened their lives. Their only salvation lay in our parents ordering us to take them back to where we'd caught them.

These days, in my maturity (or, some might say, post-maturity), I can get quite excited about butterflies, which may seem passing strange coming from a man who plays hardnosed bar-room Texas Hold 'Em poker with a crowd of amiable chancers one night a week. But butterflies can, indeed, be exciting especially when one finds relatively rare individuals or a thriving community of a threatened species, as did myself and a group of birdwatchers near a lake on the Beara Peninsula in West Cork. After a long and enjoyable trek through spectacular scenery in perfect weather — full sun with a cooling breeze — we repaired to a marsh near Barley Cove. Excitement rippled through the company as a marsh fritillary was spotted, roosting on a leaf. As with mushrooms, once you've seen one fritillary, it becomes easier to spot others. We reckoned that, altogether, there was a population of sixty in the marsh. Meanwhile, some of the group were crouched over orchids, trying valiantly to 'sort them out'. It seems to me that it would take the patience of Linnaeus to do so because orchids have a classification-unfriendly proclivity to hybridise. However, all present agreed that it was wonderful to be seeing so many orchids, butterflies, birds and wild flowers, and even if one couldn't name a single species, wasn't it great to be out in the day, admiring them, in the beautiful Beara, in lovely West Cork? Shiny, bronze lizards and fine fat frogs were found too, a heartening sight, being absent in many places now. All this because the area wasn't intensively farmed.

~

We've had bats around our house for years and, after building a new home in the garden of the old, we still have them. In the mothy nights of June, we see them in the moonlight for fleeting seconds, flitting over the garden and down the corridor of trees. They are pipistrelles, the smallest and commonest of Irish bats — but can 'common' really be applied to such exotic creations? *Fledermaus* they call them in German and, as we know, an operetta was named for them, these flying mice.

It seems that they are clever bats. Last year, they discovered that by flying on a certain trajectory, they would trigger the yard light to come on. Moths would be drawn to it, and be easy pickings for the pipistrelles. Now we deactivate the sensor when we are sitting outside.

There are seven species of bat resident in West Cork, including Leisler's — rare outside Ireland. Bats are site-faithful, like swallows. However, being resident all year round, they don't have to make an annual flight from South Africa, find their way to Ireland and then to the very shed or stable they were born in. The swallow strategy is based on evolutionary experience: if the adults were safely fledged in a nest built on its rafters, their offspring will be too.

The swifts follow the same survival tactic; they find Timoleague Abbey after a 6,000-mile flight. They come back year after year, I rejoice to say, but each year there are less, and now very few. Something is amiss in the world of swifts. Once, there were so many, they joined in packs, skimming the rooftops of the village, screaming as they hunted midges rising on the warm evening air.

Our bats stay with us winter-long, hanging out — if that's the word — in a small, wooden garden shed where they seem to live between the ceiling lining of black polythene and the tar-paper roof. They continue to reside there, despite the shed having been lifted and swung on a gantry and relocated at least twice in the last few years. They sometimes fly on warm winter days.

I remember an old bank house that I lived in as a child in Ballinrobe, County Mayo where, on long summer evenings, dozens of bats flew over the yard and we tried — bloodthirsty boys that we were — to knock them out of the sky with hurley balls pucked with ferocious force. By the grace of the gods and the agility of the bats, devil-a-one did we ever hit and the little *fledermäuse* dodged, dived and pirouetted above our heads, regardless. Well could they pitch and weave between the high-velocity *sliotar*s we hurled across their flight paths.

~

So beautiful is nature in midsummer that it's hard to resist taking photographs, especially now that we have digital cameras and can shoot away without the crippling costs of developing what turn out to be our mistakes before we know how bad they are.

Previously, we might find that our moody views of the Burren limestone pavements were spoiled by a distant washing line festooned with long johns and commodious knickers and doing absolutely nothing for the magic of the milieu. Now, however, with digital programmes on the computer, we can simply excise the offending underwear, lopping it off completely or, if we are real aficionados, copy and lift a piece of the limestone pavement, superimpose it on the long johns and, Hey, presto!, the viewer will never know they were there!

Digital cameras certainly make the identification of wild life items easier, whether a West Cork orchid or a Kerry slug. In Victorian times the rule was, if you don't know what the creature is, shoot it or, if a plant, pick it; you can then investigate it 'in the hand'. Unfortunately, this was a little profligate in the case of rare and vagrant species; they had hardly arrived when they were dead.

I was amazed to see the shots of peregrine falcons I got through the lens of a telescope on the Old Head of Kinsale cliffs when I stopped there while delivering our Scottish birder friend, Macmillan, to Cork Airport. He was certainly chuffed upon seeing the choughs, but even more pleased upon perceiving the peregrines. He was 'over the moon' as he took the plane home.

It was a marvellous sighting. In the morning light, the peregrine pair filled the lens of the telescope, so bright and clear we could almost count their feathers. In our excitement, we thought of inviting some of the sightseers on the nearby cliffs to take a look but decided we'd better not, in case they might trip over the tripod and plunge three hundred feet into the sea. While the visitors were clearly spellbound by the shimmering blue of the ocean, the Galley Head lighthouse in the distance, the clarity of the light and the freshness of the air, they seemed unaware of the huge drama of the birds on the narrow ledges of the avian metropolis beneath them.

Just below the edge of the cliff opposite us, the falcons stood as if posing for a photograph. Casually, one launched itself into space, a kittiwake hanging from its talons, the dead bird's white wing, tipped with black, fluttering like a handkerchief. Its captor disappeared behind an outcrop on the cliff face and then reappeared, mobbed by two choughs — which it ignored — its wing beats shallow and fast as it soared back onto the ledge and resumed the business of eviscerating its prey.

Through the telescope, the blood and flesh of the kittiwake were vivid red against its white, torn breast. The head, half-ripped off, lolled to one side. A few feet lower down, the other bird stood, slightly smaller and clearly not hungry. Was it a fledged youngster, we wondered, learning the territory, learning how to swoop, kill and butcher? We didn't think so; it was more likely to be the mate, the smaller, slate-grey male. The female was doing the butchering. Each time she flew out, she disappeared for a long twenty seconds behind the salient; we wondered if, at a site lost from our view, she was feeding a nest of young with kittiwake morsels. Against the background of sea pinks and brown heather under the cliff, how beautiful she and her mate looked. What magnificent birds!

Peregrines span the world, found from Arctic to Antarctic and absent only from Central and South America. As readers will know, they can reach a speed of more than 200mph (320 kph) in a stoop; they are the fastest creature in the air, apart from man in his flying machines. They beat their wings at the start of the headlong dive to gain speed, and then hold them against their sides to assume the profile of an arrowhead. Woe betide the creature that gets hit by a peregrine in a dive; they have been known to take rabbits' heads clean off.

There, at the Old Head, they nest in the midst of their prey. They will take one or two birds daily; more as their fledglings grow. The prey species cannot move their nurseries; cliffs with suitable ledges and aspect aren't found everywhere. The falcons come and live amongst them and it is a hit-and-miss who lives or dies. There are a thousand kittiwakes, fulmar and guillemot for every peregrine.

When fledged, the youngsters will disperse up and down the West Cork coast where peregrines are, again, relatively common. Here, they were not shot during World War I so as to stop them seizing pigeons that might be carrying military dispatches; nor was the population threatened by the loss of their main food source, as were American peregrines with the wholesale slaughter of the passenger pigeon in the United States. They were, however, persecuted by gamekeepers and declined hugely in number when DDT ingested in the insect diet of smaller birds accumulated to dangerous levels in the various raptor species that preyed on them, and caused their eggs to be so thin-shelled that they broke beneath the parent birds' feet.

~

'And time goes by like drifting down/ On a summer wind beyond the town . . .' were the opening lines of a verse I wrote one lazy afternoon years ago in a Dorset garden. My daughters, playing 'He loves me, loves me not' under an apple tree, were blowing the globes of dow seeds off the heads of dandelions, until the last seed, wafting away its umbrella of down, would give them their answer. Some twenty ye later, one of their sons, my grandson Jack, a precocious ten-year-old a new school, had something to say about whether girls loved him not, and wrote: 'There are no girls in my school/ I found it weird first/ But now that I am used to it/ I find it even worse!'

One recent June, I watched downy seeds from a goat willow tr waft across the garden and drift around Marie who was picking lettuc Indoors, writing my weekly column with the French windows of workroom open, I found seeds parachuting past my computer scre and continuing through the open door into the hallway. They gather in the cobwebs strung between the railing of the balcony, cobwebs had never noticed until they snared the wind-blown willow-down a were draped in white fluff. Elsewhere, fluff gathered in drifts, like sn or the tide-borne seaweed that washes into sheltered coves, and sta In corners, it formed soft, weightless balls that rolled about with t smallest movements of air and joined in chains, drifting like flotsa carried in and out by the tide.

A small girl I talked to told me that the floating seeds were fairi Where she got that notion I don't know, whether from some fancif adult or from her own fancy. For a child, the scene would certainly ha seemed enchanted, the sunny garden full of these weightless, pret things, seemingly dancing gracefully on the air, ascending, descendi but all of them moving in a general direction as if they were indeed fairy host. And they were almost impossible to capture as they flew tried it, but no matter how patiently I waited, how carefully I reach out and how quickly I grasped, they almost always escaped. For n companion, there was something magical about their escape. Wher caught one, she'd cry 'Don't crush the fairy!', and we'd enjoy conspiratorial laugh.

Goat willows, with their smooth, grey bark and leaves with sm 'teeth' at the edges, are ubiquitous in Ireland, especially where there wet ground. They are also called pussy willow, possibly because tree-huggers see the silken catkins as things they might stroke, like cats. The goat name may arise from the fact that historically the trees were coppiced to produce new shoots to feed goats.

They also feed a host of other wildlife and are the basis of a vital food web for insects, birds and small and large animals, bacteria and fungi. Male catkins are one of the first sources of nectar and pollen in springtime. It seems that when blue tits aren't gobbling caterpillars or mining peanut feeders, they live, like the gods, on ambrosia, if ambrosia is, indeed, drinkable. All the energy requirements of a blue tit are provided by feeding on willow ambrosia for less than four hours daily.

Willows, in their many forms, from weeping- to crack-willow to osier, are most beneficial trees, used for lobster pots and baskets and brooms. Many willow concoctions were precursors of modern medicines; bark infusions were used to relieve headaches before aspirin was developed. On sunny June days, when we lunch on the balcony, we regularly ingest the parachute seeds, with no ill effect. They float on the tea.

Along the garden stream, the sally osiers which, as short sticks, my son Dara had casually pushed into the ground, shot skywards at the rate of a foot per week. We cut them back annually. When we were young, my father, handing on an old skill, showed my brother, my sister and me how to make a bird trap from sallies.

With pencil-thin wands cut to decreasing lengths, he would build a perfectly shaped open-slatted pyramid, tapering from a twelve-inch square base to the apex, the whole structure held together with still lighter rods woven through the corners, and without a single tack or nail employed throughout. It was a work of art. Within it, supporting the open base and triggered to release it, was a perch made with a twig bent like a spring. The hungry sparrows and starlings, lured by food offerings to enter the trap, would hop aboard this perch, activate the spring and bring the pyramid down around them, like a cage. My good mother provided kitchen scraps for bait, and we, youngsters, whooped and hollered as we collared sparrows galore. It was an innocent pastime; we released the victims immediately; my father fed the birds every winter day and would not see them harmed. But our household sparrows never seemed to learn — or maybe they learned only too well that no harm would come to them while they enjoyed a free lunch.

My father, J.C. Enright, bank manager, calligrapher, gentleman and singer, died on 26 June 1996. He was born on the shortest day of the year in 1904. The people of his generation all had songs; now, we only have snatches of songs and I am left with half-remembered verses learned from him.

Before there were radios in cars, he would sing us all the way back from family Sunday outings to the seaside. In the close darkness of the car, he sang song after song as we passed crossroads at which country people danced at open-air platforms, or crossroads deep in the moth night where a few cigarette tips glowed. His strong voice still rises in my memory and, perhaps, he dwells in the 'marble halls' of which he sang.

July

De Camptown ladies sing dis song, Doo-dah! doo-dah!
De Camptown race-track's five miles long, Oh, de doo-dah day!

STEPHEN FOSTER (1826–1864)

~

It was a beautiful day for the Strand Races at Courtmacsherry on Sunday, 17 July 2006. As the ten horses competing in the second last race thundered past, the evening sun was slanting across the sand-spit, the improvised race-track shortly to be inundated by the tide. In a bunch, they rounded the posts at the western end and so fast was their pace and so steep their angle on the bend that we marvelled they didn't slip and fall. Then, down the straight they came, jostling as they reached the last lap, the commentator's voice racing with them and rising to near hysteria as the crowd roared and screamed in joy or despair as the lead horse passed the post to victory.

In seconds, the cheering died and a communal breath was held. The crowd stood still; then, a crackle on the Tannoy signalled a verdict. 'Winner alright!' it announced, and the lucky punters streamed towards the bookmakers like a flock of birds on the estuary, while the less lucky sat themselves down to study the card for the next race. Under straw hats and umbrellas, bookies' bag-men paid out the winners, while the bookies themselves began chalking new odds on their blackboards as they sweated in the 28 degree heat.

The village shone. All the way down the street, the sun flashed on the windscreens of the cars. It lit up the coloured façades of the houses, the white ice-cream vans and chip vans, the painted boats bobbing in the channel, the yellow jackets of the stewards and the bright summer outfits of the crowd. Gaiety was abroad, bonhomie and celebration, the street thronged with visitors in shorts and suntans, horses decanting from horse-boxes, jockeys in white jodhpurs and starry shirts, and yet more horses returning, foam-flecked, from their ferocious gallop along the sands. Holidaymakers greeted holidaymakers they hadn't met since the previous year, and racing types from all over Munster, in short-sleeved shirts and farmers' tans, crowded around the horse-boxes that stretched for a quarter of a mile at the edge of town. Earlier that day, after mass ended and the priest enjoined the congregation to 'Go forth and praise the Lord', he paused to remind them, 'And don't forget, now, the first race is at six o'clock!'

The family and I found seats on a bank of mown hay. There could hardly have been a more pleasant or diverting spot that Sunday evening as we watched the dainty horses ford fetlock-deep across the channel to the island of sand, and then gallop around it hell-for-leather to the crowd's urgings while the commentary on the Tannoy flowed as fast as they galloped.

Fintan went off to buy ice-creams, and returned with dripping cones. As we ate them, the sun slipped gently westward to the bay's upper reaches where it would throw the tall shadow of Timoleague Abbey onto the Argideen waters, as it had for more than seven hundred years.

At eight o'clock, it was all over, and we roused ourselves and headed to one of the pubs for pints, with enough to pay for the round from the evening's winnings. Half an hour later, as we drank outside, the sky began to darken and, by nine o'clock, even the hardiest of the shirt-sleeved drinkers and women-in-shorts were heading indoors, leaving the smokers to suffer alone for their unfortunate habit. Nobody complained at the change. Nature had been benevolent all day; the sun had shone and the tide hadn't rushed in until all the events were done. We'd had a week of the fine weather — more, almost a fortnight — and who could begrudge the sky for carrying a drop of rain?

Meanwhile, as Murphy's Law would have it, the plane bringing two of Marie's students from the Canary Islands to Ireland for the first time had been delayed, and as they stood out of the car that had brought them from the airport, a chill breeze blew and they wrapped their arms around themselves and shivered. I tried to tell these La Gomera girls that it had been beautiful earlier but they only nodded and smiled, as if they were hearing their first Irish fairytale. However, next morning, as I had hoped, the sun was shining again and now, singing the praises of the fields so green and the sea so blue, I could proudly take them driving down the local lanes with orange montbretia and creamy meadowsweet laid out in long acres on each side.

The sun shone that morning and continued to shine for a week afterwards. The coves at Courtmacsherry and the beaches at the Seven Heads were thronged. We took our students there in the afternoon when classes had finished. 'Fresh' might be a way of describing the water temperature but there were dozens of bathers in the sea and all seemed to be enjoying themselves without a wince or a whine. For myself, I could pleasurably spend twenty minutes swimming at Dunworley where the open Atlantic rolls in, and twice as long in the sheltered Courtmacsherry coves where, the girls agreed, the water was almost as warm as the sea around the Canary Islands — but in wintertime, of course. So, the La Gomera girls wouldn't venture in. Where they came from, only dumb or numb foreigners swam in water so cold. They were amazed that, most evenings, when they had finished work at their summer jobs, Fin and his pals would head off to swim at sunset, dashing in and out of the water until dark. Skim-boarding was the water sport of that summer however, involving, as it did, slinging a slab of plywood or fibreglass into the low surf ahead of one, then taking a short, fast run and leaping onto it. I decided that, personally, I'd give it a miss. While I could, of course, skim the surf with the grace of a ballerina, I didn't think it would be fair to embarrass the lads with my Hawaiian expertise. Someone once said that the definition of a gentleman is a person who knows how to play the bagpipes but doesn't. I felt the same about skim-boarding. And, besides, there was already sufficient overcrowding in A&E.

The overseas students who came to Language Holidays Ireland in July 2006 were fortunate; the summer was exceptionally blithe. On weekend evenings, après-races or après-beach, the groups clustered at pavement-side pub tables – all skimpy clothes and limbs shining with après-sun creams – reminded one of the Riviera, and residents held garden parties on their seaside lawns. Oh, yes, the amenities of West Cork in its summer glory can equal the Mediterranean or the Canary Islands, or indeed surpass them. Sunlight, green fields, 28 degree heat, and fresh breezes. Would the Gomera girls dare to spread the word about the Irish Riviera when they got home?

～

In July, Marie's school was at its busiest and it was possible to build classes made up of students with the same level of language skill. The entire roll of Language Holidays Ireland never amounted to more than thirty but, when groups could be made with one teacher managing a class of six or eight, it was possible to offer rates competitive with large city schools where classes might comprise up to twenty members.

It was, as business people would say (and we weren't very good business people) the 'economies of scale'. Only in summer could West Cork attract enough students to make the school viable. In other seasons, they preferred cities; in fact, many preferred cities at any time because of the cultural and social diversity plus the increased opportunity of enjoying gatherings and parties — and even, perhaps, romance — with students from many countries. For nine months of the 'low' season, the volume of students enrolling at LHI wasn't sufficient to make same-level classes possible, and teaching had to be conducted one-to-one. This made a course far more expensive than a group-class course in a city school. So, although the one-to-one fees at LHI were as low as we could make them, students who could afford one-to-one were few, and the hourly rate Marie earned was far short of that earned by a teacher in a state school.

Of great help to us and to the students was the network of family homes where the students boarded and where they had the opportunity to speak English in everyday situations. Many of the 'home-stay' hosts were farming families and when our students were young people we tried to find families who had children of the same age.

Summers were a mad rush for Marie especially. The guesthouse was at its busiest at the same time as the school. She had help at both but, nevertheless, had to supervise everything and do most of the work herself. She rose at seven o'clock, prepared freshly cooked (not micro-waved) breakfasts for the guests of the nine guesthouse rooms (more often than not they chose the full Irish, with local bacon, eggs and Clonakilty black-pudding). At nine o'clock, leaving her helper to wash up, she changed into her Director of Studies outfit, took her briefcase and drove to the school in Timoleague. There, she greeted her two or three staff and, as the students arrived — delivered to the school by their home-stay hosts— supervised their consignment into classes, and then took on the role of a teacher herself.

Three afternoons each week, when classes finished at 2.00pm, she would accompany the students, installed in a hired bus with driver, for outings to cultural venues such as Blarney Castle, Fota Island or Lisselane House. On three evenings a week we, together, took them to an Irish cultural event, a *céilí* dance, a music session, a village festival or perhaps a regatta. Afterwards, we would both ferry them to their home-stays, Marie dropping off the nearest students while, in our elderly seven-seater estate car, I did the long-distance trips for, often, the home-stays were as much as ten miles away in different directions and the long-haul driver wouldn't get to bed until 1.00am. I came to know the West Cork back roads very well.

For the students, their immersion in Irish life was as complete as we could make it. Those who came in winter, especially, lived almost Irish lives. There were, usually, young Japanese women who, having been entranced by Michael Flatley, Jean Butler and *Riverdance* when they performed in Japan, were intrigued with all things Celtic and seemed to have no problem with the relative isolation of the families with whom they lived. However, it is to be remembered that the country people in Ireland rarely lead isolated lives, unless they are elderly bachelors living alone or with an elderly mother who does not want another woman in the house. Families regularly visit cousins; there are GAA games and meetings at all times of the year. Neighbours congregate for mass stations in the houses, and there is always the Saturday or Sunday night in the pub. Also, whenever we were, ourselves, going somewhere interesting, we would take the one or two winter students along, perhaps to Clonakilty or Bandon for shopping or cinema, or to Cork city now and then. We would invite them to dinner occasionally, although, in truth, to have to speak simple, careful English in the evening after speaking it all day in class (this applied to the summer more than the winter) was a considerable strain. Before the children were born, Marie and I taught in Tokyo and lived in a house with other English-language teachers. Often, when we came home after eight or ten hours of classes, we would find ourselves addressing one another in monosyllabic English, so accustomed had we become to this during the day.

In 2006, we regretfully decided to close the school, largely because it had become impossible to find home-stay for more than a few students. Rural Ireland had changed. In the 1970s, the Irish Countrywomen's Association had promoted the concept of housewives welcoming overseas students into their homes both as a source of extra income and as a 'hands-across-the-ocean' initiative. The children of the family would be exposed to foreign visitors and ideas, and cultural exchanges might be developed on a quid pro quo basis. The idea was widely adopted and worked successfully. However, from 2004 onwards, enthusiasm began to wane. The Irish were increasingly taking holidays overseas and their children's exposure to foreign languages and cultures became a matter of course. Besides, in the Celtic Tiger years, many families grew more affluent and the small income that boarding and feeding a foreign student brought in simply wasn't worth the trouble any longer, although city schools could still find home-stay, given the larger local populations. The unavailability of homes where students could board at reasonable cost spelt the end of Language Holidays Ireland. While we were still in Travara Lodge, and once or twice afterwards, we had students live with us as part of the family but this resulted in Marie — and myself and the boys to a lesser extent — teaching, in one way or another, eighteen hours daily. When we calculated the number of hours we jointly devoted to the school and factored in the wages for teachers, bus hire and fees for cultural events in summer, we realised that, hour by hour, we were, each of us, earning less than half the national minimum wage.

However, running the school had been a joy most of the time and we had no regrets about the experience. We had been answerable to nobody but ourselves, and the income, though small, had covered living costs while the children were growing up. We'd made many friends and some of the Japanese students still write to us regularly. Some of our alumni forged permanent links with Ireland. A pretty French teenager who came in the late 1990s told me, as I drove her to her home-stay from the airport, that she had already fallen in love with Ireland during the drive. Indeed, not only did she instantly fall in love with Ireland but she later fell in love *in* Ireland and married a local boy. I often meet her wheeling their baby around the village. She has an Irish accent now.

By the time we closed the school, Marie was already getting some work as a 'supply' teacher, earning better wages, with less strain, and I was making a reasonable living at writing. I still occasionally took on a student preparing English literature for school exams, more or less as I had in London. I enjoyed doing it; it kept me in touch with the great poets and dramatists, and with young people full of hopes and aspirations. Contact with the poetry and the kids were the real profit: the money didn't much matter. I'd have done it for nothing, had the necessity been there and the pupil deserving of the time.

Sometimes, in the years of driving Language Holidays Ireland students home late at night, I would come upon road-kill bunnies. Ever the forager, I'd hop out of the car to take a look at the corpse. If it was a fine young grazer that had sustained a head injury only, I'd lay it carefully in the boot of the car for consumption the following day. Our female Japanese students, having watched the proceedings open-mouthed, invariably giggled behind their tiny hands as I climbed back into the car. This, I knew, was a sign of acute embarrassment, not because I was scavenging but because dead creatures were an embarrassment *per se*, handling them even more so, and riding with them in close proximity an excruciating experience and a cultural first.

Ignoring the giggles, I would explain that it would surely be a crime to waste nature's bounty, to let it lie there to be squashed. Yes, I was depriving the foxes or magpies but I had developed a taste for rabbit, roast or stewed, when I was a child, and was pretty sure that none of my fellow scavengers would starve as a result of my snaffling the occasional road-kill bunny before they got to it; it was the law of the wild, after all! Their faces, in the rear-view mirror, would wax deadly earnest as I spoke and one of them might timidly reply that, according to Japanese legend, rabbits were sacred moon creatures. So, I would ask them — to oohs, aah-sos and giggles — if it would be all right if I ate a fox.

Our Japanese, while hungry to ingest all they could of Irish culture, did not take to Irish stew. They firmly believed that those who ate it smelled of mutton. City Japanese are circumspect about animals, in any case. In Tokyo meat shops, you never see a whole chicken or rabbit. On the main islands, Kyūshū and Honshū, butchers' windows display only pink confections of bloodless meat, minced or cubed and arranged like cakes in a Viennese patisserie. Attitudes are different on the southern island of Okinawa, however, according to my correspondent Kaori Isizaka, who was a pupil at LHI in 1995. When she was on holiday there, she noticed that the locals — who look more like Filipinos than Japanese — enthusiastically exhibit pigs' cheeks, ears and trotters on their meat counters. Kaori was shocked at this, although she is an experienced traveller. Of course, the array of sea slugs and other bizarre denizens of the deep displayed at her local Kyoto fish markets might well give a sensitive Irish girl the vapours.

~

The Japanese, like the French, hugely enjoyed the freshness of our local fruits-de-mer. Indeed, one evening, when we had friends, including both French and Japanese students, in to dinner, marine fare arrived on our doorstep so fresh that we had to restrain it before it clambered all over the yard. It was eleven o'clock on a weekend night, and the company, what with after-dinner *digestifs* and yarn-spinning, were in 'good form' when a knock sounded on our front door and there was one of our local fishermen, Ian Howe, a giant of a man, with half a box of very large, very pink, very lively eating crabs. 'Just give us a few bob,' he said. 'I had to take in the holding pot because I was changing moorings and I know you're always partial to a few crabs.'

Partial, I am, indeed, to a few crabs, but here were twenty-five or more of the creatures in energetic fettle, and I in the middle of a dinner party. Crabs are best cooked with alacrity: they do not improve if left to die. However, Ian had been kind enough to think of me and I could hardly refuse. I paid half as much again as he asked and still paid no more than I would have for five of the creatures at a fishmonger's. As Ian drove away, I put a lid of sorts on the fish box, and, when the guests left at 1.00am, Marie and I set about cooking crabs on an industrial scale, with not enough saucepans, pots, cauldrons or gas rings to complete the process other than in relays, and with barely enough salt — which one must, literally, ladle into the water when boiling crabs — to follow the recipe we always use.

When young Fin arrived back from a party at 2.00am, he was pressed into service. Bubbling cauldrons were strained and crabs stacked up for home consumption and to be given to friends. But, by 3.00am, realising that every crab-eater in Courtmacsherry could be satiated and there would still be crabs to spare, Fin and I thought that the best answer was to drive to Broadstrand and release the survivors of our culinary marathon into the sea.

And so we went to the shore in the small hours and, by the light of the moon, emptied the fish box and let the survivors go. Off they lumbered down the strand and into the sea, the low surf breaking over them. Amongst the released was the biggest crab of all; I had never seen so big a specimen. She — for she was a hen — measured nine inches across the carapace and her claws were almost as big as my hand. However, old crabs, like old cod, lay multiples of the eggs their daughters lay. It is not simply that a three-year-old crab produces ten thousand eggs and a six-year-old twice as many. No, as with cod, the number laid is almost a geometric progression. And, as with cod hatchlings, the offspring of older females are genetically better equipped for survival. So, in the cause of conservation and future crab dinners, we forewent the claws-as-big-as-my-hand, and let the old girl go.

However, next day when I went to Broadstrand at low tide, there she lay, this mother-of-many, collapsed and dead on the sand. She was of no use to me now, having been dead for many hours, and no use to the gulls who couldn't break into her carapace. She had died, one presumes, of shock. She had crawled fifty or sixty yards along the seabed before her energy or her will to live gave out. She would feed something, for sure, in time, when the waves and rocks broke her into pieces. I could only console myself with the thought that from the sea she came, and to the sea she did return. One of the great advantages of living by salt water is not only that one gets produce from it but that one can return the leavings to the tide, there to feed other fish or sea birds. Nothing is wasted, nothing misspent.

~

It was during childhood summer holidays spent at Youghal, Ballybunion and Tramore that I first developed an interest in rock pools. When we moved from London to live beside Courtmacsherry Bay, one of my first acts was to buy a large, second-hand glass tank and rig it out as a sea aquarium. Fintan and I — his older brother was at school — would scour the pools for specimens and in summer, when my grandchildren came on holidays, I would press them into willing service too. Recently, I took my three-year-old grandchild, Luca, on holidays from the landlocked Czech Republic, rock-pooling at Dunworley, and I could see that, already, he was fascinated by the creatures his grandfather fished from the depths. He found crabs especially interesting. Perhaps, in the future, if I retire, I will find time to maintain another sea aquarium and there Luca, like his father, Dara, will witness the Miracle of the Two Crabs.

It was revealed to Dara and me when, one morning, we noticed that there were two crabs in the aquarium where, the night before, there had been only one. They were exactly the same size, and duplicates of one another in every respect. It was only when I put my hand in to try to catch one of them that we noticed the difference. One scurried away to hide in the rocks and weed while the other remained motionless. As soon as I lifted it, I noticed that it weighed almost nothing; it was, in fact, the cast-off carapace of the crab that had scuttled away. Crabs can remove themselves from their hard outer skeleton as we might take off a jersey, after which they inflate themselves with sea water and harden up into a larger version of themselves. Thus, they grow. The body, claws and legs of the carapace, right down to the 'toe' tips, is shed in perfect condition, and the skeleton left behind is a perfect replica of themselves.

Another grandchild who likes the seashore is Matilda. When Matilda was seven, I took her to the strand at Ballinglanna, and introduced her to limpets, or *lapas* as the culinary limpet is called in the Canary Islands where they are now so threatened with over-harvesting that they are a protected species. She took to them as if she were a Canary Islander born. A pretty little girl eating raw grey-brown molluscs, wet and slippery and newly prised from their native rocks, is not a common sight in Ireland, where the average small girl would turn up her nose at 'slimy' snails. However, not Matilda, who finds them irresistible.

The limpet is a snail of a marine type. The misnomer 'barnacle' is universally used by land-lubbers. With its conical shell on its back, it crawls around as the tide washes over it, grazing on seaweed and other algae. It is a sort of snail-cow. Seaweed, as we know, is highly nutritious and full of healthy trace elements, so the creatures that graze on it should be too. Furthermore, their environment is pristine, washed by the Atlantic twice daily. They are, essentially, rocky-shore dwellers, and are not found very far up estuaries.

The barnacles commonly found in Ireland — acorn barnacles, to give them their full name — inhabit the small, white, conical shells that blanket the rocks in their millions. Each shell has a kite- or diamond-shape opening on top. The limpet moves around and grazes but the barnacle stays in the same place, opening the top of its shell when the tide runs over it and extending tiny 'tentacles' which catch minute food scraps passing on the tide.

The limpet is largely solitary while the barnacles live in colonies. The same applies to goosenecked barnacles, the lovely, white-shelled mussel-like creatures that are sometimes found on storm beaches affixed to flotsam, on which they may have travelled across thousands of miles of ocean.

Limpets have been acceptable human food for millennia. Shell-middens, where Stone Age Man threw his detritus after dining on the pickings of the shore, often contain limpet shells. Also found are 'limpet hammers', rocks which, archaeologists say, were chosen or fashioned specifically for the purpose of knocking limpets off rocks. This indicates that they must have been considered a choice item — and indeed they are (as Matilda would attest) if the right type is chosen, and they are eaten raw. Certainly, a 'graspable' stone is useful when attempting to swipe a firmly stuck limpet off its hold. However, I find that, if I approach with stealth, not touching the rock whatsoever before the dastardly deed, I can slip a thin knife blade underneath the shell — there is often a slim gap between it and the rock, especially in the epicurean varieties my granddaughter and I, and the Canary Islanders, favour.

Amongst the Irish-speaking limpet-eaters of Connemara, they are called *brodírí* and *fianaigh*; the Beara people of West Cork called them, in Irish, 'sea bacons'. While the shells of the common limpet, the *glás-*

bairneach, is often thick and white, with a base as much as two inches in diameter, those of the 'sea bacons' are more delicate, smaller, darker and flatter, with deeper grooves, and, when they are turned over, are bluish or mother-of-pearl on the inside.

Eating *glás-bairneach* would have been heavy-going. Tough as boot leather, they were boiled or roasted. Some recipes suggested beating them with a meat hammer and frying them in butter, or boiling them with potatoes, onions and fish stock. However, Matilda's and her grandfather's favourite *au natural* seashore fare is the small, one-inch diameter gastronomic limpets, whisked from their shells with the same knife, their bellies discarded and the rest popped onto the tongue. They are tenderer than cooked *calamares*, and carry a delicious, salty flavour of the sea.

~

In early July 2007, William Helps, a talented wildlife artist, phoned to ask me if I would like to join him swimming amongst sharks in Rosscarbery Bay. I might have done so had I not been in the mountains of southern Spain when I received the call, swimming with ants, bugs and a dead shrew in a tiny swimming pool.

On that particular evening, William told me, eighteen baskers were feeding between Rosscarbery Pier and Galley Head, hoovering up the broad bands of red plankton that lay as distinct as the stripes on a footballer's jersey across the surface of the sea. Reports say there were possibly a thousand sharks feeding off the coasts of Cork, Kerry and Clare. Harmless to humans, and little evolved from their primitive ancestors, the basking shark is the world's second largest fish. It zigzags through the plankton fields at less than two miles per hour, its barrel-sized maw hourly ingesting two thousand tons of water, enough to fill an Olympic swimming pool. This is filtered through huge gill rakers, leaving behind tons of minute, life-sustaining plankton. While 'basking' is their usual leisurely behaviour, sometimes, in a burst of energy, they breach, like whales, and leap high out of the water. A fish as big as a single-decker bus in mid-air must be a memorable sight.

Basking shark populations in the north-east Atlantic were dangerously depleted in the past century by over-hunting and their numbers are now only a fraction of what they used to be. Ireland twice had the indecent distinction of almost putting paid to these populations altogether. Once, the largest basking shark fishery in the world was on Achill Island, processing up to 1,800 sharks per year. Having cleaned out the seas, it closed at the end of the 19th century and reopened in the early 1940s when population levels recovered. It was closed for good, owing to the scarcity of sharks, in 1975.

Nowadays, the Asian appetite for shark's fin soup targets the species — the fin can be as big as a tabletop, and fetch 500 euro a kilo. Despite the fact that basking sharks are on the Endangered Species list, the Portuguese, Chinese, Taiwanese and Japanese, amongst other nations, still hunt them. Sharks, as top predators, are essential to the oceans' health and here, again, we see an urgent reason to evolve some governance of the seas beyond national waters. Basking sharks are slow breeders. The females bear a small number of six-foot long young after a gestation of two years.

During summer holidays at Tramore, my father often took us children to The Metal Man, on a promontory above the bay, to watch basking sharks. He also took us to see waves breaking during storms when we lived in Donegal. We would sit in the car on Bloody Foreland and watch the swells sweeping in from America rising into waves and smashing on the black rocks, throwing spray and spume fifty feet high, and even splashing onto the windscreen of the car. Perhaps it was from my father that I gained an early interest in nature — and, indeed, in poetry. The words of the songs he sang were poetry — Ben Jonson's 'Drink to me only with thine eyes' and lyrics from *Moore's Melodies*, and he recited popular verses too. In his time, it was expected that any man worth his salt could stand up on his hind legs and raise a melody. Women, too, contributed. One of my earliest memories is of uncles and aunts in the shadowy drawing room in the family home at Callura House in Cratloe, County Clare, each taking their turn to give voice in a room lit by firelight and Tilley lamps. Each had a party piece: there was, of course, no television, or even radio; 'rural electrification' hadn't yet reached Cratloe, six miles outside Limerick city.

~

During our years in West Cork, the weather in July has been 'erratic' and the arrival of sunshine or rain a bagatelle. The girls from La Gomera were lucky. When we had adult Spanish students and the weather was bad, one couldn't help but apologise. However, many assured me that they had plenty of sun at home and didn't mind a diet of unmitigated shade while they were in Ireland. Others enquired about the price of thermal underwear.

More sanguine were friends of my brother's who came from Seville one July. Up to then, it had been a summer by name but not by season. June had been dismal and we hoped their investment in a holiday cottage wouldn't turn out to be money badly spent. My brother maintained, however, that for them, coming from the 'Frying pan of Spain', cool weather would be a mighty release. Temperatures in their home city had been hovering at about 40 degrees. Living in Seville in summer is like living inside a fire brick, with the fire raging fourteen hours a day. I have been there, done that, and found that even a tee-shirt was too much to wear. The buildings soak up the heat. After the sun sinks, they throw it back into the streets with a force that is almost physical; in some small, enclosed squares, one is almost struck down. The citizenry do not stir out until midnight when the whole town issues forth, and those who can do so make their way to the river. Even by the banks of the Guadalquivir, the streets and walls never entirely cool down during the five months of summer. However, a hint of a breeze is drawn up the great river from the Atlantic, past Los Palos, from where Columbus sailed.

At two, three or four am, in the cafés along the Guadalquivir's banks, trade is vibrant and noisy. The clients are in their evening best, the men elegant and polished, the women in their loveliest, scantiest clothes, many wielding fans with energy and grace. Even the grandee families, who might well have towers of air conditioners and acres of cool gardens at home, are abroad, with elderly parents and herds of well-groomed children. Nobody seems to think of going to bed. The Sevillanos have adapted their sleep patterns to siestas, long naps in cool, innermost rooms in the afternoons and evenings, and have accustomed their digestion to eating dinner at eleven at night. Needs will, if needs must.

My friend Kaori meanwhile tells me that the temperature is 32 degrees in Kyoto, and she feels she may die. It is humid and sticky; and that is worse than the dry, if searing, Andalucian heat. Heat falls on the Kanto, the central plain of Honshū, in June, July and August, like a barber's hot towel. In the underground trains, the bodies crammed together perspire onto one another. Nothing can be done; the trains have air conditioning, but as soon as the doors open, warm air is sucked in, and the platforms and underground tunnels are as humid as saunas.

I have been there, too, and done that — as they say — but I had to wear a collar and tie all day long, not a cotton T-shirt. It was worth it. There was big money to be made teaching English to 'company men' in Tokyo, and Marie and I left our rented two-tatami room at 7.30 in the morning and didn't return until 8.30 at night, travelling from office to office through the crowded, sweltering city, instructing businessmen in 'Engrish', and working at some schools too.

~

I regularly get letters from kind readers of my *Irish Examiner* column. Sometimes, I am told that a strange or exotic bird has turned up in their garden. On one occasion, my correspondent thought it was a hawk. Why did she think it was a hawk? I asked. It had feathers on its legs. Did it have a hawk's sharp, downturned beak? was my next question. Yes, was the answer, she thought so. It turned out to be a fugitive tumbler pigeon. I mentioned it in a column and — wonder of wonders! — the owner of the bird contacted me to say that when he and another fancier were exchanging birds at a lay-by in Tipperary, it had escaped and disappeared into the night. He identified it perfectly and recovered it from the finder. It's a small world, if you're a bird.

Another reader wrote to say that a pair of racing pigeons, with rings, had arrived at his farm four months before, stayed around the yard and hatched two eggs, both parents sitting. A single stray racing pigeon is not an unusual phenomenon, but two, and of opposite sexes, hinted of an elopement.

They were pretty birds, he said, but the squabs looked as hideous as only pigeon offspring can. Few wild bird offspring look attractive when hatched, while battery 'day-old chicks', all golden, fluffy-feathered and peeping shrilly, are positively 'cute' as Americans might say. How parent pigeons can love their offspring beggars belief. I realise that ascribing love to pigeons is somewhat stretching it but they, like other birds, tirelessly care for their young.

While my reader had a pair of pigeons come to stay, in recent years we have had house sparrows, two pairs, attending the peanut feeder. We hope they may, sooner or later, nest and bring blessings to the house, as is traditionally believed. House sparrows live in symbiosis with humans: they would not have been present in Ireland before the arrival of our farming ancestors, Neolithic Man. As mankind spread out of Africa, the sparrows, members of the weaver bird family, followed. In recent years, their numbers in Ireland have fallen drastically and, so, they are to be treasured all the more. Food scarcity is probably the reason. No longer do horse carts or horses' nosebags leak oats onto the road; no longer is grain spilled in the fields.

I wonder if sparrows nested in the cave near the Cape of Good Hope where, according to Simon Winchester in his book *The Atlantic*, one branch of mankind (having trekked southwards, over thousands of years, from the womb of the Great Rift Valley) saw the sea for the first time. The marks they left in the cave are still extant after 164,000 years, carbon-dated. While 'It was a brave man who ate the first oyster . . .' as Dean Swift said, seafood supplied a rich food source, easily harvested, and so early man first colonised the world via the sea coasts.

Sparrows, looking much as they do today, might well have joined them in their cave. When Lucy, *Australopithecus afarensis*, 'mother of all mankind', walked the African plains a mere four million years ago, larks and the like had, for aeons before, been climbing the skies and raining down song. Bird song may well have been the genesis of music — not that, one supposes, we ourselves couldn't sing, raising our voices to express joy or sorrow from the earliest stages of our evolution. When did the first creature that we were — out of which we would become *Homo sapiens* — string voice-sounds together and make a song? Lucy and her sisters stood a little over three feet tall, her brothers less than five feet, but perhaps they sang as well as most of us do today.

Our early ancestors clearly had a keen eye for beauty. In the caves at Chauvet, Lascaux and Altamira, the depictions of animals are breathtaking in the skill and grace with which they portray, most especially, movement. In these cave drawings, the wild bulls are charging, the antelopes leaping, the horses galloping. It is extraordinary to think that people whose technology had not developed further than the fire and the use of stone tools had evolved sensibilities equal to or surpassing our own, that they sought uncompromisingly after perfection and had, among their small numbers, artists to rival Leonardo. These were not scribbles traced by passing hunters: Lascaux and Altamira were cave temples, on the walls and roofs of which galleries of frescoes were drawn. They were occupied and visited over tens of thousands of years.

The robust, yet sublime, expression of the spirit of the animals — the power of the mammoths, the speed of the horses, the grace of the antelopes — indicates a sympathy with the creatures themselves. Did they try to capture this essence, be it courage, speed or grace to make it their own, or were the depictions a prelude to the chase? Were the creatures honoured, then hunted? In the huge frescoes, one can almost hear the hooves thundering and the cries of the stick men, with their spears, giving chase.

Humans were still rare. Herds of animals roamed the Cantabrian plains. Sometimes, the humans are drawn as rectangular boxes, with sticks for arms and legs. They stand in groups among the far finer animal portraits. There is no human portrait, or none has survived. Why not a face? In testimony of themselves, they chose to leave only palm prints, each one differing from the next in its life-lines, contours and proportions which, when first laid down, would have been clearly visible and distinct. It is ironic that, in our modern world, with terror and paranoia abroad, we again differentiate ourselves from others by hand prints and finger prints. It seems that these people left the shape of their hands to register that they had *been*, and that they were, each one, individual and different. And, in the paintings, they record not only the spirit of the animals but the quality of their own souls.

August

One August evening, after a traditional threshing, a woman from Manchester sang the beautiful lament *She moved through the fair* to the assembled crowd. One could hear a wheat straw fall, so deep was their silence as she sang. The song was a country air first collected in Donegal by the poet Padraic Colum and musicologist Herbert Hughes. It was recorded on vinyl by Count John McCormack (who, at one stage, assisted James Joyce with his budding choral aspirations). Margaret Barry, the Traveller singer, made it famous and it was popular with Travellers street-singing for the price of a drink at Fair Days.

Then she stepped away from me, and she moved through the fair
And so fondly I watched her move here and move there;
At last she turned homeward, with one star awake,
As the swan in the evening moves over the lake.

PADRAIC COLUM

~

August is the month when, in the warm nights while we are sleeping, or perhaps in the pre-dawn glow, white button mushrooms push their heads out of the earth unbeknownst to us, newly arrived aliens peeking their shiny heads over the wet grass as if trying to get a better look. For the mushroom-picker coming upon them, their beauty and innocence always presents a dilemma: pick them now before someone else finds them, or leave them to enjoy the world a bit longer and to grow larger and fatter, at the risk that they won't be there when one returns.

Mushroom pickers are secretive people. They will share knowledge of the fields with those they know, but are wary of strangers who would pillage their budding harvest and strip their acres bare.

Some years ago, when I wrote that the forest mushroom varieties — the chanterelles and ceps — seemed to be as rare as hens' teeth in my part of Ireland, a German gentleman (and he turned out to be, indeed, a gentleman) wrote to tell me that this was not the case at all, not, at least, in Kerry, and he could show me various wild fungi growing in profusion — but, on second thoughts, he wouldn't.

A retired German executive and a lover of Ireland since he was a young man, he subsequently sent me pictures of himself and his Irish wife, Rose, a Kerry woman, surrounded by baskets of mushrooms, a cornucopia of fungi of every, most delicious kind. He had repented on his decision not to show me some growing in situ. If I cared to drive to Kerry, he would take me to a few selected spots, and perhaps my wife and I might like to come to dinner afterwards.

We duly drove over the magnificent scenery of the Healy Pass, entirely obscured by the summer monsoons, and met Horst and Rose at the other side. The rain had stopped and we proceeded to woods a few miles away where he made good his promise, leading us under pines and rhododendrons to a patch of mossy ground carpeted in chanterelles, their egg-yolk colour vivid against the cushions of green.

In ten minutes, we picked nearly a gallon, leaving the smaller ones behind. We went, then, to the next secret venue — but, to Horst's dismay, found that, for the first time ever, it had been raided. Some interloper had picked it almost bare! But not to worry, said Horst, a cheerful soul — he had many other secret places and, in any case, new chanterelles would soon pop up; indeed, over the years he'd found he could harvest the same spots week after week, sometimes from June until December. From midsummer until the turn of the year, the various species of forest fungi each have their season, and Horst and I have became firm friends over the course of our mushroom excursions. I must be the only man in Ireland who receives exotic culinary mushrooms in the post — although I once sent my father a box of pristine wood blewits, beautiful purple mushrooms, and he ate them, taking my word for it that they wouldn't poison him — Oh, man of faith! — and said he had enjoyed them with gusto.

While many forest mushrooms, so-called 'toadstools', are good to eat — better than field mushrooms in many cases — some are deadly poisonous. With these varieties, as with the fruit of the arbutus tree, one of the unique Lusitanian species that occurs in south-west Ireland, it is unlikely that one will ever consume more than a single example. The Linnaean name of the tree is *Arbutus unedo*, meaning 'Arbutus, I eat one only'. This, however, is a matter of taste; the fruit, resembling small, bumpy-skinned oranges, is sweet but has a strange, off-putting texture and many seeds. It is not toxic. However, should one eat the wrong mushroom, one will not have the option of sampling another the following day.

Experts in doubt about an unfamiliar mushroom refer to the colour of the spore or 'seed'. Mushrooms grow from spore, and caps begin to deposit spore beneath them once they are half-grown. Sometimes, when one cap grows immediately above another, spore will be seen deposited on the lower cap. Finer than talcum powder, its colour depends upon the species; blewit spore is pale lilac, the spore of field mushrooms is dark brown, chanterelle spore is yellow, and clouded agaric spore is pink.

Spore prints are very beautiful and mysterious, leaving a perfect image of the underside of the mushroom, often wafted a little one way or the other by a flow of air, so that the print has a Caspar-the-Ghost-like shape. A print is made by taking a fresh cap, shortening the stem to half the length of one's thumb, and standing it on a square of black paper; one can stick a tack through the paper to keep it upright. Then a bowl or plastic tub is placed over it, one edge resting on a pencil or knife handle so as to allow a small flow of air (this also helps the phantom Caspar-effect). After twelve to twenty-four hours the cover is carefully lifted off and, if the procedure has been successful, what is revealed is truly beautiful, the mirror image of the delicate gill patterns perfectly defined in the print.

Mushrooms that might well kill you or me were traditionally used by Siberian and Laplander shamans who ingested fly agaric, *Amanita muscaria* to help them get in touch with their gods. When reindeer eat fly agaric, the shamans sometimes imbibe their urine, the toxins having been filtered out by the reindeers' livers. Such potions are not to be recommended unless one is a Lapp and knows what one is doing. As I mentioned earlier, the Vikings are said to have eaten fly agaric before going into battle.

Magic mushrooms, so called, seem to grow in almost every earthly region, and their properties have been utilised for religious rituals in most. There is a theory that the manna Moses and his fatigued followers found in the desert was actually a psychoactive fungus which gave them clarity of vision at a time when they were physically and spiritually 'lost'. The manna is described not as having fallen from the sky but as appearing overnight amongst the hoar frost, which it would have resembled. Psilocybe mushrooms of the region are, indeed, tiny and white, and appear when there is moisture in the desert. Moses instructed his followers on how to consume the bounty; some commentators believe that, as a shepherd boy, he may have inadvertently eaten such mushrooms (the vision of the Burning Bush) or learned about them from his father, an initiate and a priest.

With psychoactive mushrooms now banned — along with, perhaps, celestial visions? — are European nations becoming nanny states? I don't think so; after all, in most, citizens retain the right to drink or smoke themselves to death and cause tragedy to all around them; however, hypocrisy dictates that they should not be allowed to choose non-approved intoxicants. Legal intoxicants, proprietary-brand intoxicants, prepared-and-manufactured and properly taxed intoxicants are entirely acceptable but not those that sprout out of the ground or that nature provides free in the wild. While mind-numbing drugs, e.g. alcohol, are approved, psychoactive drugs that induce real-or-imagined introspection, thoughtfulness, universal love and spirituality are not. It is ironic that while alcohol — a by-product of which may be teenage girls lying catatonic in the street — is tolerated, stoned hippies, sitting in a field, gurgling and passing daisies one to the other is considered an affront to society. It is questionable as to whether citizens are any longer at liberty to pick a wild mushroom whose common name is the liberty cap.

When we lived in London, we often saw intense youths and their girls scouring Hampstead Heath, eyes fixed on the sward and stopping now and then to pick tiny mushrooms which may or may not have been psychoactive. In the rich silage fields of Ireland, they would not have much luck; blue-grass prairies admit no other flora. Cut as soon as it is prime, the grass is put into pits and mixed with molasses to feed and fatten the cattle in winter; most cattle, nowadays, even in our temperate region, are kept in sheds. In good weather, the huge, green tractor-trailers of the silage contractors rumble to and fro on back roads and bohreens, carrying grass from the fields to the silage pits at hair-raising speed. As soon as 'the cut' is completed in one farm, they move to the next, caravans of mobile machinery strung out along the rural roads like circuses in passage. No time to waste; onward to the next prairie!

Once the harvesters roar onto the field, an organised frenzy starts. Tractors with giant cutters move up and down the sward while a transporter, into which the mown grass is pumped, keeps pace beside each. When one transporter rushes off to discharge, it is replaced by another. From first light to moonlight, the work goes on; high-wattage headlights carve paths through the field's darkness. At midnight, men sprayed green with grass juice arrive in rural pubs ready to murder pints. With them comes the swampish bouquet of fresh-mown vegetation. If the forecast is good, it's home to bed quick, to start again in the morning. There's great money, making silage while the sun shines.

Unfortunately, hard on the heels of the cut, slurry is spread to fertilise a new crop and agricultural aromas waft fierce and pungent across the countryside. Farmers want another helping of grass and, to get it, the land must be force-fed. Slurry is a two-edged sword. It generates rich grass but it can also poison water courses, and on warm August days it generates rich smells. By and large, rural dwellers are uncomplaining about the latter: they understand it and tolerate it, although housewives, with clothes on the line, wouldn't always take that view.

A man I got talking to when I was standing, looking into the river, at Coomhola Bridge told me that, in the old days, women in the uplands found furze bushes most useful for clothes-drying; they could drape the laundry over the prickly bushes with no fear of it blowing away, and if the furze was in flower, it would have a lovely, coconutty aroma when it was dry. He also told me that the branches of furze — French gorse, in this case — provided the strongest oar-pegs 'known to man: they could withstand the strain of an oar pulled by the strongest oarsman in the wildest seas. They were resilient; like the man himself, they bent, but they could never be broken . . . .'

Besides washing the breakfast dishes, saving the laundry from a drenching is another of my domestic accomplishments. As a boy, I was well trained at bringing in the washing in a hurry, a much-to-be-admired expertise given the capricious weather we Irish live with. These days, I can write and watch out for rain at the same time, just as I can do the washing-up while watching nature in the field across the stream — multi-tasking is not the prerogative of women, as they would have one believe. When the first drops dimple the surface of the pond in the yard outside my workroom window, I accelerate into action like an Olympic athlete. My mother trained me. 'Damien, run out and bring in the washing!' she would call, and I'd sprint out into the yard and try to keep the flapping sheets off the ground as they plastered themselves around me. But, gallantly, I'd arrive back in the kitchen breathless, and she'd say, 'You're a great man — I don't know what I'd do without you!' And maybe she'd let me lick the spoon when she took it out of the chocolate cake she was mixing, never mind that I was fourteen or fifteen years old at the time. I'm still expert at disrobing a washing line, as are most sons born on this island of changeable weather. Some things one never forgets, like riding a bike.

~

In August 2005, I was asked by Séamus Ó Drisceoil of Cape Clear Island to write a book outlining walking routes on the seven inhabited islands of West Cork, the project to be backed by LEADER and the Irish Islands Federation, Comhdháil Oileáin na hÉireann. It was an enviable commission indeed. In the late summer days, I would walk island roads where the wayside flowers had never known the slipstream swish of shiny Mercs or flashy Beamers, roads where there were no cars at all. With my wife the OS map reader, and our happy hound, I would tread paths far from the endless Tiger-talk of house prices. How fortunate I was! Many more deserving souls spent their lives stuffing chickens or counting money to support their families, unsung heroes enduring, with fortitude, the postponement of dreams.

There is little money in my kind of writing but it's a fine employment, allowing me, as it does, to explore the outdoors, whether in West Cork, La Gomera or the high Alpujarras, on jungle trails in Guantánamo, Cuba or in coconut groves by the Andaman Sea. One doesn't stay in luxury hotels, but one gets by. I took on the commission, knowing that it would afford the pleasure of discovering, mapping and commenting upon byways, mass paths, school paths and milk paths previously undrawn but, of course, familiar to generations of islanders. Long ago, they were paths of necessity, often hard necessity: now, they could be itineraries of delight.

On Long Island, Dursey and Whiddy, all inhabited, there is no shop, pub or hotel — nowhere to spend money. In a nation as obsessed with grandiose houses, pretentious restaurants and over-the-top weddings as was Ireland in 2005 (spend thirty thousand on your daughter's nuptials or she'll think you don't love her; helicopter her six-year-old sister to the church for her first holy communion or she won't be able to face her friends!), how grand it would be to leave the rip-off Republic and enter a world with other values, to cross the sea to a land where no money exchanged hands, to enjoy havens of past values floating between Ireland and America, chimeras that were real and bathed in sunlight — literally or figuratively, who cared? Marie and I would be offshore, but not for tax purposes. We would explore the islands; we would take sandwiches, an OS map, a camera, binoculars and the dog.

For me, the thrill of a day on the islands always begins at the ferry, or the cable car if I am going to Dursey. As the mainland recedes, the everyday world is another country, which we have left behind. The islands ahead move in another time; for those not old enough to remember, we can say this is what Ireland was like before the traffic and the hurry, a less busy, more gracious place.

Our first venue, on a lovely August day, was Sherkin, with its ruined abbey and its story, the ruined castle of Fineen the Rover O'Driscoll and its epic tale — half-heroism, half-farce — and the Marine Station, famous worldwide, the project of a remarkable man called Matt Murphy.

When one crosses Roaringwater Bay on the ferry from Baltimore, one sees many small islands, mere scraps of land, once inhabited by a single family but long since abandoned. Those islanders who did not, or could not, settle on the mainland, or emigrate to Britain or America, had to find sustenance in the soil and the sea, and solace in religion. There was food in plenty for the spirit but not always for the stomach in the beauty that lay all around them. David S. Quin's poem 'Lucht an Oileáin' (People of the Islands) captures their spirit better than I could hope to. He says: '. . . for they dwelt upon a rock in the sea and not in a shining metropolis/ and lived off the pick of the strand, the hunt of the hill, the fish in the sea,/ the wool off sheep and packets full of dollars; [. . .] For they were full/ of sunlight and mist, wind and stone, rain and rock, but the Atlantic ocean/ would not pay them a regular salary . . .'

The spirit of the people who colonised, and turned to good use, small patches of sea-locked rock and sand all along the West Cork coast — all around the coasts of Ireland — has left a testament of lonely crofts and cottages, collapsed potato drills and lazybeds, and ruins on islands long returned to nature. It is heartening to know that, now, in a new dispensation, their world is enjoying a revival. The natives who remained are a determined people. Through centuries of often grinding hardship, they 'hung on' and now seek a vibrant future in island industry, crafts and tourism. Meanwhile, newcomers have arrived to live amongst them, new faces and new lifestyles. They bring hopes and dreams, some capital and a respect for the way of life. They come to share the peace, understanding and values of the unique environment, and the strength to be found in self-reliance.

On Cape Clear, Séamus Ó Drisceoil labours to entice visitors by arranging walks, Walking Festivals and International Storytelling Weekends. Chuck Kruger, an American who has set up home there, has generously created a trail across his clifftop land, and writes articles, books and poems about island life. Penny Durrell, an Englishwoman, has written a marvellous book about far-flung Dursey; Christine Thery, born in Hong Kong, records life on Heir in her paintings; Jeremy Irons, the actor, restored a fine castle on an islet at Kilcoe. There are many more such 'blow-ins' — it is not a pejorative term: not being West Cork-born, I am one myself.

For visitors, the islands provide superb walking and a wealth of avian and marine fauna while, beside the paths and bohreens, a profusion of wild flowers bloom. The only sound is bird song, and the hum of bees. Humans are few; traffic, on most, is all but non-existent. The air is laced with ozone, and immensities of mountain, sea and sky fill the view.

Even where there are cars, as on some of the islands, they are few, and they have little effect on the pace and serenity (there is even an oil storage-depot, unobtrusively sited, on Whiddy Island in Bantry Bay). During the research, I tried to share something of these 'other island' worlds with readers of my column and, sometimes, friends accompanied us on our island trips — Alannah Hopkin, who has also written about West Cork, or our friend Jim Buckley, a veterinary surgeon with a fine voice and a great yen for walking the untrodden ways. We could leave Ireland for the day and be home in time for supper.

The compilation of all the walks series, from the first, *Walks of Courtmacsherry Bay*, to the last, *Walks of Seven West Cork Islands* (and, in 2011, a new, updated book, *Scenic Walks in West Cork*, published by The Collins Press), owes much to Marie. I might say, 'I'd have been lost without her!' — and I also mean that in the sense of, 'At times, I wouldn't have known where I was!' In the research and walking stages, while she checked the maps, I blithely meandered along in another world, talking to myself on a recording machine, stopping to explore nature, human history or prehistory, and to photograph vistas, flowers or frogs. I found every hour of the 'work' to be a learning process and the research was half the joy — the story of the land, the lie of the fields, the rise of the hills, the colour of the lakes, the encounters with the local people I met and with the vestiges of their past that remained. Meanwhile, my geographer wife and I shared, in the case of each and every round, our admiration of the Irish countryside and the joy of walking it together.

For most of us, good company enhances our hikes but I sometimes wonder if my companions wouldn't prefer to have left me at home. I am a hopelessly unfocused walker. Putting one foot in front of the other at a hectic pace doesn't appeal to me at all. I'm intrigued by things I come across and linger over them, an interesting ruin or, even, a roadside wall, notable because of the distinctive and beautiful way the stones have been laid, and the array of plants that have colonised them. And why not stop to look? We have eyes, ears and brains to exercise, not just limbs. Wayside plants, strange bugs, sunlight shimmering on ivy, trout darting in the flow of a brown river are all absorbing and, so, I lag behind, then huff and puff to catch up with the walker-walkers who are forced to stop and wait for me. The countryside changes with each passing week and passing day and when I see folk route-marching along, arms flying, dark glasses on their eyes, headphones on their ears, I sometimes wonder why they don't stay at home and use one of those conveyor-belt walking machines. However, who knows but that they might be practising for a marathon? Meanwhile, I am conscious of the forbearance afforded me by my patient wife, children, friends and dog. They have made life's roads a pleasure and lightened my steps on the way.

~

One sunny August morning, after buying the paper at the shop (Rita's emporium, the only shop in Courtmacsherry), I strolled up the bayside path and found the ex-headmaster of the local school, Seán Barry, telling a group of thirty visitors and locals the story of the ruined monastery at Abbeymahon; I, myself, and all present, found the commentary most instructive. Great efforts are made to welcome summer visitors; the volunteers of the Tidy Towns Committee excel themselves with brushes, brooms and baskets of flowers tarting up our village, and Seán's Local History Walks are one of the diversions on offer.

August being the height of the summer season, one passes smiling faces on the street at all hours of the day and night. There's a great atmosphere of bonhomie abroad. 'Grand day!' or 'Grand night!' they declare, with the older people adding, 'Thank God.' Most of these folk have been coming here in August all their lives. Entering the pub, their faces break into smiles. 'Hello, John!', says the man who steps aside, his pint in his hand, to let them through. 'Hello, Stephen,' says John, 'It's grand to see you again.' And they move on through, the family from Cork who have come here for three generations now, meeting old friends and summer neighbours whom they haven't seen for a year, and people they see every day in Cork city, seasonal migrants like themselves, coming to their second home. Many have roots in the village and have known one another since they played with bucket and spade on the strand or went on excursions in ass carts, on bicycles or in old Morris Minors to Dunworley, out on the Seven Heads. In family albums, there are black-and-white photographs taken by a grandfather with a Baby Brownie and developed at Roche's in Patrick's Street, Cork, a family business that is still there.

August is the regatta month, too, with swimming races in The Dock, greasy-pole pillow-fights for the kids and a simulated helicopter-and-lifeboat rescue. The village holds its annual festival, as does Timoleague, at the apex of the bay. In recent years, Timoleague has been putting on class acts (not that Courtmacsherry does not have smaller-scale 'class acts' every weekend in the Anchor Bar) with famous singers like Mary Black performing in a large marquee. We are spoiled for musical choice and talent in West Cork. In Clonakilty, of a Saturday night, seven or eight pubs will host groups or individual musicians, often well-known, like Christy Moore, Sharon Shannon, Luka Bloom, Declan Sinnott, or Liam Ó Maonlaí. There are amateurs too, traditional musicians joining in the mid-week sessions in O'Donovan's Hotel, sawing their fiddles, beating their *bodhráns* and fingering their button accordions. There is punk-rock and jazz, country-and-western and honky-tonk piano, crooners and *sean-nós* singers — a musical tour of Clonakilty of a Saturday night has our visitors in awe. At home, be it the UK, the USA, Spain, France or Japan, such a variety of groups and styles in a town with a population of around 4,000 would be unknown and it is unlikely that the audience ever get nearer than twenty yards away from the performers, even when they have paid a small fortune for a ticket to attend. In Clonakilty, one may well be sitting across the table from them. The conviviality is palpable; many of these well-known names come to play in De Barra's and the other pubs because they know the owners, and they are there to enjoy themselves with fellow-musicians, often as locally famous as the stars. They come to play amongst friends, and the friends come to hear, to admire and, often, to join it. They listen with a critical ear and the silence abroad is a testimony to the quality.

~

Marie and the family and I often have our annual reunion in August, although not always in Ireland. There are nineteen in the clan now, and the cost of air fares or ferries for sons and daughters with two or three children are at their peak in high summer. With children at school, they can come at no other time — and thus are penalised, one might say, for having children. In *A Place Near Heaven*, I wrote of summer afternoons in the early 1990s when I went rock-pooling with a troop of grandchildren armed with buckets and nets. Being pre-school, their parents could bring them to Ireland in June when the car-ferries were cheaper and, so, the cars arrived crammed with children, suitcases and sleeping bags, and the bedrooms resembled Japanese dormitories with futons on the floor. Nowadays, the same children drive here in their own cars; shortly, I would imagine, those children will be bringing their own offspring — and that will be a mighty thrill which, the Great

Creator willing, I hope I will be privileged to enjoy.

Of the overseas reunions, I could give accounts of many, all memorable, with nothing but harmony and accord at each one. Remembered especially are visits of the family to La Gomera when we had the house there in the 1980s. The boys loved driving my old VW Beetle out on the dusty paths where there wasn't a living thing to harm and not a policeman within miles of us. Boy, how they whooped — and the girls too! And it did them no disservice, for they are all competent drivers now. The freedom of La Gomera was greatly to be enjoyed, the Wild West landscapes, the semi-deserts, and the lizards skittering out of our path.

In August 2006, we had an outstanding reunion in the Manchester home of my eldest son, Niall, and, some time after midnight, armed with replenished glasses, were able to stand outside his back door and watch wood mice foraging as if we weren't there. Wood mice, unlike house mice, do not smell, and do not have the scaly tail of their indoor cousins. They are sandy-brown, with white underparts and a yellow streak on the chest. In spring, they eat weed seeds, insect larvae and insects but in the garden may dine on crocus bulbs, beans, apples and even tomatoes, an imaginative diet indeed. My son's garden has none of these, except apples, but it comprises a wonderful array of shrubs and exotic trees, planted and nurtured by the previous owners over a lifetime. It perfectly complements the Victorian house; I was surprised at how leafy are the Manchester suburbs and how gracious the houses. My surprise no doubt stems from childhood geography lessons which gave me the impression that all English towns north of Watford were heavily industrialised. We learned off the names and the products: Sheffield, cutlery, Halifax, wool, Bolton, cotton and Manchester practically everything. But the factories have long since closed, the industries long since gone. One may now find them in China; and the unwelcome pollution too.

Having spent many childhood years in Spain, Niall has Mediterranean culinary skills and, on the following lunchtime, we had paella on the sunlit lawn. He had bought a paella pan, 30 inches (90 centimetres) in diameter, with a supporting stand and a gas stove with jets arranged in concentric circles. Filled to the top, the pan could feed fifty people. We only part-filled it — we numbered eighteen. What a wonderful invention is the paella, a one-pan dish based on Valencia rice cooked in oil and stock with any and every variety of fish, shellfish, meat, chicken, vegetable and fruit (tomatoes) added. In this paella, all the aforementioned were included, following the Spanish fashion, and it was a garden feast nonpareil.

On the occasion of the 2007 reunion, what marvellous tranquillity and other-worldliness we experienced on a Sunday afternoon as nineteen of us Enrights or married-into-Enrights cruised down the Grand Union Canal in Hertfordshire at duck-pace. A mallard paddled ahead, splitting the brown waters as if piloting us. Draped like a band of brigands all over the roofs and decks of two elderly seventy-foot long narrow boats lashed together, we followed that duck.

The owner and captain, my daughter Miriam's then paramour, stood stripped to the waist at the tiller, luxuriant hair falling in curls to his shoulders, as wild and hearty as any Lascar seaman who ever sailed the main with Henry Morgan. A muscular son-in-law, helped by a grandson, managed the locks as our craft, *The Euphrates*, once a tour 'package' that carried 67 sightseers, headed upstream. Canada geese passed in flotillas of twenty or thirty birds. Songbirds piped from the trees above and terns flew low against the heavenly blue — I have never had a better view of terns, with their sharp white wings and forked tails almost translucent against the bright sky. Dainty and aerodynamic, they called to one another as they patrolled the canal, every now and then plunging headlong into the brown water to rise with small fish in their beaks. The Canada geese are a nuisance on British waterways, competing with native birds, but these too were to be seen in abundance, ducks and coots, herons and kingfishers. Perhaps prettiest of all were the waterhens stepping daintily beneath the undercover of the banks. One 'hen' had six fluffy balls of down in tow, making my granddaughters shriek and want to catch and hold them.

And so we sat atop the barges, and dined and partied and drank beer or wine as we quietly chugged along the green, watery ribbon that led through market towns and conurbations with their shopping malls and spaghetti junctions, all hidden by the canopies of willows and alders so that one would never have guessed they were there. In our domain, cattle grazed in overgrown fields along the bank and buddleia bloomed over the towpaths. The verdant corridor of the Grand Union Canal is another world, removed from all semblance of hurry, remote from concrete and stress, and most of the landscapes, locks and bridges have remained little changed since the waterway, running from London to Birmingham, was built over two hundred years ago.

Dick Warner, a colleague on my *Irish Examiner* page, long ago discovered the joys of the Grand Canal in Ireland, and shared the secret via his series of programmes on RTÉ. After my canal trip on that lovely afternoon, I could well see how one could become enamoured of life on the green, tranquil corridors that run, largely unused and unsung, through the hearts of these islands. It was Andrew Marvell, the 17th-century English poet, who wrote the line 'a green thought in a green shade' previously cited. To slowly round a bend in the narrow waterway and see, ahead, through a tunnel of green light, a group of horses grazing in sunlit meadows alongside old, tile-roofed barns recalled his fresh, poetic sentiments.

Sometimes, we passed floating homes lining the banks between locks, narrow boats and house-boats of all sizes, some dinky and squeaky clean, with polished brass and varnished timbers, others growing moss and held together only by paint. The canal people seemed to be, universally, relaxed folk sitting atop their craft amongst bicycles, deck chairs, boxes of gay flowers and parasols. There was a sense of community there; all, like our captain, were refugees from the concrete jungle only a few hundred yards away, alternative people choosing life in the green ribbon rather than the fast lane. 'Here at last!' they cried to our captain as we passed, referring to the belated arrival of that year's summer. Between ourselves, Marie and I knew that we were responsible for the advent of the sun and blue skies: we had brought them with us from Spain. Up to that weekend, England had endured a month of downpours and inundation, with no break in the clouds. Then, we arrived off the ferry at Dover, opened the doors of our car, and released the Spanish sun trapped inside. It rushed out and warmed the chilly English and painted their pleasant countryside in gold.

~

Here, at home, one Sunday afternoon in late August 2003, we headed west to Rosscarbery where we knew that the fiddler Gerry Lombard and some friends were playing at the Courthouse Bar. A traditional threshing was just finishing up in the yard as we arrived, the big wheels and belts of the combine harvester still turning and a crowd watching, eating chips. A friend arrived with some visitors from Norway. When the music struck up, it was so good, and the atmosphere so friendly, that one couldn't but be proud of Ireland.

But we were in for a surprise. Suddenly, a slim girl, about ten years old, danced out into the space in front of the musicians, arms by her sides and legs flying like a miniature Jean Butler. Shortly she gave way to a friend who, in turn, gave way to two girls dancing side by side. The music of the fiddle, *uileann* pipes, banjo and guitar set all hands clapping and all feet tapping. Overwhelmed, a ruddy farmer 'in good form', with a bent-shank Kapp and Peterson pipe between his teeth, hopped out and did a brief 'batter', followed by the mother of one of the young dancers; one could see where her daughter had learned her skills. A friend joined her and they were as practised as a pair from *Riverdance* itself. The *Darby O'Gill and the Little People* farmer stood looking on, nodding to the music and beaming at the good of it.

After the dancing, one of the high-stepping party took up the microphone and sang 'She moved through the Fair'. So fine was the entertainment, it might have been professional, but it happened spontaneously on a West Cork August day. The dancers, the singer and the *uileann* pipes player all turned out to be from Manchester, of Irish stock. Since childhood, most have spent their summers in West Cork.

Someone joked, 'We send them away but they keep coming back, thank God!'

Driving home, we saw a man on a platform in Clonakilty giving a speech, and the streets crowded with listeners around him — had the statue of Michael Collins suddenly come alive on its plinth in Emmet Square? At Timoleague, the village festival was in full swing, the sounds and the lights of the 'Merries' (as funfairs are locally called) bright against the evening sky.

September

The poetry of earth is never dead:
[...]
The poetry of earth is ceasing never:

JOHN KEATS, 'On the Grasshopper and Cricket'

~

In September, our inshore seas are benevolent. Mackerel shoals riffle the surface like fairy winds, and gulls dive on sprats in the shallows. In the evenings, the waves break on the sand still warm from the sun. When the boys were young, I would often round them up and pack them into the car, sometimes with friends, and head off to Dunworley for an after-work, pre-prandial dip. It was always exciting to be in their company; their enthusiasm was infectious and their good-humoured banter kept one young. When sprats were boiling in the dock, I recall ten-year-old Fin and his pals 'dive-bombing' them off the pier, leaping down from on high and scooping up the stunned, slippery fish that came to the surface.

In recent years, a feature of September evenings has been the Polish men from the meat-processing factory cycling through the village, fishing rods strapped to their bikes. At the weekends, their wives or girlfriends keep them company but many of them have come to Ireland solo, sending money back to their familes in Poland and saving almost every penny of the wages they earn here. At weekends, Poles staying at Pad Joe's hostel in Timoleague — the provision of hostel accommodation being a timely and lucrative initiative on the part of Pad Joe's grandsons who inherited the pub — make trips to the off-licence downstairs to buy a bottle of vodka and six packs of Polish beer at very reasonable prices. They are rarely seen in the pub itself but Polish 'sklceps' or grocery stores can now be found in most country towns, catering for eastern Europeans in general. Meanwhile, the ardent anglers make good use of the fish they catch, welcoming the opportunity to avoid spending hard-earned wages on shop-bought fare — as would have the Irish emigrants to Britain in the bad old days. And it seems that the Poles like fishing. Indeed, there can be few cheaper, healthier, more productive or more inspiring ways of spending leisure time than standing on the shore in the stillness of the evening, casting a line of feathers out over the sea.

For Marie's summer students, a regular highlight of the evening fishing trips in Mark Gannon's boats was feeding the screaming clouds of seagulls with the heads, tails and viscera of the fish they had caught as we powered homeward after a couple of hours hooking mackerel and pollock off the Old Head. On one memorable evening — memorable for the sunset mirrored on the sea's surface, for all the world like a red carpet welcoming us back into the bay — a gannet appeared, beating upwind, low over the water, gaining fast on the boat which was travelling at twenty knots, more than twenty miles per hour. Suddenly, it was in amongst the gulls, close above us, its broad black-tipped wings, spear-head beak and yellow poll unmistakable in the white cloud of birds.

But it had competition in the air; the black-backed gulls, herring gulls and black-headed gulls were more agile in flight, turning and swooping and all but flying backwards or upside-down to snaffle the snacks before they ever hit the water. However, when a heavy fish head was flung high into the air, the gull cloud opened and the gannet came into its own. As the gulls screamed and plunged to the surface to retrieve the bounty, the gannet dived. With its wide wings folded close against its body, it hit the water like a torpedo from a dive bomber, raising a fountain of spray. It would have been an unfortunate gull that came between the gannet and the fish head. I can't imagine the gannet being able to put on the brakes once it was committed to the dive.

In times past, in the Irish and Scottish islands, gannets were highly valued as a resource. In the Hebrides, they were 'harvested' by tying a herring to a waterlogged board which would float just below the surface of the sea. The gannet, spotting the herring from on high, would go into dive mode. Even if it saw the board seconds before it hit it, there could have been no hope of braking. 'Solan goose' the islanders called the gannet. With a wing span of forty inches, it is larger than many geese. In those make-do days, the heavy layer of fat on its breast was used not only for cooking but for tallow for lamps, and for waterproofing wet-weather gear. The thick down was used to stuff pillows, the feathers to make brushes — indeed, I remember my father, who could have afforded the shop-bought product, using a goose wing as a brush to sweep crumbs from the tabletop after tea; he had learned such conservation economies on the home farm as a child.

From the 7th to the 12th century, the monks who then lived on Skellig Michael, the tall, black sea-stack eight miles off the Kerry coast, regularly dined on gannet, usually fat young fledglings, or 'squabs', taken from the nests of the colony on the sister rock, the Small Skelling, home to the second largest gannet colony in Europe. The rights to harvest gannets on Small Skellig was rented out until late into the 1800s, and Blasket Islanders, on occasion, raided the rock to fill sacks with toothsome squabs to take home.

Tomás Ó Crohan, in his classic first-hand account of life on the Blaskets, *The Islandman*, relates a confrontation at sea between the currachs manned by the owner's hired guardians and those of the raiders. A fierce fight ensued, and two men in the guard boat were killed. The 'Gannet Wars' were, happily, short-lived, with the guard boat taken off duty, and the harvest available free to all. One can understand why the colony was fought over. Des Lavelle, in his book *The Skellig Story*, tells us that 150 years ago gannets were fetching up to a half-crown, a big sum in those times.

Now, in this period of economic downturn, perhaps we should again be harvesting gannet squabs or mackerel, and smoking them to preserve them through the winter. With the Irish economy in the horse latitudes and the ship barely afloat, private enterprise is the best hope for many. Kitchen gardening is the new palliative; those who first encountered 'endive' in fancy restaurants during the Tiger years are now trying to grow it in their gardens. They may have to turn to spuds, and to personally 'managing' their lawns where previously they had a contract gardener 'come in' to do it. Or turn the lawns over to woolly lowland sheep.

~

When August gives way to September, one can already feel an autumnal stillness in the air. Red admiral butterflies in dramatic array flit over the fuchsia, bask on knapweed and thistles or haunt the orchards where a few apples already lie fermenting in the grass. After rain, speckled wood butterflies spiral in the sunlight spilling through the branches. On sunny days, the woods, with the sun behind them, are a canopy of pastel leaves with patches of brilliant blue in between.

Some years, when the blackthorn blooms, it so densely packs the hedges that one wonders how there will be room for other trees. But, then, as it dies off, the whitethorn comes on, even denser, whitening the same hedgerows again with another crop. Rising ground is white into the distance, hedge behind hedge, so frothy that the fields between are invisible, the landscape as white as if there had been a fall of snow. On such years, the whitethorn — also called hawthorn or May blossom — produces an exceptionally heavy crop of haws. In September, the hedges are as red and shining as if painted, with branches bent under the weight. The blackthorns, alongside, bear sloes as big and black as pickled olives. One wonders if haws could be harvested for vitamin C and sloes converted into jams, jellies and condiments, apart from flavouring sloe poteen.

Poteen — or moonshine, so-called in America — is still made here but only by the old people. The traditional poteen-makers did not take up champagne or brandy-drinking during the Tiger years. Small farmers with mountain and moorland holdings saw little of the wealth of the mid-2000s: their land was unsuitable to be zoned for development — not that unsuitability much mattered if you had the money to pay lobbyists to 'brown-envelope' those local councillors who, in exchange, would vote for the rezoning of agricultural land for housing development, making the landowner an overnight multi-millionaire. Poteen was made by rural people because it was a cheap drink, untaxed, and could also be used for medicinal purposes, whether as an embrocation to rub into calves' legs, or as a cure for a cold. Country folk swore by it, and I can confirm that, with added lemon juice and honey, it is most efficacious in relieving a cold, often overnight.

I remember a very entertaining and erudite West Cork Church of Ireland vicar, a white-haired Oxford man, who received poteen from two of his parishioners every year — the production of poteen is non-sectarian, it seems. His supply, delivered gratis, would come in bottles wrapped in copies of the *Southern Star* left at his front door. Having anticipated this annual event, my friend would have a sherry hogshead to hand ('begged', as he put it, from a wine merchant of the C of I persuasion in Cork city). After decanting the new poteen into the little barrel, he would then take, from the depths of his gardening shed, the hogshead which he had laid down ten years before. I was present on one such ceremonial occasion and we savoured the first glass of the ten-year-old together. It was crystal clear, a beautiful amber in colour and, although I am no aficionado of whiskey, it seemed to me better than any I had previously tasted.

I also recall, one sunny Sunday morning at about that time, 1970 or 1971, walking with a party of boys and girls, my youngest children and some of the parson's own, up the sloping fields behind the lovely old farmhouse we were renting in the Borlin valley, west of Bantry. It was spring, and the leaves were green on the birches and alders tracing the course of the many streams descending from the Cork and Kerry mountains above. It was wild country, the home of our nearest neighbour a quarter of a mile away.

The children ran ahead, excited. Then, led by my daughter Lydia who, at six years old, was the eldest, they took the notion to run down a steep slope to a wooded cleft in the land below. I had walked on for, perhaps, five minutes, when I heard Lydia calling. I stopped and she rushed up the slope, followed by the others, all with flushed faces and excitement in their eyes, 'Dad, we've found an Indian camp,' she cried. 'Come, come, and look!' and off they belted down the slope and I followed.

The sight I came upon was like one of those art works called 'installations'. Where the stream curved sharply around a bend thinly wooded with birch trees, there was a 'camp' indeed, a poteen-still standing in its pristine glory under the sky, everything as clean and shipshape as if it had been abandoned five minutes before. There was the barrel of mash; there was the 'cooker', comprising a half-barrel, cut horizontally, supported on a trestle of one-inch-diameter metal pipe. Beneath this was a scaffold pole bored with holes and joined to a hose leading from a gas bottle. But most ingenious, most 'organic' of all, was the constant supply of cold mountain water to cool the 'worm' and distil the vapour, this being simply a branch of the stream channelled across the 'kitchen' floor and flowing back into the main stream below.

I marvelled at the artistry; it was no Indian or fairy camp as the children imagined, but here was equal magic, equal alchemy. And what effort had been applied to carry barrels, pipes and gas bottles across steep fields a half mile from the nearest road! An Indian camp, the Borlin Indians; artisan moonshine made with branch water indeed.

At the time, we had neither cameras nor the money for film. We lived for the moment; we didn't care about keeping records. But I still have the pictures in my mind's eye.

~

In autumn 2010, Horst, our fungus-foraging friend, invited us to a

Kerry *Boletus* hunt as soon as the 'king of mushrooms' appeared. The last bumper year had been 2006; they had been all but absent in 2008 and again in 2009 and then, along came 2010, with a profusion rarely before seen. Called 'ceps' in France, 'porcini' in Italy and 'steinpilz' in Germany, *Boletus edulis* are much larger than the elegant chanterelles and have spongy, rather than fluted, gills. Two average-size ceps will provide as much eating as a pint of chanterelles and are so 'mushroomy' that they are the species used to flavour tinned soups. In small copses on Kerry hillsides, we found many with caps twice as large and fat as a bap bun, and stalks almost as thick as one's wrist at the base. How beautiful they looked, with heads the shade of tan leather and the tubes underneath the colour of fresh cream. How solid and weighty they felt in the hand, as we placed them in our baskets. How few of these giants a basket could contain!

Harvesting them, we cut the stems neatly, down low. We left a few at each site to deposit their spore for crops in the years to follow — and, in any case, inevitably, some specimens would be past their best, the tubes yellowing, the caps beginning to soften or whiten with mould, and so these remained too. Horst, visiting his secret sites every few days, had left small specimens to grow larger so that he could be sure of having a fine crop to show us when we came. It would seem that the previous year's hard winter followed by the warm summer had generated the abundance of *boletus*. The 2006 season had had similar weather go before it: and it is a fact that mainland Europe, where *boletus* have been harvested for centuries, has this weather pattern of warm summers and cold winters. The damper weather seems to favour the chanterelles.

Arriving back in West Cork after spending the night with Horst and Rose, and enjoying a fine dinner (with mushrooms, of course), we set about preserving the booty. Some we ate fresh; small ones can even be eaten raw in salads. The rest we sliced into thin strips and dried. In the forests of La Gomera, we regularly collected fine ceps: there, the strips could be dried in an hour in the strong sun. Here, we rigged up yards of lettuce-wire racks, suspended over radiators. They did the job. When dried, the volume of the caps reduce by 80 per cent. Thanks to

Horst and Rose, we had jars of pungent cep-slices to add to pastas and
risottos for the next year.

~

It is heartening to live in a country where an anonymous artist and
craftsman or woman devotes hours to constructing houses in hollow
trees solely for the wonderment of children. The story of the 'fairy
houses' in Reen Wood was retailed to me by my friend Hanly, who had
seen them with his own eyes. Kevin sports a long, white beard and looks
not unlike a woodland spirit. Walking his dogs in Reen Wood near
Castletownshend, he came upon four miniature houses built into
hollow tree-trunks, with roofs and windows — some with a miniature
cat sitting inside — and front doors with knockers and letterboxes.
They were, he said, works of art. Praise to whoever had the imagination
and love of children to create them.

The story of the houses subsequently appeared in the *Irish Examiner*
and, on the following Sunday, Reen Wood was full of parents with
children. I can imagine how my daughters, and indeed, my sons, would
have responded to these 'fairy' houses when they were young. I wished
I had a couple of small grandchildren to hand so that we could go
exploring, perhaps early in the morning or at dusk when there would be
nobody else about. When we got close to the spot, I'd let them run
ahead and they'd come charging back, breathless and full of excitement,
like Lydia and friends when they found the Indian camp in Borlin. How
wonderful it would be to see their faces, convinced that the fairy stories
we'd told them were true.

Children, when they are very young, believe all things are possible.
They don't know the world and, if they're loved, they believe the best
of everybody and everything. If a pig suddenly took flight, they would
not be surprised.

Amongst the visitors to Reen Wood that Sunday, Hanly came upon
a man shepherding four grandchildren. Clearly, he was not prepared for
sylvan excursions. As Kevin put it, he wore a stylish crombie overcoat,

collar and tie, polished town shoes and 'priest's trousers'. It had been raining the night before and the paths were slippery. While the grandchildren were obviously enchanted, their poor guardian looked seriously discomfited, his smart shoes and trouser-ends encrusted with mud.

~

High in the ridge of mountains dividing West Cork from Kerry is the Priest's Leap. One follows a road alongside the Coomhola River, which descends the mountains in leaps and bounds, resting briefly in deep-brown pools before rushing onwards through groves of silvery hazel and alder until it issues into the broad expanse of Bantry Bay.

A mile or two inland from Coomhola Bridge, on the Glengarriff Road, one turns into a bohreen, and begins to climb. When I spent a short while in Ireland in the early 1970s, the road that took one over the Priest's Leap 'pass' was unmetalled and often deeply runnelled or washed away by winter rains. It was used by drovers driving cattle to fairs but the only motorised habitué was a local veterinary surgeon: he would drive up to the hill farms to attend to sheep, and continue on into Kerry in his brave little VW Beetle car. I once tried it in a VW van. However, as we passed the last house and climbed ever higher, the family began to protest that the road edge might give way and we would tumble roly-poly down the slope alongside. I suggested they walked until I had negotiated the bits that worried them. However, I shortly abandoned the ascent. While, in the event of a spill, I was unlikely to be hurt, it would have been the end of the old van and I certainly did not want to despoil the beautiful glen below us, with its shallow little river at the bottom and a scattering of ancient Scots pines.

Mountains are uplifting to the spirits. 'My soul is in the mountains, My heart is in the land, I'm lost here in the city, There's so much I don't understand,' was the chorus of a plaintive song by Floyd Westerman that Christy Moore used to sing. I am no mountaineer, but I enjoy hills and, once, Marie and I climbed hill tracks in Nepal until we reached nine thousand feet on the Jomsom trail. Our son Dara was born three months later. Marie, the young girl who is the narrator of the first part of T.S. Eliot's *The Waste Land*, takes a different view than Westerman and says: 'In the mountains, there you feel free.'

Few of the West Cork mountains rise high enough to look bare at the summit and, in fact, there is usually a rich growth of lichen, greyish-green, or as orange-coloured as if eggs had fallen from on high and their yolks had spilt over the rocks. Mosses and ferns thrive in fissures and, on wet ground between the outcrops, orchids peek over the sphagnum and scutch grass in spring. Black-faced sheep graze the slopes and perch on sheer rock faces with no less aplomb than their near relatives, the mountain goats.

In late August and in September, the uplands burst into flower, prickly dwarf gorse covering acres as if they were on fire, with carpets of purple heather thrown in their midst. In lags, wild irises — 'yellow flags' — tell us we'll get our feet wet if we proceed. Over the banks of the small streams, the rowans, hollies and whitethorns burgeon with berries, all a different shade of red, bright in the yellow sun.

In the autumn before the millennium, Marie, the boys and I camped by a mountain stream on the green highlands near the apex of the Priest's Leap. So sultry it was that evening that at twilight, despite the fire, I was eaten alive with midges — but, as darkness fell, they went. The night that followed was enchanting, with clouds veiling a pale half-moon and then, slowly, coming down over us, blanketing us entirely until, around midnight, they lifted and revealed the lights of Bantry far below, small stars winking through the haze.

Above us, the planetary stars came out and winked at us as stars do, a reassurance surely as old as time. Someone in Shakespeare said, 'Sit, Jessica: look, how the floor of heaven is thick inlaid with patines of bright gold . . .' Those lines, which I recited half to myself, half to the boys, I had addressed once, years before, to their mother, bidding her to sit and look, for all that her name was not Jessica but Marie. Such lines had, indeed, often stood me in great stead with women, causing many a girl to pause gobsmacked by my eloquence (actually,

Shakespeare's) on a Mediterranean or Pacific beach or amongst Irish sand dunes. The children too were gobsmacked that night as we sat outside the tent on the mountains, so much closer did we seem to the 'patines of bright gold'. Patrick Kavanagh once said that school poetry was his only learning, and it was certainly the start of mine, lines that touched the heart and mind and stayed there, lines one could ever-after whisper to lovers, to children, or to oneself.

We slept to the sound of the stream's murmur, and woke to wash in its cold water. It was good to have children. We might never have spent a night on a mountain-top but for them. Later, we said we wouldn't have missed it for the world.

~

I believe that there is a great deal to be said for learning poetry's memorable lines at an early age. Great poetry is not only pleasurable but functional and in ways other than those I've explained above. Eliot's 'Let us go then, you and I . . .' and Yeats' 'I will arise and go now . . .' provide both a novel propositional and a useful exit line. Besides that, the metre and mellifluousness of such phrases are forever stored in the brain, ringing like an echo, assisting us in making our own words flow more felicitously, and that cannot be a bad thing. Facility with language is much admired amongst the Irish, and there are few higher accolades an Irishman can bestow on a neighbour than to say 'He has a great way with words!'

After breakfast, as we descended on the Kerry side of the mountain, we found a turf-road running straight and true into the purple distance of the Kenmare plains. Soon, after the stark emptiness of the mountains, there was evidence of people, stooks of black turf, and the fine, skilled marks of the turf-cutter's slane on the brown sub-soil banks. We parked the car. Our own footsteps, the bleat of mountain lambs, the heady buzz of bees and breaks of birdsong were the only sounds as we walked.

In that lovely Sunday morning landscape, signs of the human past were evident, too. The stones-upon-stones of human endeavour, the small fields walled with broken rocks, a derelict cottage, the traces of potato drills. Later that day, driving home, we marvelled at a road, high in the West Cork mountains, built with Famine Relief funds, a 'famine road' along which the doomed feet of mountain people made their way to the lowlands in the vain hope of food.

~

The butterflies of September are beautiful as they cover the verbena in the garden like a shifting tapestry, the peacocks, red admirals and tortoiseshells, with silver-washed fritillaries, too, and the occasional meadow brown that crosses the stream from the pastures of Kincragie. There are, of course, also, the large- and small- and green-veined-whites which seem all the whiter for perching on the deep-purple verbena flowers. In 2008 and 2009, the small tortoiseshell, one of the brightest of the Vanessa butterflies, were so scarce that one wondered if they were a disappearing species, but in 2010 they were present in their myriads, while the painted ladys which had arrived from North Africa in their millions in 2009, were all but absent. At times, I could count up to thirty small tortoiseshells on the verbena or buddleia. But much of the buddleia dies away early in summer, and the seedum, another honey-pot for butterflies, often does not flower until October, so the mainstay was the verbena. Once or twice a day, I couldn't resist leaving my workroom for a few minutes just to admire the butterflies.

Vikram Seth, author of *A Suitable Boy*, wrote a short poem about a Chinese administrator in his garden, admiring his koi, commenting that 'He may have got/ The means by somewhat dubious means, but now/ This is the loveliest of all gardens.' I felt rather like that gentleman, though the means by which we came to own the verbena — or the garden — was hardly dubious. Our friends the Reynolds, who live high above the bay — the bay, with its shifting channels and sandbanks, like a Google Earth map laid out below them — gave us some root stock and the following spring off it went, skywards, the stems so tall that, to photograph butterflies on the flowers, I had to perch on a set of steps. I cannot resist photographing butterflies. Like the aforementioned buds of May, their 'summer's lease hath all too short a date', and if you don't snap them today you can't snap them tomorrow.

In September, too, red admirals frequent the fuchsia and as I walk the lane down through the old village of Meelmaan — where, until 2004, the antique cottages wore distinctive roofs tipped to one side like corner-boys' caps (half of these were knocked and replaced by imposing residences during the era-of-affluence) — they flit off the hedges, while speckled woods, the most ubiquitous butterflies of all, spiral in mock battles around one in the sunlit clearings in Kincragie Woods. In the old orchards, red admirals imbibe the fermenting juices of windfall apples and grow tipsy. Ringlets frequent the briars and wall browns bask on the warm stones of the decaying walls.

Where do butterflies go when it rains? I wondered one September morning, when the light in the kitchen suddenly darkened as if Apocalypse was upon us and a hiss of hailstones hit the windows and danced two inches high on the roof below. Leaves flew horizontally from the beech trees, which churned and roiled while the roistering zephyrs passed.

As suddenly as it had arrived, the shower moved on. The trees calmed and shook themselves as if in relief and a gentle breeze stirred the still-shivering leaves. Five minutes later, one would never have known, but for the sunlight catching the pools of water in the courtyard and the scarlet stain of blossoms on the ground beneath the fuchsia bushes, that any such engine of destruction had passed. The leaves shone and water droplets hung from their tips, sparkling in the sun. And then, as I looked out, a dozen or more butterflies fluttered into the sunlight outside my workroom window. They were speckled woods, small, dark-brown creatures that normally haunt the dappled light under the beeches. At first, I thought they were beech leaves, driven by the breeze. Some spiralled, flying back and forth as if stretching their wings; some landed on the white courtyard walls and even on the drenched sheets on the line which I'd not been fast enough to rescue.

It was clear that they had, somehow, anticipated the hailstorm and taken shelter. Not like the Spanish sparrows which, my brother reported from Seville in June 2006, had been slain by a storm of hailstones, some weighing up to two pounds and almost three inches in diameter.

~

The wide expanse of the western ocean, seen from our island at the edge of Europe, is a strange and lovely place, dazzling or sober from hour to hour. On the brightest day, cloud masses can drift in from the Atlantic and sunbeams, breaking through them, are like searchlights sweeping the hills. Out over the water, the light falls in curtains. The sea sparkles like snow or glass. Around our coasts, we have many islands. Seen from the shore, some are soft folds of land, others sheer pinnacles of rock. The islands of the west are hard places, locked in battle with the sea.

On a bright September day in 2005 when Marie and I made our first trip to Dursey to research the islands book, the sky was blue and the sun warm. Dursey, set at the remote end of the Beara Peninsula, a finger of land reaching out into the Atlantic, is as far west as one can go and still be on dry land. Because of the long drive, we would stay overnight in Castletownbere and, on the following day, walk Bere Island, also to be included in the book. Dara was working in London, Fin at university in Cork; there was nothing to stop us being away as long as we pleased. Nicky the Dog would come with us and would, no doubt, enjoy the universe of new olfactory experiences she would encounter.

Dursey is reached via Ireland's only cable car, operated by Cork County Council, a stout box carrying up to six passengers — or two heifers, or four sheep — which crosses the abyss between the mainland and the island suspended on a cable 80 feet (26 metres) above the sea. In 2005, the old car was still in operation; in 2009, it was replaced by an updated model and it now rests in a local farmyard where it serves as a hen house with a difference. A range of poultry, including fine turkey cocks and geese, share the enclosure in which it stands, while spectacular peacocks roam free around about it and on the road outside. A life-size, fibreglass lamb stands in the doorway, a reminder of the fact that Dursey's transports-of-delight traditionally carry not only passengers but livestock.

In the narrow, cliff-walled channel of the Sound over which the cable car passes, two currents meet. When one reflects that Dursey is, in fact, the severed fingertip of the Beara Peninsula, it is not surprising that the waters of vast Kenmare Bay and even vaster Bantry Bay, spilling through the narrow conduit, should clash and boil. The sea far below is, most often, crystal clear. Dolphins disport within and outside the Sound, and are worth watching for. A friend tells me that he once saw nine basking sharks, some 25 feet long, cruising languidly in the strait. Their sheer bulk, and their fins breaking the surface, made them easy to spot.

The crossing is a novel and, for some, a hair-raising trip. Immediately after starting out, the car starts 'downhill', seemingly set to nose-dive onto the rocks below. Seconds later, however, it slowly and sedately rises and assumes a horizontal course to deliver one safely on the Dursey side. Like a fairground attraction, it is a ride well worthwhile for the sheer thrill; and the delights of the island await beyond. On a fine September day, I could not recommend a more uplifting experience than an airborne voyage to Dursey, followed by a road walk the length of the island and a return via sheep paths along the central ridge, with bird's eye prospects of the island below, Kenmare Bay to the south and, to the north, Bantry Bay, as far as the Skelling Rocks and even the distant Blaskets, in clear weather.

Dursey is different from the relatively sheltered islands of Roaringwater and Bantry Bay. Spectacular in a bare, ascetic way, in winter the landscape is brown, the sea grey beneath the steep cliffs, the view romantic when soft rain blows like veils across the small green fields and ruined cottages. It is sun-baked in good summers, for there are no trees, and so there is no shade. It is loveliest of all in September, when the prickly, ground-hugging Irish dwarf gorse is in flower and the island's rolling hills are dressed in brilliant gold, dramatic against the deep blue of the sea. There is no hindrance to the rambler on the trafficless roads and unfenced hills.

Nowadays, there are five or, perhaps, six, permanent or semi-permanent residents on Dursey. We were lucky enough to meet one of them on the cable car and she kindly invited us to stop at her house for tea. We sat in a flower-filled garden (the soil is wonderfully fertile, she said) while a robin hopped about our feet, so friendly that, with small encouragement, it might have alighted on the rim of one's cup. The owner, born on Sherkin Island, had grandchildren visiting from London; how wonderful for them to have come to such a remote and unspoiled place. They might tell their London friends that their granny lived on an island where there were no shops or streets and the hills were covered in gold.

Afterwards, we walked the straight, empty road to the western end. It could well have been the 1940s; little had changed but for the metalling of the road surface and an electricity power line overhead. Some slates were gone off the roofs of the abandoned houses but they still stood firm, stone-built and unrendered, growing mosses and lichens, part of the landscape on the side of the hill.

But for all its beauty, Dursey has a tragic history. In 1602, soon after the Irish defeat at Kinsale, its 300 inhabitants, all members of the O'Sullivan clan, were massacred, many thrown off the cliffs, and all of Beara was put to fire and sword. Finally, in the freezing winter of that year, the chieftain, Donal Cam O'Sullivan Beare, led what was left of his people – men, women and children – from Beara to far-off Leitrim, in the dead of winter. Walking into exile and oblivion, like the Oglala Sioux on the Ghost March, they were beset by enemies and wolves, with no shelter or quarter, raiding for provisions as they went. To cross the Shannon, they killed four horses, ate the flesh and used the skins, drawn over branches, to make currachs. Harried and attacked by both English and Irish every mile of the way, many died in skirmishes or from hunger and exposure. Some fell behind and were given succour, being no longer a threat. Fourteen days later, of the thousand who had started out, only thirty-five reached the safe haven of Breffni and refuge with their kinsmen, the O'Rourkes. It was a lovely land they had left, and they must have been heartbroken for the loss of family, friends and fields they would never again see.

That day, as Marie and I picnicked on the farthest headland, gannets dived on the stiff, blue sea far below us, their white plumage catching the sunlight. There was a small breeze, welcome in the heat but, out of the wind, it was as warm as the Mediterranean in autumn. No shops, no cars, no sound; white waves breaking in silent animation on black rocks under the Bull Island lighthouse, two miles to the north — and across the sea, beyond it, the Iveragh Peninsula, blue mountains behind blue mountains. To the south, the Muntervary Peninsula, with the Sheep's Head at the tip. Sitting on a flat rock between golden gorse and purple heather, we lunched on our sandwiches and a field mushroom we'd found, cut into slivers, with larks in the clear air and choughs soaring above.

~

On warm September days, lizards bask on the walls of the collapsed 15th-century bawn at Three Castles Head, beyond Barley Cove, golden lizards, sharp-eyed and fast, disappearing between the stones at the hint of a footfall or shadow. Along the south coast, swallows gather in reed beds as they prepare to leave for Africa. One afternoon, when Marie and I sat enjoying the view above Foilarea Bay with my brother and his friend Claudine, a thousand or more skimmed low over the headland all around us, dashing back and forth in great excitement. Which would be first to set out over the sea, we wondered; which would lead the way?

Later, as we walked inland, we saw hundreds more swallows perched on telephone wires and through the binoculars I saw that most were young birds, as yet without the long, needle-feather tails of the adults, and with fledgling gapes. A keen observer of such things tells me that he has seen swallows barely three days out of the nest joining the flock for the 3,000-mile flight south to Botswana and Lesotho. After leaving Ireland, they would fly over Biscay, then over the Straits of Gibraltar. Next, it would be the warm thermals over the Sahara and, after that, the humid air above the rain forests of the Congo. Finally, those that survived would arrive in Botswana and Lesotho, these being of the tribe of swallows that had been born in Irish barns.

It is a journey fraught with danger. Eleonora's falcons, whose chicks are timed to hatch as the migrant flocks fly over, stand ready to ambush them as they cross from Spain to Africa. South of the Sahara, swallows from all over Europe break their journey to roost in reed beds and locals will, literally, pick the exhausted birds as they would fruit, pluck them and pop them in the pot. Their epic trek fires the imagination. One September day, I was having a drink with a friend, now passed away, when he called me to come and look out the window at swallows gathering on the telephone wires over the sea. He'd travelled all his life, and missed the thrill of it. He sorely wished he too could go south but, sadly, his wings were clipped by age.

October

The white boats on the channel catch the sunlight. Out on the sandbanks, shelduck walk between the pools left by the tide. Here, on the village street, nothing stirs. As Wordsworth wrote about London on some lovely long-ago morning, 'Ne'er saw I, never felt, a calm so deep!'

~

In some years, summer can extend into October in that most pleasant of weathers, the 'Indian summer' named, it is said, for the time when the native Americans hunted game and harvested crops in preparation for the winter. Perhaps, in the recently straitened times, we should harvest the windfalls in the orchards and the crabapples and rosehips in the hedges. Others say the 'Indian summer' was so called because it was a period of good sailing weather for ships en route to India during the British Raj. Some had the letters 'I.S.' burnt into their hulls to indicate the high level to which they could be loaded in this clement weather. When summer thus lingers along this coast, one can swim in October — indeed, one year, I noted that the boys were still swimming in November.

But October can be a harbinger of winter, too, as in the equinoctial storm of late October 2004. The first I heard of the drama was when

Fin phoned to tell me that one of nature's spectaculars was in full swing. 'Hurry and bring your camera down to the pier!' he said. Most of the three miles of road between Courtmac and Timoleague was under water, with waves breaking over it and into the fields on the other side, especially where the old earth-and-stone ditches had been stripped of briars, ivy and weeds in the cause of neatness and road safety. As Murphy's Law would have it, our well-worn 4x4 was in the garage for servicing, so I had no alternative if I wanted to see the sights but to walk. It was getting darker by the minute; it had been no more than half-light all day. Donning a waterproof and calling up the dog, I set off.

All afternoon, I'd been sitting in front of a computer screen in my workroom. Sheltered as we are, I had no idea of the battle royal raging between sea and wind two hundred yards below the house, on the bay.

The tops of the pines swung like saplings seventy feet above me as I hurried down our road, rutted by streams rushing towards the sea. As I neared the water, I saw, through the wind-driven rain, a ghostly trawler, moving up the channel, its mast lights jumping and rolling as it tossed like a straw in a millrace, running for shelter before the storm. When I turned on to the village street, waves were breaking over the sea wall, leaping to the height of the lamp-posts, dashing over the globes, a grey and sandy sea flooding across the tarmac like dish-water thrown from a basin. Nicky yelped in alarm as it suddenly swirled around us, nine inches deep and, too late, I found my new walking boots swamped and my trousers wet to the knees.

Along the length of the street, the sea poured ashore, unfettered, leaping the sea wall opposite the house fronts, inundating gardens, laying layers of green seaweed over the lawns. Slabs of concrete, eight inches thick and three foot square, lay broken on the verge, part of the sea-side path uplifted and demolished. Heads down and plugging onward, the hound and I marched into the pelting rain and screaming wind, the pier our destination.

In the dock, protected on three sides, the water was bucking and churning, tossing two thirty-foot fishing boats about as if they were driftwood which, indeed, one of them was shortly to become. Gusts of stinging hail swept the pier while waves swept across the concrete, leaping like demented animals over the bollards and rushing on. So high was the tide that the metal and wood pontoon, normally lying twenty feet below the pier surface, was lifted level with it, tossing and jumping alongside it like a moored barge.

In a hut above the slipway, half of the Courtmacsherry lifeboat volunteers were gathered ready to go to sea in a matter of minutes, if called. Through the spray-lashed window, I saw the 'ghost ship' once more and now recognised it as the O'Donovan trawler, with Barry at the wheel. It was beating upwind not more than fifty yards off, tossing and pitching, the wind throwing waves over its stern. I watched as it swung around in a wide sweep and set off towards the bay mouth. 'Why?' I asked, shouting above the din. 'No mooring,' someone yelled. 'The only answer is to keep driving up and down!' And drive up and down he did, passing the pier every ten or fifteen minutes, beating into the gale or into the waves, like a cork on the bucking-bronco sea.

Many amongst those present in the hut had seen storms before but none that had inundated the village like this one. Some had been crew on the lifeboat that had gone to the aid of a flotilla of high-speed yachts caught in the eye of the deadliest storm in the history of ocean racing during the Fastnet Race of August 1979. Dozens of boats had been wrecked and fifteen yachtsmen drowned, with over a hundred more rescued from the violence of the seas. Sammy Mearns was the coxswain of the Courtmacsherry boat when it powered out to the rescue, all aboard knowing that they were risking their lives for strangers. Sammy, a squadron leader in the Fleet Air Arm during World War II, passed away in 2009, aged eighty-eight. He and his wife Anne had moved to Courtmacsherry from Hampshire in 1970, and in the years that followed, Sammy became an outstanding example of an English 'blow-in' who was respected and, indeed, honoured in the community.

The Fastnet Rock around which the yachts intended to sail is a single pinnacle of slate-veined quartz rising one hundred feet out of the ocean more than four miles south of Cape Clear. The Norsemen called it Hvasstan-ait (the sharp tooth) and from their charts the present name evolved. Looking out at it from the mainland, Carraig Aonair (the lonely rock), its name in Irish, seems more descriptive and appropriate. Around it, tides rise twelve feet and currents can run at three knots. On only a dozen tides a year is the water calm enough to allow a boat to pull alongside.

Since that local storm of 2004, we have seen the terrible toll of the Asian tsunami of St Stephen's Day (Boxing Day) 2004 and of the tsunami that hit the coast of Japan in March 2011. On Stephen's Day 2004, my son Dara was on the beach on the east coast of Thailand. Happily, that coast escaped. As a child in the womb, he had been transported over the Phuket beaches which were devastated by the 2004 event. In 1977, Marie and I spent idyllic weeks living in a rattan hut on those, then undeveloped, shores. I subsequently learned, from a reader of an article I had written about tidal waves, that tsunamis can occur in Ireland too. An incidence of such a wave that occurred in Timoleague in the early 1930s was fresh in the memory of a local man who was then only thirteen. He well remembered the evening when he was standing with an old man on the bridge over the river Argideen, fishing for bass on a spring tide when, to their alarm, all the water in the vast, tidal estuary, save for the river, was suddenly 'sucked' out of view, leaving sand and mudflats exposed beneath the sky. 'It was as if the tide drew itself back in the space of a few minutes,' he said. 'It was like a miracle and we were very frightened. We thought it was the end of the world.'

They stood frozen on the spot, and minutes passed before they heard a far-off roar and saw the sea charging back up the estuary towards them, preceded by a three-foot high wave. It swept up the almost waterless bed of the Argideen and hit the piles of the bridge beneath them 'with a mighty slap'. Onward it rushed, full of weed and sand and debris, all the way to Inchy Bridge, half a mile upriver. After writing about this in the paper, I heard reports of other Irish tsunamis..

In Kylemore Quay, County Wexford, in 1854, experienced divers reliably reported a series of five or six enormous waves travelling at over ten miles per hour. On a fine day in August 1852, twelve men, fishing off Glassaun Rock on the Aran Islands, were drowned by a huge wave which a boy — sent ashore to get more bait — reported to be thirty foot high coming in from the ocean. In August 1979, J.G. Farrell, the author of *The Siege of Krishnapur*, was swept off a rock in West Cork by a freak wave, a great loss to literature.

~

In October, the Virginia creeper on the walls of Lisheen, our first house in Ireland, would turn every shade of red. The same glorious transformation could be seen on house fronts in Emmet Square in Clonakilty, one of the finest Georgian squares in any country town in Ireland, where I spent seven years of my childhood and where my brother and sister were born. Dylan Thomas in his 'Poem in October' says, 'the town below lay leaved with October blood'. Those verses were in celebration of his birthday, his 'thirtieth year to heaven', but I marvel at how uncannily he could, as an adult, in 'Fern Hill' and elsewhere, recall and convey the innocence of childhood when the world was all new, 'In the first, spinning place, the spellbound horses walking warm/ Out of the whinnying green stable/ On to the fields of praise.'

Other poets also had this gift of recall. Wordsworth remembers his childhood vision and laments its loss: 'There was a time when meadow, grove, and stream,/ The earth, and every common sight,/ To me did seem/ Apparelled in celestial light,/ The glory and the freshness of a dream./ It is not now as it hath been of yore; —/ Turn wheresoe'er I may,/ By night or day,/ The things that I have seen I now can see no more.'

Thomas Hardy, too, bemoaned its passing: 'Childlike, I danced in a dream;/ Blessings emblazoned that day;/ Everything glowed with a gleam;/ Yet we were looking away!', and R.S. Thomas, a Welshman like his namesake, Dylan, addresses adults in his poem 'Children's Song', and writes, 'We live in our own world [. . .] Where we dance, where we play,/ Where life is still asleep/ Under the closed flower,/ Under the smooth shell/ Of eggs in the cupped nest/ That mock the faded blue/

Of your remoter heaven.'

But few poets have ever caught the innocence of childhood as well as our own gruff, intemperate Patrick Kavanagh in 'A Christmas Childhood', when he remembers Christmas on his father's small farm in County Monaghan, 'I nicked six nicks on the door-post/ With my penknife's big blade —/ There was a little one for cutting tobacco./ And I was six Christmases of age./ My father played the melodion,/ My mother milked the cows,/ And I had a prayer like a white rose pinned/ On the Virgin Mary's blouse.'

While Virginia creeper and Japanese maples (both 'introductions' to our flora) light up October gardens, their glory has long since gone when our native ivy still catches the slivers of winter sunlight pouring through the leafless trees. When they were young, my daughters, Lydia and Miriam, and their brother Matthew, would sometimes thread together a series of the silver, red or gold milk-bottle caps and hang them from trees in the garden where, as they turned in the breeze, they reflected the sun like so many small mirrors. I am reminded of this when I see the leaves of the ivy on an old stump in our garden shine like silver milk-bottle tops or polished silver dollars in the sun. All winter, on mornings when the clouds part and a few beams break through, this stump lights up like a truncated Christmas tree. If there is a breeze, the leaves dance like mad things, and glitter like shards of glass. No wonder our pagan ancestors held this familiar plant in awe.

An ivy-bedecked tree on our lawn is similarly resplendent when the sun touches its branches. A few years ago, someone told us we should tear it all off but we ignored the instruction and I'm glad we did. In spring and summer the flowers and the foliage of the tree, a flowering cherry, are lovely, but in winter, without its jacket of ivy, it would be a dark and depressing sight. The bare limbs of big deciduous trees, standing alone in parkland, can be striking in winter, but not our cherry. So we decided on a moratorium or, rather, a compromise. We removed some of the ivy, but not all.

A popular song of the 1940s, performed by Bing Crosby and by The Andrews Sisters, went, 'Mares eat oats and does eat oats and little lambs eat ivy / A kid'll eat ivy too, wouldn't you?' Personally, I wouldn't, although ivy was once used medicinally, in small doses, for coughs and fever. A so-called 'novelty' song, the first verses were written to be sung as 'Mairzy doats and dozy doats and liddle lamzy divey / A kiddley divey too / Wouldn't you?' Even with the real words, it sounds like nonsense. However, I learn that sheep do, in fact, sometimes eat ivy leaves and berries in winter — as will goats which, as we know, will eat anything, including one's socks off the line.

We were also reluctant to chop the ivy not only for its silvery opulence and glitter in winter sunlight, but because its berries provide sustenance for the birds when other food is scarce. Its foliage supplies sheltered roosts on stormy or bone-chilling nights, and its dense cover provides safe nesting sites, especially favoured by wrens. Red admiral butterflies love to bask on its leaves as late as the end of October, when they are often still flying. Few sights are more striking than an admiral perched on a shining, dark-green ivy leaf with its glorious red, black and white wings spread open in the sun.

A common misapprehension is that ivy is parasitic and kills trees; even Thomas Hardy, one of the finest English nature poets, made this mistake. In *Tess of the d'Urbervilles: A Pure Woman*, he says, 'The house was overrun with ivy, its chimney being enlarged by the boughs of the parasite.' Ivy is not parasitic; it dries out the walls it grows on, and it does not kill trees. However, its roots can, unquestionably, undermine the mortar in old houses and its foliage can significantly increase the 'sail effect', so that, in storms, the wind can the better catch, throw about and ultimately knock ivy-festooned walls or trees.

A parasite feeds on its host while contributing nothing to its survival. Ivy is an epiphyte; it grows on, but does not feed on, the host. Unlike mistletoe, whose roots tap directly into the resources of the host plant, ivy has its feeding roots anchored in the ground and simply uses the tree as a support to climb to the light. The masses of tiny, hair-like roots sprouting from the under-surface of the stems merely enable the plant to climb.

Ivy flowers appear in late autumn when most other flowers are gone.

They provide nectar for a range of butterflies, and for bees, a last chance to gather honey for the winter. An ivy bush in warm autumn sunlight swarms with insects. They are like jewels on wings, foraging or basking in the sun. Because ivy flowers so late in the year, its small, black fruits fatten throughout the winter and are available when other food is scarce. In springtime, ivy bushes are laden with swollen, purple berries bunched in tight clumps. A few days later, they may well be gone, having been discovered by a band of foraging thrushes. Realising all this, I'm more convinced than ever that we shouldn't remove the good old pagan ivy from trees that remain healthy. It would be a sin.

~

The stone walls on Cape Clear Island give little succour to ivy, although they are often rich in stonecrop which forms mats on the wall tops and, from June until early October, put up white, star-like flowers, frequently tinged with pink. A Cork University study of Irish field-wall building noted that walls on Cape displayed specialised characteristics relative to their location on the island. While comparing the different patterns, the researchers discovered that families traditionally built their field walls in an individual family style. Story has it that one could tell an Aran Islander's family origins from the pattern of his *báinín* jersey, an important plot point in J.M. Synge's *Riders to the Sea*. Now it seems that one can still tell the ownership, past or present, of Cape Clear fields from the pattern of the stone walls that enclose them.

One day, as we crossed to Cape on the ferry, I came to the conclusion that shags, despite their prejudicial name, are very elegant birds, very much more attractive than their cousins, the cormorants. A fishing party of some thirty birds bobbed on the swells as we approached the island. In the sunlight, their plumage shone glossy black with a bottle-green iridescence, and their top-knots, like crew-cuts coaxed over their foreheads, gave them a rakish look. A gorgeous gannet (I describe it thus not for the onomatopoeia but because no other adjective could do it justice) floated so close to the ferry, the *Dun Aengus* from Baltimore, that we could see the dark-blue ring around the yellow eye set in its bright orange head. And then it rose, cruised fifty feet above us and, of a sudden, rocketed down into the sea.

For the folk who find intimations of the divine in West Cork's rugged beauty, Cape Clear Island is as near to heaven as they might hope to experience on earth. Few could fail to be awed by the beauty of the island, its empty spaces, its quiet roads, its bright-blue bays. To the east, the other islands of Roaringwater Bay — the Calfs, Heir, Sherkin; too many to name — lie between Cape and the 'blue remembered hills' of Ireland, especially 'remembered' in our case because on the previous weekend we had walked them and viewed the bay from the high, rounded pate of Mount Gabriel.

On Cape, we looked down on cliffs and rock platforms from the headland of Pointanbuillig. Fulmar drifted on stiff, outstretched wings below us: they seemed not to need to beat their wings at all. Guillemots and razorbills, hunting in parties, were black spots on the silver sea. It was impossible not to admire the glory of the panorama laid out before us. There, to the north, was Mount Gabriel, rising behind Schull, the golf-ball-like domes of the Radar Tracking Station under which we had stood shining like artefacts on another planet.

To the south-west, black and alone, the Fastnet Rock floated on the horizon. In the years when emigrants sailed for America from Cobh, the Fastnet was called 'Ireland's Teardrop'; for many, it was the last sight of Ireland they would ever have. Fastnet was a lonely and dangerous station indeed for the men who lived there and manned the light from when it was built in 1904 until 1989. Its light is 60 feet (48.5 metres) above the sea; yet, as one former keeper put it, in severe storms the 'big seas would come sailing up over the entire building like the field of horses in the Grand National'. One keeper recalled a storm in 1985 when a wave reached as high as the light and came crashing through the glass, overturning its vat of mercury and sending the poisonous liquid pouring down the stairs. He doubted that the tower would have withstood another such wave, but it never came. Suddenly, a great calmness fell over the sea.

On the south-western shore of Cape Clear is a sight best seen as the sun sets, although it is memorable at any time of the day. Then, the ruined O'Driscoll castle called Dún an Óir, 'The Fort of Gold', is indeed gold, hazed in motes of gold when the sun is sinking on the horizon behind it, a trick of the light over the sea. Captain Richard Tyrell, one of Hugh O'Neill's ablest commanders, took refuge there after the defeat of O'Neill and the Irish forces at Kinsale in 1601 and it was bombarded by English cannon, hauled from ships to the hill above it. The land side is in ruins, while the sea side is unscathed but for the toll of time and weather. Acres of bracken have subsumed the fallen stones. It was one of the last castles left to Fineen, 'the Rover', chieftain of the O'Driscolls, who had supported the doomed Irish-Spanish cause. He lost his lands for his trouble and died destitute in his castle beside beautiful Lough Hyne.

On those islands, be it Cape or Sherkin, Heir or Long, on a clear day one can, as the cliché has it, 'see for ever'. Eternity is out on the horizon where sky meets sea; there is not a single human artefact to snare one in time. Looking out over the 'undeveloped' land, where any trace of fields has long been covered by furze and heather, one can forget oneself completely, a sensation which, however contented one may be, is refreshing, and one wonders if one wants to ever set foot on the mainland again.

~

An Irish monk called Augustin wrote the first natural history of Ireland in 655; his text survives only because he was confused with St Augustine of Hippo and his writings were collected and published along with those of the great saint. The latter lived in the 4th century, and the former in the 7th. The first was sainted while the second wasn't but, to a natural philosopher, what's in a few centuries and a halo anyway?

Both speculated about the origins of the species; how land animals came to be on remote islands. Had they swum there? Had they risen from the clay when God decreed that the earth be populated by living creatures? Had they been brought there on the Ark? And, in the Great Flood, why were land animals singled out for extinction, while fish, patently, were not? And how did seals — say — manage, which needed dry land on which to breed, or otters — or duck-billed platypuses, I might ask. And where did amphibians fit in?

The Irish Augustin was clearly a man of introspection and speculation; he did not accept things simply as they were but saw the hand of God or evolution. He asked, 'Who could have brought wolves, deer, swine, foxes, badgers, little hares and squirrels to Ireland?' This gives us the first list of what one might expect to meet in the Irish woods in 655.

The monks of the Celtic church, living close to nature in such redoubts as the Skellig Rocks and Iona, wrote poetry about the natural world. Of the birds, they especially mentioned the blackbird. In Gerard Murphy's *Early Irish lyrics, eighth to twelfth century*, we find two poems attesting to its significance, 'The Blackbird Calling from the Willow' and 'The Blackbird by Belfast Lough'.

In the 12th century, Giraldus Cambrensis, Giraldus de Barri, a Fitzgerald on his mother's side, crossed from Wales on a military expedition with the future King John and updated Irish natural history in a major medieval treatise on the island and its people.

In 1183, wild boar roamed the extensive Irish forests; wolves howled in the night; red deer were widespread. There were no poisonous reptiles. There were frogs but no toads. However, Cambrensis probably did not visit remote Castlemaine Harbour in County Kerry, where the natterjack toad may, even then, have naturalised, arriving in sand brought as ship's ballast from continental Europe. Or perhaps the natterjacks were 'always' there having, like other Lusitanian species, crossed on the ancient, later-to-be-drowned land bridge between Iberia and Ireland and survived the Ice Age on the relatively mild Kerry shores.

The Welshman's assertion that there were frogs in Ireland at that time may owe more to propaganda than to fact. That he devotes a whole chapter to it is suspicious in itself. Entitled *Of a Frog lately seen in Ireland*, Cambrensis writes that shortly after the Normans arrived, one

Robert le Poer showed a frog to an Irish prince, Donall Mac Giolla Patrick, and the prince, never having seen a frog before, was greatly demoralised, taking it as a sign that newcomers, i.e. frogs and Normans, would soon colonise all Ireland.

I cannot believe that 'frog' was already a pejorative term for a Frenchman and that the prince saw this event as a portent that Frenchmen would breed and multiply on Irish soil as, indeed, did the actual amphibians themselves when, in 1696, a Fellow of Trinity College poured a jar of spawn brought from England into the ditches in Dublin's Phoenix Park and frogs became an indigenous Irish species for the first time. It now seems clear that le Poer had a 'hidden agenda' — an English frog in his pocket — and Cambrensis made much of the story so as to show the Irish that the world was in flux, the natural order awry and the invasion of Normans, like the frog, was already a *fait accompli*. It must be remembered that Cambrensis was the chaplin of Henry II, the Plantagenet ruler of England, and that *The Conquest of Ireland* was penned by the same man.

Cambrensis believed that barnacle geese hatched from goosenecked barnacles, the shellfish that adhere with their long, rubbery necks to driftwood in the sea. The antiquarian Roderic O'Flaherty, writing in 1684, held that gannets were engendered from floating logs and that they maliciously flew through ships' sails, piercing them with their beaks. The ideas of these writers were indeed strange but hardly more so than those that still obtained into the post-Renaissance period, as evidenced in the 1768 diary of the naturalist Gilbert White, Vicar of Selborne in Hampshire.

Parson White still divined signs of the weather like a medieval soothsayer and, as we all know, he thought swallows spent the winter snug in the mud in the bottom of ponds, a theory similar to that put forward, centuries earlier, by Giraldus to explain the absence of certain birds in winter and their reappearance in spring. What is strange is that science had moved so little in the intervening six hundred years. When I hear this story, I cannot but ask why it was that sailors did not report regular annual falls of migrating swallows onto their riggings far out at sea. Local fishermen tell me this happens today.

～

The immense importance of nature's humble creatures was once again brought home to me one October night as I strolled meditatively along the tide line of the beach in front of the Courtmacsherry hotel and found sand-hoppers in their millions, perhaps trillions, busy consuming the three-foot wide swathe of washed-in sea lettuce like crustacean cows. They seemed to feel the disturbance of my footsteps from six feet away as I walked, and this sent them leaping knee high in front of me, a haze of shiny bodies frantically trying to move out of the path of the giant with his monstrous ten-league boots, actually size eight-and-a-half.

When I'd suddenly stop and stand, they would rain onto my toecaps for an interval of thirty seconds and then, suddenly, all activity would cease and nothing stir. Hundreds, in their panic, had flung themselves suicidally into the surf or on to the dry sand, but others had found the burrows which they'd already made and disappeared down them, pulling a trapdoor of sand overhead.

How myriad and how useful the sand-hopper beach-cleaners are! They clear the beach of washed-in sea lettuce; they feed the sea bass and the birds. The bass, in turn, feed our digestive systems and the birds our imaginations. For a physical flight of hope and glory it is hard to beat that of 'E7', a female bar-tailed godwit, a species of wading bird that is sustained, at least in part, by consuming fat sand-hoppers on Irish estuaries.

In 2010, scientists tracked E7 on her migratory round. The name E7 hardly fires the imagination, but it's better than Bessie or Bertha, for sure. The results of the tracking were truly awesome and gives a whole new meaning to the phrase 'as free as a bird'.

E7 first made a non-stop 6,400-mile seven-day flight over water from New Zealand to the Yellow Sea in China in March; then, in May, she left China and made a five-day, 4,000-mile flight to her Alaska breeding grounds. Having bred and hatched chicks, she made a non-stop eight-day return flight to New Zealand in autumn, a distance of 7,300 miles entirely over water.

What can E7 have been thinking about as she flew on and on, tireless wing-beat after tireless wing-beat, or did she think at all? Clearly, she knew where she was going. After seemingly endless miles of open ocean, the New Zealand islands at last hove into sight. She hadn't eaten or drunk for eight days.

Godwits undertake the longest non-stop over-water migrations of any bird species; they fly farther than the swallow, farther than the knot or the Arctic tern. E7, weighing just eight ounces, flew almost a thousand miles a day. Unlike seabirds, which feed and rest on their journeys or swifts which feed on the wing, godwits make their epic sky-treks without eating or drinking. They cover the vast distance without a compass. When godwit juveniles are only two months old, they fly from Alaska to New Zealand alone.

During the seven months she was monitored, E7 flew eighteen thousand miles. She will fly 300,000 miles during her lifetime. She does this without oil or aviation fuel; all she needs are protected sites at the Kuskokwim Shoals in Alaska, where she can breed, and at the Yellow Sea in China and in New Zealand where she can rest and feed. Surely she deserves it; surely, in our supremacy, we cannot deny her that.

~

One October morning, walking down the decaying, tree-lined driveway of Kincragie, I found some magnificent — indeed majestic — mushrooms under a majestic tree. The Prince, the mushroom is called, *Agaricus augustus*, given this Linnaean name because it was the favourite of Caesar Augustus. The Caesars, apparently, liked their mushrooms, and I thought them excellent too.

They were certainly a princely and an august fungi, big and solid, white, with scaly tops. I hadn't come across the species before and was concerned to be sure that they were 'right' — it would have been unacceptable to poison the family or, indeed, myself. Although there was no 'ring' around the stem, in all other respects they matched the descriptions in the four separate books I consulted. They were robust; the spore print was dark; they bruised yellow on the cap (but, please, let no reader assume these characteristics alone identify a mushroom as *Agaricus augustus*). In any case, I decided to try a sliver, making myself the guinea pig. Gently fried in butter, with no additions, it was delicious, with a fine, firm texture, neither too chewy nor too soft. Finding myself still alive twenty -four hours later, I decided to have the rest for lunch. My wife, brave woman, joined me. She pronounced them as tasting of vanilla and being exceptionally good.

With a view to a future lunch, I had left three small princelings unpicked. The intention was to let the caps reach five inches across before I picked two, leaving the third remain so that it would lay down spore for a new crop the following year. I was disappointed when I later found all three kicked — not picked — by a passer-by. The kicker was obviously ignorant of their worth and blind to their beauty. He or she had seen these lovely mushrooms in full health and vigour and decided to uproot them — murder, on an autumn day! However, I realised that the instinct might have been well-intentioned; perhaps by tradition country folk kicked over toadstools, thinking them dangerous to man and beast, and the resorts of witches.

The trunk of the majestic Monterey cypress beneath which the royal group held court has a circumference of 36.5 feet (11.5 metres), a stately tree for stately fungi indeed.

~

There are storms and storms; the equinoctial tempest of 2004 was frightening and destructive, while the gales that blew one October day in 2001 were an invitation to go abroad on land or sea and enjoy the sheer force of air.

We woke to the sound of the wind. Far below our top-floor bedroom window, the garden swayed like an underwater jungle and shifted like the floor of the sea. The leaves of the gunnera — like giant rhubarb or elephant ears — tossed in lazy slow motion. The heads of the cabbage palms rippled and frilled like enormous, green anemones. Shoals of small fish — wind-thrown beech leaves — scudded past in their thousands. The familiar garden had become surreal and unworldly, a submarine planet, viewed from a submersible. Over the treetops, the bay was shrouded in strange, brown light.

Later in the morning, Dara, by then grown to a strapping six foot two, went wind surfing. He was repeatedly blown off his board. He resorted to a smaller sail but the result was much the same. He would find a steady wind; then a gust would strike and flatten him. Far out on the bay, between the white caps, he'd climb aboard again, only to be blown off once more. At last, he and the other wind sailors abandoned the day.

Out on the cliffs, it was wild, the wind buffeting the ears, the sea in chaos, hurling itself over the black rocks, battering the coast with white water, drawing back and battering it again. Cormorants dived between the teams of white horses. Headlands were lost to view in the grainy air. Overhead, cormorants, with a tail wind behind them, rocketed up the inlet like missiles — one wondered how they could manage to stop. When one faced into it, the wind blew the breath out of one's mouth. On the cliff fields, horses grazed with tails blown between their legs. Ravens were thrown about the sky like swallows. It was exhilarating and almost frightening to be out.

However, beyond the point, when I took a few paces into the woods, I found that all went still, as if I'd entered a deep bunker with a war raging outside. A robin sat on a branch by the path. Robins are always tame but this bird didn't move as I passed only a yard away; wild creatures often behave strangely during storms. The lee shore of the bay, sheltered by the woods, was surprisingly calm, while farther out, where Dara had been, the white waves still raced and tumbled.

The village, facing north, basked in a micro climate as I walked down through the meadow into it. Had fires been going in the houses, the smoke would have risen from the chimneys straight as a die. Soon, the sun shone through the clouds, so warm that I took off my jacket and walked in shirt sleeves. A half-mile away, at the bay head, the gale raged, although all one could know of it was a distant, constant sound of the seas breaking on the shore.

November

Thomas Hood, disenchanted by November in 19th-century smoggy London, took his revenge by writing:

> No sun — no moon!
> No morn — no noon —
> No dawn — no dusk — no proper time of day.
> No sky — no earthly view —
> No distance looking blue . . .

and so on. Like ourselves, he should have moved to West Cork. Here, November, while damp and sometimes grey, is certainly not depressing.

~

On early November days, bass fishers, men and women, are seen standing in the channel up to their oxters in waders, casting-rods extended and landing-nets to hand. Small boats drift up and down on the tide, trolling lures behind them. Our friend Gillian, small but prettily made, is one of them. The bass are 'in' and, while weight and bag limits are conscientiously observed, some big fish are caught. Lugworm and ragworm are favourite baits.

I notice that a farmer cleaning his ploughshare by dragging it along a local beach is careful to avoid areas where lugworm casts spot the sand in dense profusion. Heaven help the poor, fat, ugly finger-thick lugs if a plough blade carved through them and their homes. They are the humble stuff that feeds the fishes, the bass and flats, the smooth hounds and dragonets, and the birds too, those that have beaks long enough to reach them and strong enough to extract them. I imagine a curlew could manage it; certainly curlews take ragworms.

Ragworms have an unfortunate name; anyone who has ever seen them swimming — which they do — will remember them as beautiful, iridescent creatures, amazing when they take to the water and often twelve inches long. We do not expect to see worms swimming, with frills (actually legs) rippling along their sides. Even less do we expect to see pieces of worms swimming, but this will happen with ragworm because their undulating motions are controlled by their nervous systems, not their brains. We've heard of chickens running around with their heads cut off. Ragworms go one better; even after they have lost their heads and are cut into segments, each segment continues to swim.

~

As I set out one November day for a forty-minute hike to shake off the cobwebs and reduce the corporation, the weather seemed set fair — but in the words of Dylan Thomas, 'the weather turned around/ It turned away from the blithe country. . . .' and, suddenly, the sky was stained as blue as a bruised damson when a squall swept in off the sea.

Bad timing, I thought, and retreated indoors just before the heavens bucketed down and raindrops were suddenly hopping on the yard. So dense was the downpour that I could no longer see the horses, let alone the rabbits, in Kincragie fields. Five minutes later, however, the shower had passed and the same fields were as bright as if the grass had spouted out of the ground minutes before. Down at the strand in front of the hotel, a rainbow materialised and spanned the bay, its bands of colour as distinct as the stripes on a football supporter's scarf. The sand flats shone like buffed gunmetal and beyond them, on the other shore, the fields were pastel perfect, as if freshly painted by a giant brush. On the mud, the redshanks' legs shone as if they'd been varnished and the greenshanks' breasts were pristine white. A cormorant displayed a chest as snowy as a penguin's and a cowl as black as coal. What a handsome bird, it was, suddenly, this normally reptilian-looking creature with its voracious beak and pelican-like gullet! Nearby, a couple of hundred lapwing stood facing into the fresh wind, their topknots flying and their iridescent feathers catching the sun. Over the bridge at Timoleague, gulls hung in the sky, riding the wind, white pennants against the turquoise blue. The lichens on the walls of the abbey glowed rust-red in the light and, on the waterside, I found green lichens wrapped like lagging on a water-pipe around the branches of a silver birch.

It's amazing, the Irish weather: in the blink of an eye, it changes from fair to foul and foul to fair. Can our new government perform the latter miracle? Under the last incumbents, our financial vista darkened with the same alacrity as our blue skies when clouds sweep in off the Atlantic. Not that the fiscal clouds drenching us in gloom all emanated from across the Atlantic; no, they were seeded at home with our self-serving leaders vaporising our assets in cloud-capped towers and gorgeous palaces and promising us crocks of gold at the end of their Dulux rainbows. Their assurances were, of course, as fickle as the November weather.

~

However, we have much to be thankful for. In contrast to Thomas Hood's gloomy London November, autumn sun often lights the village street and, now and then, I see a couple of boys with hurley sticks pucking a ball back and forth after school, and no one to gainsay them. Faded tortoiseshell and brilliant red admiral butterflies flit about in the yellow sunlight. The tortoiseshells will soon seek indoor shelter in which to hibernate behind wardrobes or curtains. The admirals will die off, to be replaced by newcomers from mainland Europe in spring. Meanwhile, back at the potting shed, the spiders are eating their mates. Female spiders consuming their husbands is hardly an edifying spectacle, but it would be the height of presumption to interrupt their meal. This is the order of things in the long-legged spider world. Big mammy-long-legs eats little daddy-long-legs after the nuptials. He's had his excitement; now she has her dinner. And so when she lays her eggs, strong, well-nurtured spiderlets will be born. Mammy-long-legs is a 'widow-maker'. Such behaviour is not unique in the insect world.

~

November in West Cork offers exciting sights. Where else could two overseas visitors, my son Matthew, and his partner, Caroline, touch down at an airport and forty minutes later watch salmon, some as long as one's arm, leap up a wall of tumbling water and squirm into a deep brown pool above? A stately young heron stood beneath, as if posed for a photo opportunity; I snapped it myself. This was the scene at Bandon Weir, less than half an hour from Cork Airport, one November Sunday morning. The salmon run happens in November every year.

While similar scenes might be viewed not far from airports elsewhere — for example, in Oregon, British Columbia or Alaska — the setting at Bandon that morning could hardly be bettered, with the cascade over the wide weir catching the morning sun, the backdrop of big trees in full leaf and the quaint, stone building that houses the hydroelectric turbine like a riverside cottage perched above the rushing water.

I had decided I would take the riverside route through Bandon as we drove home. The renovation of the quayside on both sides of the river is lapidary evidence of one positive result of the Celtic Tiger debacle, the quality of the architecture and design sometimes initiated. On the Bandon riverside, where old stone buildings with blocked-up windows and crumbling walls did sad disservice to the river's beauty, there are now fine new apartments, with balconies over the water and much glass, while, opposite, where the street and pavement run along the bank, the derelict warehouses have been renovated, the stone-fronts cleaned and repointed and arches and in-character windows installed.

~

When Fintan was a boy, attending Hamilton High School in Bandon, he and his friends regularly spent their November lunch breaks watching the salmon, new from the sea, struggle upstream at the Bandon Weir. After a few days of heavy rain, the river would be crammed with fish that had waited out the drought in lower pools and now, following the rise of water, were on the move. The boys watched in awe as the fish hurled themselves up the salmon ladder only a few yards from where they stood — and watched in dismay as some missed the water and, instead, smacked themselves off the concrete walls and were thrown back. But they tried again. And the valiant triers often won cheers from the boys.

Many fish would attempt the vertical weir itself. Most failed, smashing against its face and falling back into the turbulence below. Some, having managed the vertical leap of six feet, reached the sloping lip at the top only to be swept down again by the force of the current as they tried to reach the pool beyond. Some few, having gained this slope, hung on with mighty effort and struggled forward, inch by inch against the torrent, to finally reach the upper edge and gain safety in the deep, brown water above it. And the Hammy boys cheered.

Perhaps there was a lunchtime lesson in this, of the Robert-the-Bruce-and-the-persistent-spider kind: try and try again, undaunted by failure, because destiny and one's duty to the species calls. 'But I have promises to keep, / And miles to go before I sleep', Robert Frost, the poet, said. I suppose the boys themselves, like the salmon, have many miles to travel. And the tests at Bandon are only the first of many, over which, we hope, they will each, at their own pace, prevail.

On Fintan's urging, I went to see the spectacle for myself and found members of the public lining the river wall, as they did in June 2001 at Passage West, when the pod of killer whales came into Cork. Cork people are partial to spectacles of natural phenomena. Many had cameras. What an opportunity to film the sheer strength and poetry of nature! It is a tragic story of self-sacrifice, the salmon fighting its way upriver, beaten against rocks and shoals but finally attaining a gravel bed high up the watercourse, there to lay its eggs and die.

～

By November, the peanuts feeder has a regular queue of diners, but not all are birds. When we lived in our previous house and my workroom window looked out on the garden backed by a stand of sycamore, ash and alder, I was often distracted by the antics of a trio of ambitious young rats trying to trapeze themselves from the sycamore branches onto the bird table, thirty feet from where I sat. I should have poisoned them, I suppose, but they were intriguing creatures, tough, resourceful and intelligent, in many ways like ourselves. I wished a stoat would arrive and take up residence. Stoats will not abide rats within their range.

Many people are instinctively repulsed by rats. As we know, they can be hugely destructive and carry fatal disease. For all the downside, I couldn't help but admire the agility, intelligence and even the beauty of my garden rats. Country rats, they had thick, furry pelts, and in the November sunlight their guard hairs shone like gold. Climbing the limbs of the sycamore tree that stood near the bird table, they were more like mischievous squirrels than dangerous vermin (not that squirrels can't be vermin, too).

The three raiders were clearly juveniles of the same family. This was confirmed not only by comparing their size with a much larger adult that sometimes showed up — and, seeing no prospect of success, wisely left without delay — but by their playful behaviour as they chased one another amongst the dead leaves in games of hide and seek. The rest of the time they busily scrambled all over the tree and crept to the very tip of the branches which ended close enough to the surface of the bird table to make reaching it possible in a daring leap. However, the branch tips weren't thick enough to provide a solid launch pad and so, after sniffing the air and vainly reaching out with their front paws, they had to retreat and clamber off to try another branch, above or below the first.

On these branch tips, often thinner than a pencil, they clung and balanced, swaying and dipping, sometimes losing their footing and frantically hanging upside down. Sometimes, they fell off altogether and landed six or eight feet below, on the leaf-strewn lawn. They were fascinating. Would they risk the jump? Would they make it, if they did? Despite our age-old — and understandable — prejudice, most fellow observers were quickly won over by their tenacity, bravery and brains. And when one or the other poked a furry face through the escalonia leaves, some watchers even thought them pretty, too.

However, before that November was out, I wrote the following in an *Irish Examiner* column: 'For our merry little rats the game is up. No more trying to swing from the sycamore tree onto the bird table, no more dancing and prancing amongst the leaves on the lawn. A stoat arrived, and it was curtains for the rats thereafter.'

We saw it only once; weasels, as they are incorrectly called (or 'waesals' in the local vernacular — and why not?) are shy. Perhaps it was there all the time, but otherwise engaged while the rat family cavorted. A small, sleek creature with a white chest and beady eyes, the stoat was standing on its hind legs amongst the ferns across our stream, straining to look over the rampant vegetation. Was it the same stoat I had seen the day we first came to 'view' the house? Quite possibly. Now, suddenly, here it was again, a close neighbour, and one that just wouldn't tolerate rats!

~

After storms, yet more trees have slipped down the eroding clay slopes onto the beach from the old wood above. The estuary broadens — it is always so with rivers, widening their throats, carving away their chins. But it is a great pity to see the beeches and alders lying dead on the shore and to watch the sea come in and wash over them as they lie amongst their comrades, long stripped, blackened and salted, skeletal figures facing the sea. It is well that recently a villager has begun to harvest some of them, cutting them into logs to take away.

In the wild weather, the seagulls sweep and soar and their cries are lost on the wind. The great northern divers swim in small flotillas close to shore. Godwits, curlews, redshank and greenshank take to the fields. The little dunlin crouch together in the shelter of the salt marsh grasses on humps of ground that aren't yet wet. The philibín or lapwing stand amidst comrades in tight-knit bunches, their topknots dancing in the blast. How far are grey November skies and the odour of decaying leaves from the sweet smell of new-mown hay in summer! Nevertheless, it is worth venturing out. Indeed, rain or mist regardless, nature continues its day-to-day round. In fact, it is as if some creatures know that mankind won't be abroad and, as at dawn and dusk, they will have the world to themselves. From the kitchen, I see a fox crossing Kincragie field in curtains of rain, and rabbits sitting in the rain until the fox is almost upon them. Wet rabbits feed, and even groom, as nonchalantly as if the sun was shining. A cock pheasant struts beside our stream — what with the deluges, it could almost be called a 'river'. It pecks along the banks, its dazzling colours somewhat muted by the water vapour in the air.

~

When I leave the house to go for an hour's walk, there is always the choice of the woods, the cliff fields or the sea shore. 'I must go down to the seas again', as John Masefield said — 'to the lonely sea and the sky.' When the tide is out, it is always a pleasure, in any month and in almost any weather, to walk along the beach two hundred yards below the house. Sea birds' footprints mark the line of the surf. Cockle-shells lie on the sand, like button mushrooms. In November, there were still small fish in the rock pools, shannies and Montague blennies, the latter with little top knots on their heads. One windy day, with the sky blue and the wind sharp, I was bending over a pool when, behind me, Nicky suddenly barked in alarm, and I turned to see a huge red kite against the sky, buffeted in the wind, with a wave surfer scudding over the broken sea forty feet below it.

Poor dog; no wonder she was scared. Perhaps images of pterodactyls swooping from the sky are imprinted in some ancient recess of canine memory. Humans, too, respond defensively when a shadow suddenly blocks out the sun. But, in fact, the kites and the wind surfers — for there were half a dozen of them — were a wonderful sight amongst the long waves rolling into the bay, the gale off the land lifting their crests so that they were like serried lines of horses, plunging towards the shore. What a thrill it must be to find oneself airborne, and in motion, over friendly water. Surely, it is as near as man has yet come to flying.

Vis-à-vis the ancient reactions of animals and humans to danger, one can see this in the response of young cattle to a dog. They rush forward, as one, to mob it. This behaviour is apparently a herd instinct in cattle (and, sometimes, in horses too) in defence against wolves. Long may such survival instincts survive in their DNA and in our own.

~

When the sun shines in November and the wind blows away the clouds, it is easy to forget the fiscal gloom. On such days, like the Americans on the November 2008 morning of the Obama victory, we wake in another country. Dark days are part of the natural cycle in Ireland, and they would return. But we hoped that across the Atlantic, whatever the weather, the glittering future would not fade. It is a great country, America, and it was tragic to see its ideals traduced by the Bush-Cheney gang. An America that achieves the ideals of its own constitution would be a beacon of hope for humanity.

Meanwhile, out on the mudflats of the bay on warm November mornings, how companionable are the birds! Knot, which may have come from the Canadian Arctic, feed alongside whimbrels from northern Scandinavia and Russia; they are all on their way south and the Irish coastline is a grub-stop en route. As I watch, a squadron of tiny dunlin comes winging fast and low down the estuary. They flick over and, for a second, their white breasts flash in the sun. They swoop, bank and set down amongst the knot as lightly as feathers falling.

On such mornings, it is wonderful to be alive and to be out and about. The slob still has acres of sea lettuce and enteromorpha plastered across the mud but it is dark-green now and shining, easy on the eye and no apparent problem for the birds. The shelduck in the distance appear as moving flecks of brilliant white. Through the binoculars, they are seen to be gorgeously patterned, with chestnut collars, black heads and red beaks vivid against the snowy white of their backs and breasts. Beaks close to the mud, they hoover up shrimps and sand-hoppers between the tide pools, bright mirrors in the sward of green.

Along the channels carved in the mud by the falling tide, flotillas of widgeon and teal cruise slowly by, while others roost, head under wing, along the banks. Teams of oystercatchers and godwits pick over the shining grass in fields opposite the water. Here, by the sea, is 'The Peaceful Kingdom', as the American folk painter and Quaker minister, Edward Hicks (1780–1849) called a painting of wild and domestic animals lying down together, the lion and the lamb. In the background, we see the Pilgrim Fathers in amicable parley with the native Americans.

Like myself and the walkers I meet, all living things seem to be glorying in the sun and sharp air.

~

But on still, grey November days, the storm beaches, in contrast, can be bleak places. Then the oystercatchers are the only splash of colour, foraging along the surf with their bright black and white plumage, orange beaks and legs. A few grey crows are always about, seeking stranded shellfish: as we approach, they lift and float downwind a short distance before settling again. Sometimes, we see a small flock of turnstones. They are busy birds, turning over seaweed hour after hour, never stopping to rest, as if their lives depended upon it — which, of course, they do. The Little egrets out on the mud, their snowy feathers dishevelled by the wind, seem incongruous under our grey skies; somehow, we think of them as birds of warmer places. However, they are well established in Ireland now.

~

Walking a lonely shore one afternoon in November 2005, I saw, in the distance, a pale object on the beach about the size of a white-coat baby seal. However, the weather had been settled, with no storms, and grey seal pups normally wash in only during wild weather. Besides, by November, those pups that have survived their rough weaning are strong. I hauled out my binoculars to have a look.

It was, in fact, an old, plastic drum, weathered by long immersion in the sea. A second thought occurred to me: it might have brought quite different seafarers ashore, not fat, furry seals, with endearing baby-eyes, but a species we find only when it is washed up out of the deep ocean. I decided to investigate.

As I suspected, the drum was the floating home of a colony of pelagic gooseneck barnacles. Turning it over, I found them on the underside, an exotic macaroni of three-inch long yellow necks attached to the barrel, with the white, porcelain-like shells of the animals at the end of each. These shells, up to two inches long, have plates that open to allow delicate fronds (cirri) to emerge and filter the sea for plankton. The necks are the 'holdfasts' that anchor the barnacles to the log or flotsam upon which they sail. Thus, they travel with the currents and tides, or as the wind takes them. They sail the oceans, and generations live their lives without ever coming ashore. Indeed, to be washed ashore often spells disaster. In this case, many of the creatures had already been scoured off by the rocks as the drum washed up and down in the low surf, and only stumps of the necks remained. Some, however, had survived and were complete; when I stood the barrel on end, the barnacles hung like bells, some moving, expanding or contracting, the necks like roots, black at the sucker end, pink or yellow in the length, as tough and flexible as the holdfasts of a kelp forest. Amongst them was a small, pink crab, lying doggo but clearly alive, an inch across, with formidable pincers for its size. I took a photo and have tried to identify it, but couldn't. It may have been a deep-sea species or a creature symbiotic with gooseneck barnacles — a life on the ocean wave, perhaps, for this crab.

Before I left, I put the drum lower down the shoreline to ensure that it would be lifted by the incoming tide. Years before, on Inch Strand in Kerry, I had come across a tree trunk blanketed in goose barnacles that had dried out so that when the breeze touched them, the shells knocked together and tinkled like tiny bells.

Next afternoon, I walked again to the same lonely shore in the gathering dusk. There was not a human soul to be seen, only the oystercatchers and, as the light went, a grey mist came rolling in from the sea, shrouding the headlands, muffling the oystercatchers' calls. The drum, with its crew of barnacles, was nowhere on the sand. I was glad that my efforts may have helped the goosenecked sailors and the mariner crab back to sea.

~

The crab reminds me of another November incident, this in 2009, when, walking the scoured sands of Courtmacsherry Bay after a storm, I came upon many full, fat cockles. Ever the forager, I put three dozen in my hat — the only available receptacle — and took them home. Once again, it would be shellfish tagliatelli, food half for free!

I kept my eyes open for cockles as I walked. When they are stranded, they catch the glint of the low sun or cast a crescent shadow easily seen. Later, when we put them on a hot pan for twenty seconds and they opened, we found pea crabs inside them, creatures I'd never come upon before. Pea crabs are the size of one's small fingernail, and they live their entire lives within the shells of the living cockles; at least, the female does. The male swims about and, upon finding an open cockle with a receptive hen inside, he dives through the gape. Inside, he waits, his cold paramour beside him, until she lays her eggs. Then, he fertilises them, leaves her and travels on.

The crabs were not only a surprise but a touching sight when we saw them, nestled beside the cockles, their small, dead bodies shining in the kitchen light. Having been steamed within the shells, they had changed to a vivid red, as crustaceans do when they are steamed. The male had ten tiny yellow nodules on his coppery back and the female's carapace was a startling blood-red, with translucent margins. They looked like gems.

Their steaming was inadvertent and regrettable. To eat the cockles, we had to open them, and steaming them briefly was the most humane means we knew. As with the omelette and the eggs, one can't make seafood tagliatelli without opening the cockles. From the moment I met them, their fate was un-sealed. Of course, the shell might, in any case, have been broken open by an oystercatcher or a hammer-billed grey crow and they would have met their end just the same. I was simply the first — or last — of the beach scavengers. The early oystercatcher catches the cockle, but perhaps so many had been washed up in the agitation of sand by wind and sea that the shore birds, already replete, had stopped feeding.

After consuming the succulent cockles, I took a glass of wine and went to review again their crustacean companions in misadventure. I photographed them, partly in apology and partly in gratitude for their enhancement of my evening and enlargement of my mind. Having established what they were from a book on my shelves, I turned to the internet.

'This is the crab that can be seen swimming in estuaries over mussel beds,' a British Marine Life Study Society website obligingly told me. 'It is the most active swimmer of all the British [and, I might add, Irish] crabs. The female is quite different. She is almost twice the size of the male and usually yellow with a bright red blob on its soft shell. She is hardly able to crawl and cannot swim. She does not need to, because she spends her whole life inside a live mussel [or cockle] shell. The male fertilises her eggs by swimming inside the mussel when it opens to feed.' I assume there is some symbiotic relationship between crab and mollusc. I scratch your back, you scratch mine?

∼

The leaves on the beech trees across our stream are resplendent in the autumn sun. They have a sort of luminosity, a sheer brilliance, the reds and golds shot through by sunlight. If one subscribed to the concept of a celestial vision, one could seek it in the woods on these bright November days.

It is about the middle of the month when the beech leaves begin to fall but, if there is a breeze, they rise or even fly horizontally, like a shoal of small fish past the window. Later, they carpet the yard. 'Look at all the leaves!' I said to a young person, as we looked out on the yard. 'Twenty-five-hundred million!' cried the child, with delight. Numbers are new to her, and have infinite possibilities. I hope there will be as many leaves in the world when she is my age.

Unfortunately she wasn't there when, one day, I looked up from my desk and saw a mound of leaves in the yard suddenly rise in a spiral, going round and round, as high as the roof of the annex, caught in a *sheegaoite*. Marie tells me that such 'fairy winds' would sometimes arrive in the hayfields in her home place, and lift the cut hay into a twister against the blue sky.

By November, the leaves on the sycamore hang grey and ragged but their red stems are still bright in the autumn sun. The lower branches of the big ash trees behind our house are still green but the crowns are entirely bare. The cones on the alders are green, while the female catkins are brown and woody. A piece of rough ground near us was colonised by alder and, in two short years, the sapling were ten feet tall. When they were felled, the trunks went reddish-orange, as if they were bleeding. For this reason, legends arose that alder was evil. It certainly is not; its roots fix nitrogen in boggy soil and thus allow other trees to grow. However, the evil Alder King, or Elf King, legend arose, inspiring works by Goethe and Schubert.

Sweet chestnut leaves are pastel yellow, long and elegant, and the green, spiky husks that contain the nuts are now scattered around the trunks. This year, there is a fine, fat crop and we have already toasted some by the fire. November is a good time for those with cuisine ambitions to harvest some to use as chestnut stuffing at Christmas.

~

As the leaves go, we begin to see the birds. Tiny goldcrest wrens flit through the branches, smaller than the falling leaves. Killarney National

Park, about two hours from here, is in its glory. The landscape is a palette of colour and Torc Mountain, seen across Lough Leane, is ablaze in the evening light. As we walk through the woods, the yellow leaves of limes, brown leaves of oaks and beech leaves that rustle litter the paths.

I cannot remember an autumn month of such abundance as November 2004, when the hedgerows were laden with haws, holly berries, rowan berries, crabapples and sloes, and the woodland floors littered with beech mast, hazel nuts and sweet chestnuts. Sometimes, I would gather a few hazels, find a stone and break them, using a fence post as an anvil — but the shells are empty as often as not. Recalling the children's rhyme 'Here we go gathering nuts in May', I think to myself that surely the only place you'd find nuts in May would be in Brazil or Australia. I later discover that the original words were 'knots of May', referring to the custom of gathering 'knots' of hawthorn blossom to celebrate spring — in Ireland, Bealtaine, the old pagan knees-up falls on 1st May.

Crossing parkland near the Deenagh river in Killarney, we noticed many spiny shells open and empty some hundreds of yards away from a solitary sweet chestnut tree that stood alongside a path. Foraging rooks were the reason. They carried the husks away for privacy, and then hammered them open with their stout beaks. We saw them at it, hammering away; they looked like donkey pumps in an oil field. It was good to see some use made of the delicious nuts inside; in Ireland, only the crows and ourselves seem to value sweet chestnuts, although, every few years, they swell large enough to be well worthwhile, and one could fill a sack under some trees near our home.

The tree is also called the Spanish chestnut. A native of southern Europe, it is often up to a hundred feet tall, with a huge trunk and leaves that are amongst the largest of all the trees in these islands. They were introduced to Britain by the Romans; when they came to Ireland, I'm not sure. Initially planted as ornamentals, they have long since naturalised.

Were sweet chestnut trees around during the Famine? If so, one can only hope that they saved lives. The Romans made *polenta* from the nuts; this is now usually made with maize, except in Corsica, where chestnuts are still favoured. The nuts are slowly dried by the fireside and then ground up and mixed with milk. A porridge is made and, when it cools, cut into shapes and baked, toasted or fried.

In Cillmanistir, there are many sweet chestnut trees. Did the monks plant them and harvest them, and are the present trees descendants from the first? The nearby monasteries were established in the medieval period, so that there may well have been a sweet chestnut crop to feed the starving 165 years ago.

In November, on Tomies Mountain, in Killarney, we heard the bellowing of many red deer stags but saw only one. The ability of large animals to hide themselves in woodland is uncanny. As we returned to the car via forest paths in near darkness, the sudden, loud whistles of sika stags in the woods on both sides were unnerving. During the afternoon, we had now and then seen small groups of animals on the path ahead of us in full sunlight, but they walked into the trees and disappeared. No fuss, no panic: soundlessly, they faded into the shadows.

~

On a 2004 November whale-watching trip from Reen Pier, skippered by our old friend Colin Barnes, we logged three pods of humpbacks twelve miles out, with fin whales up to seventy foot long everywhere, possibly the highest concentration of this species anywhere in the world — as one tripper said, 'The sea was erupting with whales.' Three young American girls at the rail could hardly contain themselves, jumping up and down and screaming like ra-ra girls every time a new whale was spotted.

At sunset, the 'blows' of the fins, vertical columns rising afar off against the painted sky, were wonderful to see, but one blow amongst them sent a frisson of excitement through the watchers. The column of water was almost twice as tall as the blows of the fins, which rise to about 20 feet. Was it, therefore, that unprecedented, sought-after sighting, most treasured of all, of a blue whale in Irish waters? They were once relatively common, an average of fifteen taken each year at whaling stations on the west coast in the first two decades of the last century. Recently their 'songs' had been detected acoustically in the same area; perhaps they were making a come-back. Meanwhile, the screen of the on-board fish-finder showed the sea almost solid with sprat for three miles from Rosscarbery, going west, at a depth of about 250 feet. Occasionally, the big 'blob' of a whale could be seen moving through their midst.

~

On 'pet' November days, I sometimes climb down to the sea and stand or sit with my back against the cliff face opposite where the ravens nest and where poor old Nicky came a cropper and lost her life. The rocks are as flat as the bed of a billiard table, and incline at about 70 degrees — they are made for leaning against, sitting or standing. Catching the full force of the sun, by eleven in the morning they are as warm as toast. The view is magnificent, with the Old Head of Kinsale off to the east, the lighthouse white and shining against the clear blue of sky and water. The only sound is the sea. When far-flung family members tell me it's been raining nonstop in Andalucía, miserable in Hertfordshire and minus eleven in the Czech Republic, I cannot but consider how lucky we are!

~

The garden and all about our house is so absolutely silent that, one November night, when Dara heard something rustling amongst the leaves across the stream, he took it to be one of the horses that graze in Kincragie fields. However, it turned out to be a hedgehog.

What a racket a hedgehog can make, sniffling around amongst dry leaves! We brought a flashlight. However, the hedgehog curled up, of course, so there was no hope of seeing the cute face with the beady black eyes. We didn't pick it up. It would have terrified the creature, besides the fact that hedgehogs often crawl with fleas and are hardly cuddly. It was nice to find one near the house. They are great consumers of slugs, so a hedgehog family would be welcome in the garden. Perhaps we should have tried to entice it. So far, we had stoats, a fox that passes regularly (we have no chickens), a badger, probably just passing through while looking for a mate, and now a hedgehog. Hedgehogs move about a great deal. The home range of a male is about sixty acres. Some are entirely nomadic and have no fixed home or territory at all. Most travel between one and three miles at night; this must take considerable effort on such short legs. In summer, they often don't bother to return home but bed down in temporary nests, holiday homes used by peripatetic cousins and strangers; two or three may gather together of a summer night.

Our neighbour said hedgehogs grunt like pigs. I haven't heard one but will take her word for it. They could, then, as accurately be called hedgepigs as hedgehogs. When hibernating, they should not be disturbed, but here, in the mild south-west, garden hedgehogs are seen occasionally in all the winter months.

Bats are seen too, flitting between the hedge in the bohreens as we return, in the dark, from weekend walks. They are pipistrelles, one assumes, the common, and garden, bat. While in Ireland we have only one shrew species, against Britain's three, and one vole species, against Britain's four, we have bats not found or very rarely found in Britain. This is Leisler's bat, and the world's largest roost is in West Cork. They are half as big again as pipistrelles, and the last time I saw one, I thought it was a moonlighting blackbird. However, when it whizzed overhead a second time, and I ducked, its flight clearly indicated that it was no bird.

We have no vampire bats in Ireland, although it was an Irishman who made them the stuff of nightmares. Dublin's Bram Stoker created Dracula, the human blood-sucker who would drain the corpse of a pretty girl so improvidently that there'd be no coming back for seconds.

Vampire bats do not do this; they take blood from animals, and not from people. They do not take much and do not leave empty cows or horses lying around after a meal.

The largest vampire bat is only four inches long, so they are hardly nightmare material. Fruit bats are larger, but are dangerous only when they're drunk and fly into things. They get drunk when the fruit they feed on has fermented in the sun. I have seen drunken fruit bats in India. On one memorable occasion, when we sojourned on a beach in Goa in 1975 (Bhaga beach, then pristine, but now overrun with tourists and hustlers), a Japanese girl visiting our rented hut went to the shed to fetch some green peppers which had been hung on a clothesline to dry. The peppers were dusty, and it was dark. She carried a dozen into our candle-lit kitchen, held tight against her breast. As she poured a jug of water over them to wash them, one pepper suddenly exploded into a mini-umbrella on wings. She screamed. Her husband chased it with a rolled-up *Time* magazine. We opened the windows and it found its way out.

It had been drinking all day. We'd seen it and its companions, under a loquat tree, making merry. Such bibulous behaviour was typical of bats in Catholic Goa. It would never have happened in next-door Karnataka, an alcohol-free Hindu state!

December

Herons against the moon, and whales beneath the boat, singing. Night-lights in saucers leading down corridors. No electricity, but no darkness either. No TV or Playstation but the thrills and spills of Snakes and Ladders and the shrieks and squeals of Blind Man's Bluff!

~

n Italy, I found the place-names a joy to pronounce, but we have a lexicon of romantic place-names in Ireland — Lough Allua and Gortnamona, Shanagarry and Shanagolden, Lisheenaleen and Ahakista, Avoca and Coomanore. Dozens of such names are found on every OS sheet; they are in every parish. The old Gaelic names, they have meaning; they are not, like the anglicised versions, simply sounds.

Italy sings with opera, but not with birds. The sound we most often heard along the fringes of a famous National Park was the banging of twelve-bore shotguns. Birds enter Italian airspace at their peril. Arriving home, I hear a heartening story of bird-friendliness. My pal Hanly, chugging up Courtmacsherry Bay in his boat, noticed a black guillemot hanging around the moored craft in the channel. This was strange. They are mainly seen in the outer harbour, hunting at least a hundred yards from shore. Small fish-hunters, waterhen-size, with vivid-red legs, they are coal black with a white wing patch in summer, and in winter are mainly white. They have the typical short wings of auks, moving in a blur as they fly low over the water.

A few days later, Mr Hanly was talking to a friend on the pier when they saw the bird close in. The friend said it had sometimes followed his yacht up and down the channel. Next day, as Hanly was preparing to row out to his boat, it popped up six feet away from him and cried out 'Peep-peep-peep!' Curious, he tapped the side of his punt and made noises 'like calling a cat'. The bird came forward, and he reached out and picked it gently from the water. It made no attempt to escape.

Its craw seemed full, and it appeared to be perfectly healthy. There was no sign of a ring on its leg. It stood up and clapped its wings and, when put back in the water, swam casually away.

That evening, as he chugged back up the channel, the bird followed him. 'Peep-peep-peep!' it went, and answered to his call. Later, he and others watched it in the inner dock, swimming after large, five-pound-weight mullet, causing consternation amongst them, presumably for fun. Swimming with wings and feet, it shot like a torpedo through the clear water and was a joy to behold.

Similarly human-friendly was a Little auk found on a road in West Cork two weeks before Christmas 2001 — in the February chapter, I mentioned that another of this High Arctic species was found beneath a car in Ballinspittle in 2005. Driven off course and ashore by storms, it was in bad nick indeed, and was taken home by an official of the local chapter of BirdWatch Ireland. After careful feeding, it was released, local twitchers, interested in a tick to add to their 'life lists', having been alerted in advance. However, instead of heading out to sea, it came directly back to its birder benefactor. Research then revealed that this seems to be standard behaviour with sea-wrecked Little auks which, until they have fattened up to a minimum of 30 ounces, return again and again to the hand that feeds them.

A few months ago, I had, nestling in my hand, one of prettiest birds I've ever seen, and one of the most elusive, a storm petrel. It had flown into the lighted window of the house of a friend, a barrister, and his consort, a fudge-maker. They live in an extremely remote house on the Seven Heads.

When the bird struck the glass, they both heard it, despite the wind and driving rain, and rushed out into the storm to rescue it. It is well named indeed, a storm petrel. Large numbers of rare Madeiran petrels and Wilson's petrels were seen passing the Old Head of Kinsale on those storm-bound days, driven inshore by the tempest. The tiniest of all the family, the little storm petrel, smaller than a swallow, is our only native species.

It nests on islands far offshore, coming to land only during the mating season, and then only at night. A bird of the open ocean, rarely seen and having no contact with our species, it is quite unafraid of man, so unafraid that it happily sat in my wife's hand while we took photographs.

Mother Carey's chickens was the old sea dog's name for petrels: they literally dance on the waves, seeming to peck plankton from the ocean surface like chickens picking feed in a yard. 'Petrel' comes from Peter, for walking on water: Mother Carey from Mater Cara, the Virgin Mary, because they were said to forewarn sailors of impending storms.

Bird ringers, attempting to count them, stand mist nets in front of scree slopes — and stone walls where there are any — on islands like the Blaskets and the Skelligs. They ply their expertise at night, in the nesting season, especially when there is little moonlight. Shearwaters also arrive, another oceanic species, but much larger. Just as swifts come to earth only to nest, petrels and shearwaters come to land only to lay their eggs in crevices under rocks or in rabbit burrows. Indeed, the storm petrel's black, scythe-like wings are very similar to those of a swift, long and narrow, reaching to the end of its tail.

The petrel was the loveliest of creatures, all the more because it was so tame and unafraid. On its short, black legs and webbed feet, it hobbled around the dark-red carpet of the dining room. It wasn't good at walking: shearwaters are, perhaps, even worse. Both have webbed feet, designed for riding the roughest seas. No wonder they rarely meet us. The open ocean is their element. They ride out whatever the weather brings, perhaps a thousand miles from shore.

The shiny hooked beak, with breathing tubes or nostrils mounted above, the jet-black, downy plumage and the striking white band above the tail contrasted vividly with the carpet. The bird made no attempt to scuttle away or hide. Placed on a shelf, it seemed as at home there as a pigeon in a dovecote.

One night, a Manx shearwater crash-landed in the village street, drawn in by the strobe lights which, on holiday weekends, pierce the darkness, attracting visitors to the disco amenities of the hotel. As I was walking home from the pub, I met a man carrying it. Shearwaters, also a tubenose species, are equally attractive birds, but are not to be messed with. It had already drawn blood from its rescuer's young companion and, as I checked it for damage, it set about nipping me. Cory shearwaters regularly crash into the harbour lights in La Gomera: there, a 'shearwater rescue service' supplies the harbour personnel with 'recovery boxes' — and stout gloves. Manx shearwaters have wingspans of almost three feet and, while petrels dance on the waves, shearwaters skim them like mini-albatrosses in the course of epic oceanic flights.

Both our nocturnal visitors were released as soon as they seemed recovered — the petrels in the dark of night, for fear the gulls would attack and eat it, the shearwater the following morning. Those who released them tell me it was wonderful to watch them fly out to sea, the far horizon their destination, their encounter with man unique.

～

Badgers and the seaside don't really go together. Otters are at home by the sea and are regularly seen cavorting on the village pier by late-night dog-walkers. Yet, only twenty yards from the home of the aforementioned barrister and the sweetmeat-maker, an ancient sett of badgers flourishes on the shore where the waves, when high, must all but come flushing down the tunnels. On summer nights, they have been seen rolling down the banks and nosing the weed along the tide line. Badgers, not uncommonly, may have 350 yards of tunnels, eight to twelve inches from roof to floor, and displace twenty-five tons of earth during the digging.

Certain otters seem not the least disconcerted by urban life. A reader of my column wrote to tell me about an otter he had seen in the Lee in the centre of Cork city and wondered if people thought him daft as he stood pointing at the river, calling attention to an otter that sometimes was there and sometimes wasn't, because it had dived, leaving nothing to see.

Either Corkonians were too busy to stop or a man pointing excitedly at the surface of the river is a common sight in Cork. Far from being daft, the sharp-eyed observer had spotted, as he said, 'The biggest otter I've ever seen, four feet long, hunting between Nano Nagle footbridge and the Southgate Bridge, oblivious to people passing on the footpath, and the traffic.'

It was a Saturday morning, at half-tide. The observer, who had worked all his life beside the river at Union Quay, was surprised that he alone seemed exercised by the sight of this elusive animal in the very heart of his city. So am I. If close-ups of a hunting otter were shown on David Attenborough TV, viewers would be gasping at the charm of it. Equally, if a disgraced politician or banker appeared on the streets of Cork, passers-by would fall over one another staring at him — yet such creatures have recently become commonplace in town and country. Poor otter! However he might duck and dive, however sleek, however slippery, he could not hope to compete with those humans who are talented in these arts.

But the otter's skill and fearlessness weren't wasted. A father, walking with some small children, saw my correspondent's excitement and stopped and stared and marvelled, enjoying a riverside lesson in animal behaviour, thanks to this Mr Healy, a keen-eyed observer of the Lee.

Not long afterwards, a lady told me that she had seen an otter on busy Merchants Quay. It had, apparently, emerged from the river and ascended to street level for a quick look around. Satisfied that there was nothing of otter interest, it returned to the Lee's salubrious stream.

The lady was overwhelmed to be sitting in her first-floor office and seeing the sleek, wild creature in the street below. Will otters soon be raiding the bins in Patrick Street? Surely not!

～

Past midnight on the night of a December full moon, I was intrigued to see two herons flying across the dark-blue sky squawking to one another. Earlier that day, my brother Gerry and I had been listening to whales clicking and crooning beneath the boat in which we rode on a calm sea five miles off the Galley Head in West Cork. Such is the magic of Ireland.

Whales were all around us. To port, two sportive humpbacks, to starboard two enormous finbacks. The fin whales passed us in majesty, over seventy foot long, the second largest creatures on earth. So numerous are whales along the West Cork coast, and so many are the species present, that it is now amongst the best venues for whale-watching on earth. It is as if the whales heard that in 1991 Ireland unilaterally declared Europe's first whale sanctuary within its 200-mile fishery limit. Hunting of all whale species, including dolphins and porpoises, was banned.

We had located the pods by pinpointing pillars of spume rising out of the sea, and by the bird-clouds. As Colin Barnes, our skipper, drove us at high speed from bird-cloud to bird-cloud, dolphins raced the boat as if for sport. 'Footprints' left on the surface showed where the whales had dived — smooth water, like in the wake of a boat. Where they had fed, luminescent spots floated down into the deep, scales from the sprat they had swallowed. Finbacks eat two tons per day, humpbacks in excess of a ton. That day, there were some forty whales between the Old Head of Kinsale and Galley. Some had been there for months. How fecund is our sea!

As we drifted gently, time and again whales rose from the depths and rolled their massive backs out of the water only yards away. Sometimes, a humpback, making a steep dive, would raise its tail against the sky. It was awesome not only to witness the reality of that iconic image but to be so close to it, lifting out of the ocean, a tail fifteen feet across. The serrations on the fluke are recorded by experts like marks on an ogham stone. Thus are individual whales identified, and humpbacks monitored on their migration. The movements of fin whales, however, are less well known.

The bird-clouds, too, were spectacular. Dicing with death, the seabirds feed on the sprat, herded into balls by the whales and driven to the surface. Seagulls snap, kittiwakes plunge-dive and gannets rocket into the shoal even as the huge maw of the whale drives up from the deep to engulf it. But on that glorious winter's day of high-seas adventure, we witnessed something Colin Barnes has never before seen in forty-three years at sea.

In a small area of water, twenty kittiwakes and gulls lay floating lifeless, two gannets amongst them. We took one gannet aboard, a beautiful bird, snow-white with black wingtips, its body still warm beneath the dense feathers of its breast. What could have happened to these birds, newly dead? They could not have been poisoned; we were miles offshore on the open ocean. A whale could be the only explanation: inadvertent slaughter by a whale.

A humpback powering up from the deep sees the ball of sprat against the light and gulps it down. A fin whale, in a burst of speed, envelops the shoal in a lunge. Called the 'greyhounds of the sea', fins can swim at 23 mph (37 kph). Clearly, a whale had engulfed the birds accidentally, found it had a mouthful of alien, feathery things and spat them out.

Colin explained that the first action of the whale upon taking in a fish shoal is to squeeze out the water through the baleen plates in its jaws. Then it swallows the fish like a living river of oil running down a plug-hole. The birds would have been drowned and crushed as the water was expelled. However, a single herring gull on the surface still showed signs of life. Brought aboard, clearly in shock and shaking from fear and cold, it lay wrapped in a towel until, well recovered, we released it over the side. Swept away on the wake, I watched it through binoculars.

No worse for its Jonah experience, it flapped its wings and took to the air.

A man who had driven from Dublin for the outing wondered should he remove the gannet's head and present the bird to his mother, saying it was a Christmas goose. As I mentioned earlier, Scottish islanders hunted gannet which they called the solan goose, and the early Christian monks on Skellig Michael harvested the squabs. However, we committed our snowy gannet to the sea.

~

When I started writing my *Examiner* column in 1991, the business of getting the news of such events to my newspaper in Cork city sometimes took on the complexion of Paul Revere's ride. Nowadays, from wherever I am in the world — be it La Gomera, Cuba or Senegal — I can send word by email at the click of a button. Then, I would try to meet the *Echo* van which whizzed around West Cork delivering the *Evening Echo* newspaper. The driver would collect my lapidary dispatches, left in an envelope at the filling station in Timoleague, and deliver them to the *Examiner*, the *Echo*'s parent paper, when he arrived back in the city. I see that in my column of 2 March 1993, I noted that 'Last week, for the first time ever, my dispatches failed to get through . . .' Something had gone wrong — a spider stuck in the ointment, a Spaniard in the works. The column had disappeared — the horror, the horror! Too late, its absence was discovered: the deadline had passed! It had been full of good news, fair tidings of spring. 'Beautiful are the feet of those who bring good news', the Bible says. But the *Echo* van didn't travel on feet, and spring arrived anyway.

Living in a rural village can present challenges in communication. However, should the computer or the car fail to start, good neighbours will willingly assist: indeed, there is always someone who will help with almost anything at a moment's notice and, usually, at no fee. We try to reciprocate: I am happy to edit an advertisement for insertion in a newspaper or the wording of a brochure for the internet. Thus, we rub along. If the car fails totally, there is the daily bus to Cork and, if the computer has a tantrum, I can dispatch my column from a friend's. However, one winter, the weather went against us, and there was little anyone could do to help.

It was 1998, and 'A dark Christmas we had of it', to paraphrase T.S. Eliot's 'Journey of the Magi'. It was a memorable Christmas, nevertheless, gathered around fires and candles, with night-lights in saucers leading down corridors and oil lamps in windows.

On our coast, storms raged and left us without electricity for forty-six hours. Power lines were flying like flitters all over West Cork, all over Ireland, whistling and flapping in 100mph gusts. Above our heads, in our then home, Travara Lodge, the forest roared like a hundred express trains passing, all day and all night. The dog cowed, the new kitten mewed. Birds flew backwards over the bay. The wind, meeting the incoming waves, threw them back in walls of water. Squalls, like alien raiders, moved down the estuary in wild, grey ranks. Nature was king, and the might of the wind wreaked havoc on all man's puny works and sent him skulking back into his cave.

On Christmas Eve, at lunchtime, Marie and I sat in our cave contemplating the fact that the 'quality' presents we'd planned for young Fintan, then eleven years old, had turned out to be unavailable and there was nothing to be done but to get him what he really wanted, one of the new 'electronic games'.

For those not feckless enough to have young children, let me explain that such games cost the price of a Christmas dinner for four at a Grand Hotel, or four pairs of decent shoes. They also obsess the owner, who will spend hundreds of hours prostrate in front of the screen, a world unto himself, exercising nothing but the fast responses of three fingers.

But we surrendered. We had failed in our good intentions; however, now the problem was where to get one of these infernal games. We learned that Cork city was sold out; finally, we found a shop with two left in a suburban shopping arcade. Thus, at the height of the tempest, at 1.00pm on Christmas Eve afternoon, Marie and I set off for the city, nothing to save us from annihilation by a toppling forest giant but the thin roof of the car. As we drove, bushes, hoardings and sportive tar barrels flew all around us and, for a stretch outside Bandon town, a galvanised shed, somersaulting along the outside lane, kept pace with us for a hundred yards. However, we arrived in Cork alive and the shop lady had kept the game as she had promised on the phone.

But, when we arrived home at nightfall and switched on the lights, a cruel irony became clear. *There would be no electricity with which to play the game.* We had risked wife and limb for nothing. Fortunate was the child who, for Christmas, would receive a plain football or a hurley stick for, without electricity, the Playstations and Nintendo 64s were so much plastic scrap. For Christmas Day entertainment, there would be no option but to take out the forgotten deck of cards or the ancient Ludo board, anachronisms the electronic kids had never before encountered, the old interactive games for adults and children, the thrills and spills of Snakes and Ladders, the shrieks and squeals of Blind Man's Bluff!

On Christmas Eve, midnight mass in the village was cancelled. The priest stood outside the church with a large flashlight, apologetically sending people home. A candle-lit service might have been lovely but there were the steep steps to the church and, as someone said, the occasional parishioner might have overindulged in Christmas cheer.

As we walked home along the edge of the bay, the night was as black as it had been at The Beginning. Not a light showed in the village street, nor across the bay on the deep, black hump of the opposite shore. No stars pierced the cowl of clouds above it: over there, all signs of human settlement had vanished. Human activity, for which there hadn't been enough hours in the pre-Christmas days, had stopped. The light had gone out and all noise by night had ceased. The world sank into silence. It rested; we rested. We concluded that we should have two whole days and nights without electricity every year.

Later, reading by candlelight, we marvelled at how much light a single candle throws. We remembered the farmhouses in the Balearic Islands lit by candlelight, the rattan hut on the beach at Ni Han on the Andaman Sea, the first house we rented in La Gomera. Interiors look more beautiful by candlelight, softening the contours of our man-made walls. The walls around us, nearly two centuries old, had been built when there was no light but flame. That night, soot gently blew down the drawing room chimney while we blissfully sat in the fireside glow, unaware that our liver-and-white dog, stretched on the carpet, was slowly turning black.

It was a memorable Christmas, 1998; no electricity, but no darkness either. Circles of light encompassed us, and we gathered, like humans of millennia past, around the fire. Television programmes didn't schedule our days. Time passed slowly. At night, the world was a gentler place, without glare or noise, hushed, as if listening.

~

In the pub of a winter night, I hear local stories of the good old days when there was the railway and there were three shops in the villages — and of the 'bad old days', when many a village boy emigrated to America, sometimes leaving before his younger siblings were born and meeting them for the first time as forty-year-olds when he came home for his mother's funeral, aged going-on sixty himself.

As I step out into the street, the night is silent and the sea is calm. The pier lights are like four candle flames on the still water. Above, the sky is crystal clear and the stars are sharp, glittering cut-outs against the deep blue of space. Are they all rock, or burning orbs, or iceballs? Or is there one like ours? On this tiny globe, we have the miracle of a hundred climates and a million microclimates. Why not elsewhere?

~

As I near the end of this book, there is new hope for Ireland. The party whose *folie de grandeur* and dedicated self-interest took grievous toll of the lives of many innocent people has been drummed out, in disgrace and disarray. Its legacy still stalks the land, but we are a resilient race. We will overcome. Honest government and intelligent management —

if this is to be the new order, as we have been promised — can create an Ireland to which its children, forced to emigrate, can come home, and wherein its cruelly dispossessed will again have homes to go to.

~

Amongst the changes in the village in these last twenty years, the post office is gone, and we have to drive to Timoleague. Billy Drake, our postman, is still here; he tells us there's no need to fix a letterbox to a tree at the end of the drive — walking the fifty yards back and forth to the house is good for him.

The Golden Pheasant, a substantial Georgian house facing the sea on Courtmacsherry's single street, has had a marvellous makeover by new owners and now provides the village with a garden café, set amongst the owleries and pheasantries, these being commodious aviaries where the dramatic birds (all cage-bred, I'm assured) are displayed. The eagle owls sit on their perches, with one eye open. A foolish fox cub set about digging its way into one owl-house and narrowly escaped with its life. Meanwhile, the eponymous pheasants, along with their cousins, the equally flamboyant Lady Amherst pheasants, strut about, their spectacular plumage shimmering in the dappled light, or roam between the exotic shrubs and trees on the sloping terraces with the old Earl of Shannon woods behind. The hotel, once the earl's summer house, is also much improved, with its grounds and ancient cork tree, the beach in front and new apartments built around, most tastefully all agree. West Cork tourist facilities have improved exponentially but aren't brash or overcrowded. I doubt this will ever happen here: the attractions are, inherently, organic and ambient. What attracts the visitor is warmth of welcome, peace and beauty, the opportunity to walk, or fish, to loiter on pristine sands or swim in an unpolluted sea.

Some things remain the same. The Anchor Bar puts on live music every Saturday night, with bands from Cork and elsewhere, and the Barryroe women — and some men — dance in good-humoured relays to their tunes. The Lifeboat provides good pub food and is an alternative Saturday night music venue with a warm welcome extended to drinkers, diners, poker-players et al by Margaret O'Donovan and her family. Equally warm is the welcome at The Pier House, where John and Breda Young have handed over the reins — or rather, the beers taps — to their sons. Our village pubs and the Courtmacsherry Hotel are all family owned and the hospitality personally offered to strangers reflects this.

There is a Saturday market in the village now. Country markets have sprung up all over West Cork, and at some (such as Bantry Market, which fills the entirety of the broad square facing the bay) one can buy anything 'from a needle to an anchor'. Clonakilty, Skibbereen and Dunmanway markets all present artisan food-products, fish and home-grown vegetables on their open-air stalls. More exotic fare is also offered: chorizos and olives, sundried tomatoes and imported olive oil. Irish cheeses are hugely popular and, over the past twenty years, more than two dozen artisan brands have become available. Here in Courtmacsherry, with its few hundred native souls, the market offerings are more modest, but hardly are the tables set up than there are queues for Brendan's brown bread and Kathleen Finn's home-made scones.

Arts festivals have become part of the West Cork year. A three day-and-night literary festival is held in Bantry every summer with festivals both literary and jazz at Kinsale, a guitar festival in Clonakilty and a fiddle festival at Baltimore. Attendees at the West Cork Literary Festival are treated to workshops and exhibitions, and readings by such literary luminaries as Eavan Boland, Dame Margaret Drabble and Dame Fay Weldon. 'There is nothin' like a dame!' according to the song from *South Pacific*: it seems literary dames are greatly appreciated in West Cork. Despite the talented company, the organiser, Denyse Woods, herself a distinguished author, has been kind enough to ask me to get up on my hind legs and talk about my writing. I've been gratified by the sympathetic hearing and extraordinary patience of my listeners.

A few Irish resorts offer casinos and ballrooms-of-romance, Brighton Belles or hurdy-gurdys, but in West Cork, fishing, swimming or horse-riding are more likely attractions. We have the scenery, the wild life, and the fresh air. World-class walking paths have been opened to the public; urban folk do not come to the country to sit on a ditch and watch the bees buzz by. The Beara Way and the Sheep's Head Way have been joined and offer circuits taking not hours but days, with scenery and wilderness to rival anywhere, the sea a constant presence and the typical Irish diversity of rough and smooth, clifftop, riverine, pastoral and mountain scenery, each with its specific flora and fauna to be enjoyed. International walking festivals have evolved. The pay-back to tourism is obvious.

The swifts that once split the air and shrieked like Valkyries when we sat in the backyard of Dillon's pub in Timoleague are less numerous than before. In recent summers, there were no more than two pairs nesting in the abbey. Their scarcity is hardly to do with any cataclysm they have suffered here in Ireland: the nesting niches have not been blocked up in the abbey so they have not suffered the fate of swifts where latter-day 'neatness' and 'efficiency' has led to the loss of nesting sites, as it did in a block of Victorian flats which we know well near Parliament Hill Fields in London. There, flocks of 300 birds provided evenings 'full of swifts' wings' and great excitement for us tenants who would sit on our balconies and watch them swoop and dive until the light went from the sky: such sights are now no more. It is to be hoped that they will return in their previous numbers to Timoleague Abbey; they have been nesting there for centuries.

However, as I mentioned earlier, we have egrets nesting in Cillmanistir just across the bay and in the trees behind Timoleague House on the banks of the Argideen. Spoonbills are again here this year, so they, like the egrets, may establish colonies. They may well, like the egrets, learn the best sites from the herons which, even in December, stand up to their knees in the sea at half past midnight — I first noticed them years ago as I returned from a stroll, my breath making clouds in the air, and the hirsute dog shivering. Although their legs have evolved convectionally-heated veins, they look permanently cold. Maybe that is why they are blue.

Sparrows and martins still nest in the eaves of village houses. I put up a specially designed sparrow nest box last spring, hoping two pairs might move in. It took me two days, and I spent hours up a ladder, twenty feet off the ground. However, they ignored it. Perhaps next spring they may appreciate my efforts.

While many changes are welcome — the Golden Pheasant Tea Rooms, the new pontoon giving easier access to the pier, the renovation of the primary school looking out on the bay and birds beside Timoleague Abbey — it is fascinating to think how ancient and unchanged some everyday things remain in this secluded corner as the world spins in flux about us. The bay is millions of years old but the birds, having been around for 150 million years, colonised the sky above it long before it ever spread to its present size. Our human presence is, of course, like a drop of water in the bay of time; our oldest ancestors date back only three million years and *Homo sapiens* evolved just 250,000 years ago. In comparison with the bay and the birds, we, and our ancient abbey, are recent phenomena.

On the mudbanks, nothing has changed. If the windows of the abbey had eyes, if the ghosts of the monks were watching, it would surely be hard for them to tell whether a century, a year or only a single night had passed since they last looked, since light came and went from the sky, and the tide rose and fell. Another day ends, another tide withdraws. The lapwings hunch their shoulders and draw their wings close against the night. All is still, until a car passes. All is the same until they raise their eyes and see the new second-homes that have sprung up, white and gleaming, down the bay.

When our grandchildren are driving spaceships — or are back in the coracles, if the energy runs out — the mudflats, with the birds, will, likely, still be there. Meanwhile, the new developments that did, indeed, gleam like coveted pearls on the green velvet of the village outskirts, are for the most part inhabited — but there are, also, fine newly built houses which lie empty and are unlikely to enjoy the warmth of human occupancy for some years to come.

As for our own accommodation, I have related how our first house in West Cork was beautiful indeed, with its gracious gardens and gracious Georgian rooms, but it was really not the place for me, rather too squire-archical, rather too grand: 'The house of the planter is known by the trees', as Austin Clarke so perceptively put it. I am not a planter, so much as 'planted', and I really could not go in for cravat-wearing and playing the part of the mansion owner, nor could Marie. Perhaps, I couldn't 'live up to it' — I was brought up in one of the finest Georgian houses in one of the finest Georgian squares in Ireland in Clonakilty, but nevertheless, it is not my style. Now, five houses and seven moves later, we have built the house in which I believe we will stay. Marie says that if we sell it, she goes with it. So, you can offer me a million, but I won't do a deal.

Our needs are built into this home. Dara's design and workmanship is evident in every room, the spaces divided as we wanted and the colours, the height of the ceilings, the size of the windows and their views all as we hoped they would be. This upside-down dwelling suits us perfectly with its big balconies, gravelled 'courtyard' and garden front and back, its fruit trees and beds of dark earth where the spuds fatten in spring, its stream, with watercress, the line of beech trees on the other side and the rough pasture beyond with horses grazing and rabbits jumping and humping in their season, the birds that nest in the ivy, the stoat that lives in the woodpile, the fox that visits at night, the flocks of winter thrushes that move in serried ranks across the field.

How fortunate we've been, how lucky we were to ride the waves and troughs of the Celtic Tiger and not flounder. It was pure good fortune; we moved because family circumstances and financial constraints dictated: there was no master plan, no 'investment portfolio'. Somebody up there was looking after us, some bird of fate, some guardian angel — perhaps it was our parents' prayers, if such prayers are heard. Meanwhile, even as we are etherially transported by the loveliness and gentleness of this place, our earthly transport continues to be a twelve-year-old estate-car that has seen better days, most of them long before we bought it. But, as I said before, it motors, and aren't we lucky to have a car at all?

The twentieth anniversary of our return to Ireland fell in late

September 2009. In that twenty years, we haven't once regretted leaving London — a great city where we spent wonderful years, had many friends and felt absolutely at home. However, in the last decade of the millennium, it was no longer the upbeat city of the Swinging Sixties, and the heady inspiration of Wordsworth's 'Ships, towers, domes, theatres, and temples lie/ Open unto the fields, and to the sky;/ All bright and glittering in the smokeless air' was no longer there. Neither was it the bustling, coffee-house-London upon which the great doctor so memorably pronounced — however, we left it not because we were 'tired of life' but because we were tired of traffic, the polluted air and the incipient dog-eat-dogdom that prevailed in the Thatcher years. We find that now, again, the warmth is returning to the city. The traffic becomes tolerable and we enjoy our visits and meeting old friends.

Without doubt, the move from London proved immensely positive for the children and for ourselves. *A Place Near Heaven: A Year in West Cork* was a great joy to write and it has been gratifying and inspiring to be told by strangers that they have enjoyed it and found it inspiring too. Launched in 2003, it is still floating — some great bird of fate, some guardian angel, indeed! Besides, there is the weekly column, the poetry and other books to write. The boys have achieved their academic aims and have strong roots here. Marie has renewed her bonds with friends and family. We are at home. And so, I find the T.S. Eliot lines, used too often, are yet worth repeating: 'And the end of all our exploring/ Will be to arrive where we started/ And know the place for the first time.'

The Heron Diaries

etween the writing of this book and its publication, the family and I were blessed with the arrival of a new member whom, while fascinating for family and visitors alike, we hope can be dissuaded from settling with us indefinitely.

This, for its own sake — for the moment, I'd better call it an 'it', although I will be giving away the fact that it is not human. It would be amusing to call it 'he' and prolong the reader's curiosity about this new family member but, then, 'he' might not be the right pronoun anyway.

In fact, it's impossible to tell to which sex our adopted heron — or any heron — belongs on sight alone. To establish this, we would have to examine it 'in hand' and, while we are on extended-family terms with the bird, we have avoided physical contact, except when it was a fledgling and we had no option.

A grey heron indeed it was. In its early days as part of the family, it became known as 'Ron', taken from the word 'heron', and conferred upon him by our son Fintan's English girlfriend, Stephanie, who did sterling work in the first encounters and could not be gainsaid when it came to naming the bird. For me, 'Ron', however, was rather too English and too matey and, privately, I address him as 'Bird'. If 'Bird' was good enough for Charlie Parker, it was surely good enough for a creature that not only could not play the saxophone but could not even sing.

We first met Ron one Saturday morning — 26 March 2011 — when Susan, our neighbour, found him on the lane below our house after he had fallen some seventy feet from a nest in a Scots pine behind the hotel. She had had the courage, despite his snapping his long, spear-like beak defiantly at her, to usher him into the woods, for fear he'd be flattened by a car. There we found him beneath his nursery tree, a creature like a hirsute Looney Tunes Road Runner, his topknot a mass of wiry hairs, his neck and breast like a dishevelled bottle-brush of grey feathers streaked with black and white. When we approached, he fixed us with his yellow eyes, close together on either side of his long, dagger-like beak, darted his head forward and snapped noisily. This was defensive; but we later learned that the snapping was also a demand for food.

We were faced with a dilemma. Leaving young birds to their parents' ministrations is always best; however, it was clear that it would be weeks before this bird would be ready to fly. In the meantime, he would certainly fall victim to a cat, dog or fox — twenty-four inches tall, he couldn't hide as a song-bird fledgling might, and the parents would not feed him on the ground as songbirds do their young. In the event, it was seven weeks before Bird took wing. He hadn't been ready to leave the nest; he had simply fallen out of it.

A second option was to return him to the nest high above the forest floor. A local tree surgeon would have done this, but he was away at the time and wouldn't be back for a week. Fin volunteered to climb thirty feet up the trunk on a ladder, carrying the bird in a basket like a heron's twig nest and to fix the basket to the tree. There, it would be safe from predators, and the parents might feed it until it could fly. However, if the parents didn't take to this idea (which was very likely), the creature would certainly starve. The only safe solution was to adopt it and, so, we found ourselves parenting a heron.

We picked him up, staying wary of the beak which was so pointed it could take one's eye out. In fact, he wasn't stabbing but snapping: and the snapping proved useful and saved his inelegant carcass from an untimely demise. As Fintan carried him home, he snapped at Stephanie's finger and caught it in his beak. The beak, however, wasn't sharp-edged and the pressure wasn't great, so when we reached home, Steph allowed him to do it again while I poked defrosted razorfish down his gullet. After just three or four such efforts, there was no longer any need to hold his beak open; he opened it himself and gobbled down whatever seafood was offered. A young heron is not like a baby robin, wren or song thrush which requires specialised, largely invertebrate diets. Our foundling, we soon discovered, could put away food like an eating machine.

In the following days, housed in a large, open shed off the courtyard, he ate with great gusto and expressed the leavings — a sort of whitewash — with equal aplomb, making it something of a chore to keep his makeshift quarters clean. He was not in danger of dehydration, as would be most young birds, because the water-content of fish supplied his needs. We provided him with a turf-creel, a basket of woven willow saplings, as a roost, and he seemed perfectly happy sitting on a bed of straw within it or standing on the rim.

As days became weeks, he took to flapping about the shed, perching on tool boxes, old suitcases and a wheelbarrow, leading to more cleaning up for Marie and me. Then came a problem. Fin and Steph had gone back to college and Marie and I were scheduled to leave home for a fortnight. What would become of Ron?

In the event, young Ron went on holidays to Galway, to stay with Steph and Fin. They made the four-hour journey south to collect him, and it was a surreal scene as they prepared to leave. Ron stood in the turf creel in the open hatchback of Steph's small, blue Ford Ka, looking at us with his large yellow eyes with their black irises, his scrawny neck fully extended and his still-wiry topknot raised. Herons' eyes appear to be almost crossed, situated at the front of the head immediately above the beak and focused on the beak-tip like the sights of a gun. One eye observes what is to the left of the beak, the other what is to the right. When the subject of interest is above it, it lays its head on one side and watches it with a single eye.

In Galway, Fintan arranged an aviary on the balcony of his apartment above the dock in the middle of the city. Happily, his landlady didn't know that he was boarding a heron on the amenities of her des. res. Ron must have felt in his element, the open sky above him and the tides pouring in and out of the basin just across the road. A local fishmonger obligingly supplied his carers with daily off-cuts, and so the privileged Ron dined on salmon, turbot and bass.

When Marie and I came home to West Cork, Ron was duly returned and now took up residence on our own wooden balcony-cum-deck, again open to the sky and, in this case, affording fine views of the courtyard pond, the stream, the leafy beeches and rabbity field on the other side, and, below the house, the wide bay and the tides coming and going, flooding or uncovering the sandbanks where his kindred, and no doubt his parents, fished. A grid at the top of the balcony steps disbarred foxes, and a four-foot-tall trellis divided his spacious aviary from the rest of the deck. There, he lived in a fish box on an outdoor table, the box borrowed from a pal at the pier and labelled 'Union Hall Fishermens Co. Ltd. No Unauthorised Use'. When the sun was strong, we rigged up a large, black, funeral umbrella over it, and Ron would sit beneath, like a hen sitting on eggs.

The grub was good too; the O'Donovan brothers kindly kept by-catch from their trawler for Ron's exclusive delectation. More than once, tides dictated that they docked at midnight and I was to be seen climbing down the iron ladder set into the pier wall, bucket in hand, to collect a bountiful mix of dragonets, gurnard, small plaice, witch, dabs, megrim, poor cod and red bandfish, an orange-red species as thin as a snake and a foot long. Ron, with his expandable throat, had no trouble in swallowing such exotica. One could see their progress down his reptilian neck, now covered in pretty black-and-white feathers, regularly preened and groomed. After his dinner, there would be the standing-still-and-digesting period, then the preening period, and then a period sitting on the shredded paper in his 'nest'.

One day in late April, five weeks after we had become his surrogate parents, Ron suddenly made a daring, five-foot, flapping leap onto the wide railing of the balcony. After rocking dangerously forward, he regained his balance and, straightening, stood framed and composed against the vault of the sky and the bay below us. Later, we found him standing on one leg, neck drawn down into his shoulders, a heron at rest.

Now, of a sudden, he adopted a rigorous daily regime, spending hours on the rail flapping his wings to strengthen them for flight. The sooner he could fly, the better, we agreed. He would be less vulnerable to predators and we could remove the barriers and recover the balcony for our own use. However, for the moment, we made do with a small table nearby and on fine days he would watch us, as we lunched, a few yards away.

Ron was, indeed, becoming a fine-looking bird, and a lot more interesting than a canary, but the need to feed him was taxing at times. At the old Tanner's Pier, in front of the hotel, I saw an adult and a juvenile heron fishing, the juvenile watching attentively and being fed by the parent as they stalked the shallows in a team. However, since I wasn't ready to don rubber boots and an imitation beak and provide our youngster with lessons, the next best thing was to put a live fish into a long-disused baby-bath half-filled with sea water, and see if it could learn for itself. Off to the rock pools I went, and came back with a shanny, a small fish. I deliberately dropped a sliver of plaice into the bath beside it. Ron first grabbed the morsel and then the shanny, turning it neatly around before swallowing it head-first, poor fish. I have an affection for shannies, and I didn't like this, but Ron had to learn to hunt and no parent herons had come to teach him. After ingesting the shanny, he bathed in the bath, perhaps not yet confident enough to risk the garden pond.

By May, when I was watching vultures in Extremadura, messages from home told me that Ron had stretched his wings and flown all of ten yards to the extension roof. Soon, he had gained sufficient confidence to flap down off the balcony into the yard, returning to his balcony roost via the extension.

After I returned home, he would sometimes step daintily across the courtyard to the ground-floor French windows of my work-room in mid-afternoon and tap with his beak on the glass. I wasn't sure if the tapping was to remind me to include him in that week's column or to fetch him a meal. The tap-tap-tap was uncannily like Morse code.

In mid-May, I wrote:

Out household heron is knocking on the glass of my work-room window and seriously disrupting my efforts to write comprehensible prose. He stretches his long neck up the glass pane, and he's a metre tall looking in at me with one beady eye. It's feeding time at the heronry and I have no option but to go to the pool-room fridge and fetch him a meal. He eats twice a day, and this is afternoon tea. Sometimes, he follows me into the pool-room and even flies up and perches on the pool table. However, I discourage this; accidents might happen, and Ron would not replace the green baize.

In the mornings, when we open the bedroom curtains, we see him 'hunting' in the stream running across the courtyard but there is nothing to catch. However, he assumes the drawn-back-neck, poised-to-stab posture of a real hunting heron, and when he steps into the water does so stealthily without a splash or even a ripple. He seems to know how to hunt; now, we wish he'd go and do it. I think he will, before long. He's taken to disappearing from the garden for a few hours daily. We don't know where he goes, but he continues to return.

Sometimes, when Marie is gardening he follows her about and even plucks gently at her cardigan. Would he eat worms? Certainly; herons will eat fish, frogs, bugs, mice, rats and even ducklings. I hope he doesn't get fixated on her as did our ill-starred dog and pine when she isn't here. A cacophonous dog howling for its emotional beacon was bad enough; a heron squawking for the return of its 'mother hen' would drive me demented.

~

Dawn Chorus Week came and, while the garden was full of warbling songsters, Ron's dawn chorus was nothing but a squawk and a tap at the window for breakfast. Once he'd reminded us that he was there, he was amenable in waiting. However, a crisis arose when wild weather prevented the fishing boats from going out and we suddenly ran out of supplies.

We bought him some processed fish — there was no other fish available —at the supermarket but he wasn't partial to this, so there was nothing for it but to take our octopus out of the freezer, defrost it and feed it to him in bits. Happily, after a few days, the weather changed and the boats went out again. I went down to the pier at midnight when they 'landed', and came home with a bag of by-catch as heavy as a Ryanair take-aboard suitcase. However, when I looked out the sitting-room window, no spectral figure stood shoulders-hunched and head-under-wing on the balcony railing. The fish box roost was empty. We had lots of fish but no heron to eat it.

Perhaps, we said, he had decided it was time to exchange free lunches for the hard life, a future in nature with all its hazards and insecurities; perhaps the wild heron that had come earlier that day had wooed him away. It was probably a sibling, possibly from the same treetop nest from which Ron — whom I still intimately addressed as Bird — had fallen seven weeks before.

The drama had begun that morning. I had seen a heron gracefully alight in the grass under the beeches across our stream. While young Ron, as yet, had no more than flapped or glided, the visitor was an adept flyer, but I could tell that it was also a juvenile because, like Ron, it had grey legs and a clump of wiry-looking feathers on its crown. In adults, this tangle of wires develops into a sleek, glossy pigtail which twirls in the breeze and shines in the sunlight; perhaps it is the origin of the local name, Curly-the-Bogs. The stranger was, no doubt, hoping to share in the wholesome cuisine dispensed by those obliging two-legged creatures, my family and me.

It flew onto the woodpile under the trees and, from that vantage-point, surveyed the courtyard. Ron, immediately aware of its arrival, flapped across the stream and, for five minutes, both birds stalked about on neutral ground, keeping a distance between them. Then, the stranger 'casually' crossed the small bridge and entered the courtyard. He was now in Ron territory and Ron was quick to follow. Reaching the edge of the courtyard pond, he took up a station by the water, his shoulders hunched and neck drawn down, as if roosting. Meanwhile, ignoring me as if I weren't there, the invader walked the yard with measured tread, observed by Ron's single yellow eye. Minutes later, it set off around the side of the house towards the front garden and the broad tarmac apron where we park the car. Ron followed; I assumed it was to see the trespasser off the premises via the front entrance but there were more acts to unfold before the drama's end.

While 'our' Ron stalked it, the interloper strolled about the yard with pretended innocence as if to say 'I'm just out for a walk, and what's your problem anyway?' Then, of a sudden, it flew onto the eight-foot high wall bordering the garden and looked down. Ron, in turn, flapped onto the closed cover of a garden refuse bin directly beneath — a favourite roost of his — and, in stalemate, the two roosted in the sun for half an hour, Ron every now and then inclining his head to stare up at the interloper with a baleful eye. So they roosted together briefly; this proved to be significant later on.

In the final act, the stranger flew onto the gravel of the drive and

Ron hastened to follow. Near the driveway entrance, repeated stand-offs ensued. Sometimes, the two described cautious minuets about one another, a sort of 'Dance of the Herons', with occasional rear-ups and wing-flapping. For an hour, Ron stood sentinel in the middle of the drive, between the stranger and the house. At last, the invader left.

That night, for the first time, Ron was absent from the balcony. We assumed that having met another heron, he had returned to the wild and was consorting with his kind as we had hoped. But at noon next day, he was back again, waiting for a late breakfast.

One sunny morning, a week later, the interloper appeared again in the field across the stream, close to the house, and he and Ron interacted as before, this time standing tall and long-necked in the carpets of meadow buttercups. However, on this occasion, the stranger didn't stay long.

From then on, Ron spent some nights with us, and some not. At times, he stood with shoulders hunched on the balcony rail outside the sitting-room window, in the teeming rain. Occasionally, he would look in at us. When curious, his neck would stretch eighteen inches above his shoulders, and then drop back again like an elevator going down a shaft. When the night was warm, we would open the French windows and he could enjoy concerts or TV shows from his balcony-rail perch. His daytime roost became the bonnet of my elderly Mercedes; I wasn't too happy about that but at least when there was an 'accident', it took only minutes to hose down. One afternoon, as I lifted the hose, he rose on capacious wings and I stood enthralled as our one-time scraggly orphan soared over the treetops, a master of the air.

Ron's behaviour on warm days — rare last summer — informed me of an interesting anatomical feature of herons. Having stood by the pond with his beak wide open, panting vigorously for minutes at a time — like dogs, birds pant as a method of cooling down — he would sometimes hop into the water and lower himself so that he appeared to be floating on the surface as might a duck; however, his feet were on the bottom. When he did this, a white slick would float on the water around him, oil and dust from his feathers, we thought.

In fact, herons have relatively small preen glands, the oil-emitting glands situated like a nipple on the 'parson's' or 'pope's' nose in other birds. Instead, herons have 'powder-down' patches, furry mats of short feathers on the breast and rump that are not moulted but continuously grow and disintegrate into powder.

The heron uses its head and bill to spread this powder over its feathers to clean them. It employs its large middle toe, which has a comb-like underside, to preen the crown and upper neck, impossible to reach with the bill.

Most birds lack powder-down and instead use oil secreted by the preen gland to clean and waterproof their plumage, stimulating the gland with the bill and then using the bill to spread the oil over their feathers. Other birds take dust baths to clean themselves up!

By early June, Ron was approaching four months old (assuming he was a month old when we found him) and had matured into a singularly beautiful bird. If we were away, our neighbour Beth Hanly kindly looked in and, if he was there, gave him a fish from the pool-room fridge. Those who came to view him oohed-and-aahed at his elegance while he posed by the courtyard pond as relaxed as a domestic fowl. He had also become something of a performer.

His evening grooming ritual and tai-chi exercises were fascinating to watch. Perched high on the pergola above the balcony, silhouetted against the sky, or standing on the balcony rail, silhouetted against the bay, he would stretch out one wing, then the other, with the slow, measured motion of a tai-chi master. Next, he would extend each leg behind him in slow motion, and draw it back into his body, and extend it again. He would then open both wings at once and, holding them half-folded, stand motionless for minutes, his neck at full stretch, his beak pointing at the sky.

Grooming followed. The breast feathers were the first to receive attention, the beak laid flat against the throat and then combing downwards, again and again, with a careful grace. Next, fully extending a wing, he would stretch his neck below it and preen the flight feathers, his head looking up at them, his reptilian neck so flexible that it could bend like a snake in, seemingly, any direction.

Feeding time provided further dramatic evidence of the elasticity of the heron oesophagus. I could drop a sand dab almost the size of my hand into the shallow stream and Ron, without a moment's hesitation, would leap in, grab it and gullet it with the alacrity of a politician 'trousering' after-dinner contributions.

Once, having eaten — he always knew when to stop — he picked up a light, but long, twig, blown off the beech trees during a summer gale. After carrying it around the corner of the house, he returned and picked up another, this one longer than himself, and set off again. I followed, and found that he had placed both on top of the Mercedes which was parked in a favourite spot where the sun struck the garden wall and reflected the heat. Not wanting him to commence nest-building on top of my car, I reached out to remove the twig nearest me. Immediately, he stretched out his long neck and 'beaked' it out of my grasp as if to say, 'That's mine, hands off!' Then, to my surprise, he rose on his huge wings, twig and all, and soared onto the roof peak of the extension. There, he uttered a squawk which I could only describe as triumphal.

Soon afterwards, having posed there for a photo opportunity, he flapped a further twenty feet onto our balcony where he laid the twig on the outdoor table. Some minutes later, I noticed that he had broken his trophy in half and now had two twigs. Was he playing? Was he practising for nesting? Was 'he' a female then, our bird Ron?

I thought that were I a gypsy or itinerant huckster, I might have trained him to pick up and turn over cards at a fairground — 'Roll up, roll up, name your card and if Cassandra here selects it, you win the prize!'

Ron then got himself on TV. One lovely morning, I was sitting in the courtyard being interviewed for a *Nationwide* programme, when Ron, pursued by my three-year-old grandson, Luca, who was, in turn, pursued by Stephanie, ran behind me and got into shot. Surreal as this was, David Bickley, the director, decided to include the footage. I had been talking about my good fortune in being surrounded by nature and family, and it confirmed the theme.

Having seen him on TV, one of my poker-school pals unkindly suggested that we fatten up the good Ron and enjoy an unusual Christmas dinner. Herons were certainly eaten in fifteenth-century England when they were hawked with falcons. However, the family and I had no intention of consuming Ron, even though by Christmas, if he continued to eat at his usual rate, he would weigh as much as a goose.

By now, a form of communication had developed between us. Strutting about our courtyard like an articulated farmyard chicken, he would sometimes squawk as if he had something to say. Perhaps he was complaining that, as time went by, we fed him more sparingly; this in order to encourage him to go back to the wild and cease relying on perfidious human beings. We had, at this stage, become used to his disappearing for as long as sixteen hours at a time. But then, one June weekend, it seemed that he had left us forever.

He had been fed by Fintan at about ten o'clock on the Friday night. Soon afterwards, he disappeared from the yard. He didn't show up as usual the next morning, and was still absent at midday. By nightfall, he still hadn't returned. This was his first full twenty-four-hour absence. We wondered where he could be.

When he hadn't shown up by breakfast the next morning, Marie and I talked about it. Could harm have befallen him? That Friday evening, after being fed, could he have been taken by a fox? Earlier in the week, when Fin and I were playing pool and Ron was standing in the gathering dusk looking in at us through the French windows, Fin had seen a fox in the long grass under the trees only twenty feet away from him. When we went out, the fox hadn't run off but had stared boldly at us before casually trotting away. It wasn't the first time we'd seen him, but never so close to the house. Perhaps he had ambushed Ron in the courtyard; by ten o'clock, it was growing dark.

On the other hand, Ron might have simply gone to his non-domestic roost, probably in one of the hundreds of tall trees within a few hundred yards of the house. Next day, fishing along the bay, perhaps some animal had got him? I'd seen both cats and foxes hunting along the village shoreline where herons and egrets regularly fish. My son

Matt, in Rickmansworth, Hertfordshire, told me on the phone that he'd once found a heron beside his local canal 'with its head chewed off'. As time went on, Marie and I feared the worst. 'All our efforts may have been for nothing,' she said. However, we agreed that had poor Ron been killed by a predator, it wasn't because he had become tame. In fact, when a cat or dog entered the courtyard he immediately fled, and was even wary of humans other than ourselves.

At noon, our fears were laid to rest when Ron winged in over the rooftop and alighted daintily in the yard. So, he had survived for more than thirty-six hours without our intervention! It was comforting to know he wouldn't starve if we went away.

On 27 June 2011, I wrote:

It is, apparently, a fact of life that wherever one finds oneself, there is a rat no more than a dozen feet away. However, if one has a heron for company, it will soon be a dead rat. The other afternoon, as our adopted heron followed me across the yard in expectation of a ration of fish, it suddenly stopped by a clump of tall grasses alongside the pond, stared intensely into the foliage, stepped forward as if walking on thin ice, stretched its neck and then, like lightning, shot its head into the greenery and withdrew it, holding a rat.

Gripped by the scruff of the neck, the unhappy rat struggled. Herr Heron dropped it, only to get a better grip, this time clasping the whole neck in its beak. Then, calm and unhurried, he walked to the garden stream, and dunked his prey. After dunking it three or four times, the rat was quite lifeless, and our bird proceeded to swallow it, not without difficulty, but in a series of gulps. I was privileged to witness its slow disappearance and then its passage down the long neck in a series of bumps. It was a three-quarters-grown rat, young, like the heron itself, now about sixteen weeks old.

Herons, clever birds, drown captured mammals before attempting to eat them and they hold fish too large to swallow out of the water until they expire, and then eat them in bits. We are glad to see our foundling apparently knows this by instinct and can, clearly, hunt for himself. A useful bird, Ron the Ratter — who needs a terrier when one has a heron?

~

Most readers will agree that herons must eat, and that dispatching vermin is preferable to gobbling fluffy ducklings which, we know, herons will do if they get half a chance. Liquidating rodents (*rat*-ions takes on a new meaning) is a useful service, although perhaps *liquidising* rodents would be a more fitting description in the case of herons' digestive feats.

Children sometimes came to see Ron, raising their awareness of nature as they watched him from a comfortable distance; if they came too close, he would fly away. They were always intrigued, as were their adult minders. However, while nature, as the adage puts it, is 'red in tooth and claw', it was probably better that admiring visitors didn't see Ron with the rat.

Little Luca, my grandchild, visiting us from Bohemia in the Czech Republic, was the only child we allowed near Ron, and then only under supervision. He delighted in feeding the bird, which stood as tall as himself. The heron wasn't quite as delighted and regarded Luca with a wary eye.

Luca holds forth the fish — he insists on holding it by the tail, rather than using a tongs — and the heron advances. In the blink of an eye, the heron seizes the fish and gobbles it. Luca cries out with glee.

Ron was circumspect about small boys and would more readily approach an adult, although he sensibly stayed clear of all humans unless he was hungry and they came bearing fish. 'Timeo Danaos et dona ferentes,' said Virgil, a very wise Roman, meaning 'I fear the Greeks, even when they come bearing gifts.' For Ron, it was 'Timeo pueros et pisces ferentes,' by which I mean to say, in my bog Latin, 'I distrust (small) boys, even when they come bearing fish.'

Regrettably, little Luca, normally an exceptionally good-natured child, once decided to see how the heron would react if he tossed the wire fish tongs at it. The tongs fells short, but the bird took great umbrage, ruffled its feathers and flew onto the balcony from where it glared down at the small boy.

Luca and the bird are probably, in heron-span — grey herons live to be thirty — about the same age. Perhaps the boy tossed the fish tongs by instinct, in order to establish human territorial imperative, while the bird, by instinct, realised that youth is unpredictable and should be given a wide berth. Maybe Luca, unknowingly, taught it an important lesson: 'Don't trust mankind, however seemingly innocent its manifestation!'

Soon after Luca returned to Czech, Dara, his father, told us that he had been asking after the bird. I hardly dared tell the boy that but a few mornings before, I had seen Ron snaffle an unfortunate butterfly — a meadow brown, for those who may savour such detail.

The butterfly lay on a paving slab outside my workroom window, Herr Heron picking at it. I noticed that it was still alive. The heron stood back as I approached to see if the butterfly could still rise and fly. Too late; this stimulated Ron into action, perhaps fearing that I would make his captive mine. With a dart of his head and a snap of his beak he lifted it and swallowed it. Butterflies for breakfast — how could I tell the child?

~

It is September, as I write this end piece, and the 'nest' which Ron has made on the balcony table now comprises half-a-dozen twigs two or three feet long laid parallel to one another. He moves them around occasionally. The other day, Marie took them off the table in order to clean it but, as soon as she left, he put them back in place, parallel, as before. Does he/she propose to nest there? we ask. Herons do not breed in their first year, so we would have to surrender the table to his occupancy until 2013.

It would be very nice indeed to have a pair of herons raise a family a yard from our sitting-room window, but could he/she persuade a mate to do so in such close proximity to humans? What a wildlife film it would make, were we able to monitor the entire event! It is highly unlikely that it will happen, of course. But I do regret that, from Ron's Day One, I didn't regularly use the video on my camera to film his progress. I have photographs enough for a slide show, but a video would have been the thing!

On 12 September — a few days ago — Fintan spotted a magnificent adult heron atop the naked crown of a tall tree below the garden, while on a lower limb, Ron stood on one leg, neck hunched into his shoulders. The beech had been recently thinned, so visibility was good. As we watched through binoculars, a third heron alighted on a leafy tree farther down the hill. It was easy to see that it was a juvenile, about Ron's age, although not quite as sleek as our well-fed adoptee.

Seeing the three together, we suddenly understood where Ron went during his absences, and what company he kept. The juvenile was, almost certainly, the bird that had twice come to the house. The adult on the treetop was its parent — and, very likely, Ron's parent too. All were, in fact, part of the family from the pine tree behind the hotel, the tree under which we had found Ron on the first day. It was to join his real family that he regularly left us.

The three stayed on the high trees in the bright September sunlight for most of that morning, sometimes preening, sometimes standing statuesquely still. Then, one after another they left — first the parent, then the juvenile, then Ron — all flying in the same direction, towards the sea.

Ron would return, of course, although not of necessity; he didn't need humans now. As for bringing a mate to nest on our balcony in the spring of 2013, we would wait and see. Nothing is impossible. As the poet Emily Dickinson said, 'Hope is the thing with feathers/ That perches in the soul . . .'

Index